KB237059

개혁의
정치경제학

Structural Adjustment and The Political Economy of Reform: Egypt 1990-98
개혁의
정치경제학
주동주 지음
1990년대 이집트의 구조조정정책을 중심으로
한국학술정보[주]

개혁의 정치경제학
1990 년대 이집트의 구조조정정책을 중심으로

이 책은 필자가 영국의 맨체스터대학에 박사 학위 논문으로 제출했던 글을 딱딱한 학위 논문의 형식적 부분들을 일부 제외하고 일반 출판물의 형식으로 각색한 것이다. 원 논문은 2001년 10월에 초고를 탈고했는데, 지도교수의 감수가 늦어져 2003년 10월에 학위 심사를 받았다. 그 후 수정작업을 거쳐 2004년 10월에 최종 학위가 나왔다.

본 연구의 주제는 국제통화기금(International Monetary Fund: IMF)과 세계은행(World Bank)이 주도한 구조조정정책(Structural Adjustment Programme: SAP)의 정치경제학적 함의를 1990년대 이집트의 사례를 중심으로 연구한 것이다. 필자는 대학과 대학원에서 아랍어와 정치학, 경영학을 공부했고, 국책연구기관인 산업연구원(Korea Institute for Industrial Economics and Trade: KIET)에서 중동경제를 중심으로 개발도상국 문제를 오랫동안 연구해 왔다. 필자가 나중에 국제개발학을 공부하면서 이집트의 사례를 연구 주제로 선택하게 된 데에는 이러한 학문적, 직업적 배경이 작용했다고 할 수 있다.

구조조정정책

구조조정정책은 1980년대 개발도상국들의 외채 위기 발생 이후 IMF와 세계은행이 긴급한 자금을 꾸어주는 대가로 개발도상국들에 요구해온 광범위한 거시경제 조정정책을 말한다. IMF의 구제금융은 원래 대부를 받는 국가의 경제정책에 대한 간섭을 수반해 왔다. 그렇지만 1980년대 이후로는 "구조조정대부"라는 새로운 형태의 자금 지원과 함께 보다 광범위한 조건들(conditionalities)이 요구되었으며, 이러한 조건들이 구조조정정책이라는 이름으로 수행되어온 것이다.[1] 이 정책은 최근에 이르기까지 아시아, 아프리카, 중동, 중남미 등 제3세계 전 지역에 걸쳐 거의 대부분의 개발도상국들에서 광범위하게 시행되었고, 개발도상국들의 경제와 사회발전에 막대한 영향을 초래했다. 1997년 외환위기를 겪었던 우리나라도 역시 IMF와 세계은행의 구제금융을 제공 받는 대가로 이러한 구조조정정책을 시행한 바 있다.[2]

1980년대 후반 이후 사회주의의 몰락으로 동서냉전체제가 와해되면서 과거 소련과 미국의 중간지대에서 한쪽을 선택하거나 독자적인 노선을 추구하기도 했던 개발도상국들은 더 이상 선택의 여지없이 미국 주도하의 자본주의 시장경제체제로 편입되는 과정을 겪어 왔다. 미국이 주도하는 브레튼 우즈(Bretton Woods) 체제의 양대 국제금융기구인 IMF와 세계은행은 구조조정정책을 통해 개발도상국들의 이러한 이행

---

[1] 통상적인 IMF의 자금 대출은 대부받는 국가와 IMF 사이에 대기성 차관 협정(Standy-by Agreement)을 통해 이루어지며, 이 협정은 IMF가 요구하는 각종 정책을 수행한다는 조건이 들어있기 마련이다. 그런데 1980년 세계은행이 "구조조정차관(Structural Adjustment Loan: SAL)"이라는 대부 계정을 처음 만들었으며, IMF도 1986년에 "구조조정대부"(Structural Adjustment Facility: SAF)라는 계정을 새로 만들었다. 그 후 이러한 자금들을 대부받는 조건으로 행해지는 정책개혁을 흔히 구조조정정책이라고 부르게 되었다.

[2] 구조조정대부를 받은 나라들의 누적 통계는 제3장에서 간략하게 설명하고 있다. 정확한 통계가 발표된 바는 없지만, Tony Killick (1995)에 따르면 1979-1993년 사이 IMF의 대부건수는 353건에 달했다. 세계은행은 1992년까지 75개 국가에서 267건의 구조조정대부를 수행한 것으로 알려지고 있다 (Reed, 1996:10).

과정을 촉진해 왔다. 양 기구의 조건부 대부를 받은 개발도상국들은 독자적인 경제정책을 사실상 포기하고 양 기구가 요구하는 광범위한 거시경제정책의 조정을 실행해야 했다. 이 과정은 각 나라별로 기존의 정책과 제도에 대한 개혁이라는 이름하에 진행되었다.

워싱턴 컨센서스 (Washington Consensus)

구조조정정책은 보통 IMF가 선도하고 세계은행이 뒤따라가면서 자금 지원을 받는 국가들과 일정한 기간에 걸쳐 두 기구가 요구하는 내용으로 경제정책을 조정한다는 계약을 맺으면서 진행된다. 자금 지원을 받는 국가들은 대부분 절박한 경제위기 상황에서 두 기구가 제공하는 외화자금을 필요로 하기 때문에 이러한 정책 요구를 받아들이게 된다. 구조조정정책을 실행하는 과정에서는 분명하게 선이 그어지는 것은 아니지만, 두 기구가 일종의 역할 분담을 하게 된다. IMF는 거시경제의 안정화에 초점을 맞추고, 세계은행은 무역 및 투자 자유화, 국영기업 민영화 등 제도적 측면의 개혁에 역점을 둔다. 양 기구는 수원국가의 정책 이행 과정을 수시로 점검하면서 그 결과가 만족스럽다고 판정할 때 약속한 금액을 일정 부분씩 추가로 제공한다.

벌써 20여 년이 지나는 동안 두 기구가 개발도상국에 요구해 온 정책은 매우 공통적인 특징을 지녀왔다. 그것은 많은 제3세계 국가들이 오랜 동안 유지해 온 국가 중심의 사회주의적 경제정책과 제도들을 혁파하고 민간 중심의 시장경제체제와 정책을 도입한다는 것이다. 또한 대외적으로는 무역과 투자, 금융거래 등의 자유화를 유도하여 개발도상국들을 세계경제에 통합시키는 방향으로 나아간다는 것이다. 구조조정정책이 매우 많은 나라에서 시행되어 왔음에도 그 정책적 특징이 일관된 공통점을 지녀 왔다는 점은 이미 수많은 전문가들에 의해 지적되고, 비판의 대상이 되어 왔다. 즉 개별 국가의 다양한 여건들을 무시하고 획일적으로 정형화된 정책들을 요구하여 부작용과 실패를 가져온 사례가 너무나 많다는 것이다.

　두 기구가 미국의 워싱턴에 위치하고 미국 재무부의 압력을 강하게 받는다는 점에서 전문가들은 구조조정정책의 이러한 공통적 특징을 흔히 "워싱턴 합의"라는 표현으로 묘사해 왔다. 이것은 정부 역할 축소와 시장 역할 강화, 대외적 개방을 지향하는 일련의 정책들을 지칭하는 표현으로서 이 용어를 처음 사용한 미국의 경제학자 존 윌리엄슨(John Williamson)(1994: 26-28)에 의해 잘 정리되고 있다. 윌리엄슨이 정리한 워싱턴 합의의 정책 특징들은 다음과 점들로 요약된다.[3]

- 재정 규율: 재정 적자 축소, 국영기업과 중앙은행의 역할 축소
- 재정지출의 우선순위 조정: 경제적 효율성보다 정치적 동기가 더 중요하게 고려되는 행정비용, 국방비, 보조금 등의 경비 삭감
- 조세 개혁: 세수 기반을 확대하고 세율 조정
- 금융자율화: 시장에 의한 금리 결정
- 환율 조정 및 외환자유화: 복수 환율의 단일화 및 외환거래 자유화
- 무역자유화: 수량 규제를 관세로 대체하고 관세율 인하
- 외국인투자 자유화: 외국기업의 투자 및 활동을 제약하는 장애요인 철폐
- 국영기업 민영화
- 각종 규제 완화 및 철폐

---

[3] 윌리엄슨은 1989년 미국 재무부와 국제기구의 전문가들이 라틴 아메리카의 경제문제에 대한 처방책으로서 공감대를 형성하고 있는 정책들을 표현하기 위해 이 용어를 처음 사용하였다. 그 자신은 그 후 이 용어가 본인의 의도와 다르게 사용되는 점에 대해 불만을 표시하였다.

윌리엄슨이 당초 구조조정정책의 특징을 표현하기 위해 이러한 용어를 사용한 것은 아니었지만, 많은 개발도상국에서 시행된 구조조정정책이 현저하게 이러한 정책적 특징을 지녀 온 점은 분명하다.

개혁의 정치경제학

구조조정정책은 공식적으로는 경제문제에 대한 처방을 제시하는 정책이며, 정치적인 문제를 다루는 정책은 아니다. 그러나 이 정책의 시행과정과 결과가 다양한 사회적, 정치적 영향과 충격을 가져오기 때문에 많은 학자들은 이 문제를 순수하게 경제적 영역에만 한정해서 보려하기보다 정치경제학적인 관점에서 분석해 왔다. 구조조정정책을 정치경제학적 관점에서 분석하고 비판한 글은 현재까지 무수히 많은데, 이러한 글에는 좌파와 우파 진영의 다양한 시각들이 드러나고 있다.

인간의 역사가 가진 자들과 못 가진 자들의 계급투쟁의 역사라고 규정하는 마르크스주의(Marxism)는 경제문제란 그 자체가 정치문제라고 생각하는 정치경제학이다. 이러한 관점에 기반을 둔 종속이론(Dependency Theory) 등의 좌파적 이론들은 국제문제도 착취하는 "중심"(Center)과 착취당하는 "주변"(Periphery)의 관계로 현상을 설명하며, 구조조정정책에 대해서도 그러한 관점에서 해석한다. 즉 미국을 위주로 한 자본주의의 중심 세계가 국제기구들을 내세워 주변세계를 착취하기 좋은 구조로 만드는 것이 구조조정정책의 본질이라는 것이다. 본 연구를 위해 인터뷰한 이집트의 저명한 경제학자 나데르 페르가니(Nader Fergany)의 말에서도 그러한 시각이 드러나고 있다 (본문 5-3-2절 참조).

우파 진영에서 경제문제가 정치문제로 변화하는 과정을 가장 잘 분석한 이론은 제임스 부캐넌(James Buchanan) 등이 주장한 공공선택이론

(Public Choice Theory)으로 간주되고 있다. 이 이론은 자신들의 이해를 추구하는 다양한 "이해집단"(interest group)이 정부의 정책 결정과정에 영향을 끼치며, 결국 정부의 정책은 순수하게 경제적인 효율성을 고려하기보다 이해집단의 로비에 의해 좌우된다고 주장한다. 이 이론은 현대 자본주의 세계의 정치경제 현상을 분석하는 유용한 개념틀을 제공하고 있으며, 흔히 신정치경제학(New Political Economy: NPE)이라는 용어로 불리고 있다. 본 연구는 일단 이러한 관점에서 이집트의 구조조정과정에 이해집단의 역할을 전제하고, 이를 분석하고자 한다는 점을 서론에서 제시하고 있다.

한 나라의 기본적인 정책이나 제도가 크게 바뀌는 이른 바 "개혁" (Reform)에 관해 정치와 경제의 상관관계를 분석하고 정형화하려는 다양한 시도가 있었는데, 그 가운데 흔히 다뤄져 온 주제들이 제1장에서 소개되고 있다. IMF의 부총재를 역임한 앤 크루거(Anne Krueger, 1995)는 이와 같은 주제들이 크게 세 가지 범주로 유형화된다고 말하고 있는데, 실제로는 더욱 다양한 주제들이 논의되어 왔다. 개혁이 어떤 동기에서 시작하는가 하는 "위기 가설"(Crisis hypothesis)에서부터, 어떤 형태의 정부가 개혁을 더 적절히 수행하는가 하는 문제, 그 과정에서 이해집단들의 역할은 어떠한가 하는 문제, IMF 등 외부 세력은 어떤 영향을 끼치는가 하는 문제 등이 많은 학자들에 의해 다루어져 왔다.

구조조정정책과 보다 더 직접적으로 관련해서는 이 정책의 경제적 성과를 중심으로 그 결과가 초래한 다양한 사회적, 정치적 영향들이 많은 나라의 사례를 통해 연구되어 왔다. 구조조정정책에 수반되는 다양한 정책개혁은 많은 경제 집단의 이해에 직접적인 영향을 가져오고, 그 과정에서 이득을 보는 집단과 손해를 보는 집단이 생기게 된다. 특히 IMF는 흔히 "충격요법"(Shock therapy)이라 불리는 빠른 개혁을 요구해 왔으며, 이로 인해 변화에 따른 충격이 더욱 크게 느껴지는 경우가 많았다. 재정긴축에 따른 보조금 삭감으로 생필품의 물가가 상승하거나, 공기업의 민영화 과정에서 발생하는 실직자와 이로 인한 저항 등은 경제정책이 곧 바로 정치 문제화되는 과정을 보여준다.

무리한 개혁에 따른 이해당사자들과 일반 국민들의 저항으로 많은 개도국에서 이른바 "IMF 폭동"(IMF Riots)이 발생하여 구조조정정책의 악명을 높이는 사례가 되기도 하였다. 세계은행의 수석 부총재를 역임한 조셉 스티글리쯔(Joseph Stiglitz) 교수는 특히 IMF의 무리한 정책 요구가 많은 개도국의 경제를 심각하게 훼손하였다고 비판해 오면서 화제를 모으고 있다.

개도국들은 구조조정정책이 지닌 이러한 정치적 파급 효과를 우려하여 대외적으로는 원조기구들과 개혁의 범위 및 속도를 조절하고자 노력하는 한편, 대내적으로는 국민들에 대한 일종의 위장을 하기도 한다. 이집트의 경우 1990년대 초반 경제사정 악화로 IMF와 차관 협상을 벌이면서 갑자기 "이집트 경제 개방을 위한 1,000일 개혁"을 선언하였다. 이것은 IMF의 요구에 따른 구조조정이 불가피하다고 판단하면서도 외세 간섭에 대한 국민감정이나 그 정치적 영향을 고려하여 "개혁"이 국민경제의 자율적 요구에 따른 것인 양 위장하기 위함이었다(본문 7-2-5절 참조).

이집트의 구조조정

이집트는 1980년대 이후 중반 이후 경제사정이 지속적으로 악화되면서 심각한 외환위기를 맞게 되었다. 무역수지와 경상수지의 만성적인 적자로 해외차입이 증대하여 1987년에는 외채 규모가 GDP의 206%에 달하였고, 원리금 상환비율(Debt Service Ratio: DSR)이 92%에 달하여

한 해 수출액의 거의 전부가 외채를 상환하는 데 쓰여야 하는 형편이 되었다. 이와 같은 사정으로 이집트 정부는 1987년 IMF로부터 대기성 차관(Stand-by Loan)을 도입하는 협정을 맺었으나, IMF가 요구한 개혁을 제대로 이행하지 않아 이 협정은 6개월 만에 효력을 상실하게 되었다. 이집트는 사다트(Anwar Sadat) 대통령 시절인 1977년에 IMF가 권장한 안정화정책을 추진하다가 식료품과 가스 등 생필품 가격 인상에 항의하는 대규모 군중 폭동이 발생한 경험이 있어, 정부로서는 IMF가 요구하는 개혁안을 이행하는 데 주저할 수밖에 없는 입장이었다.

그러나 1990년 8월 이라크의 쿠웨이트 침공에 따른 걸프 사태의 여파로 경제위기가 더욱 심화되자 무바라크(Mubarak) 대통령의 이집트 정부는 다시 한 번 IMF에 손을 벌리지 않을 수 없게 되었다. 걸프 사태는 중동지역의 정세 불안으로 이집트 경제의 주 수입원인 관광 수입을 크게 줄어들게 만들었다. 또한 쿠웨이트, 사우디아라비아 등의 부유한 걸프 산유국들에 취업해 있던 약 70만 명의 이집트 노동자들이 일시에 귀국하여 이들이 보내주던 외화송금도 끊어지게 되었다.

이러한 상황에서 미국이 주도하는 반이라크 연합군에 참여하는 조건으로 대규모 외채 탕감 등의 유인이 주어지자 이집트정부는 1991년 5월 IMF와 18개월에 걸쳐 2억 7,800만 SDR(3억 7,200만 달러)의 대기성 차관을 도입하는 협정을 맺게 되었다. 곧 이어 같은 달에 서방국가들의 채권단 모임인 파리 클럽(Paris Club)은 이집트의 채무 중 50%를 탕감한다고 발표하였고, 다음 달에는 세계은행도 3억 달러의 구조조정 융자를 승인하였다(본문 6-1-1절 참조). 이러한 일련의 협정들에 따라 이집트는 본격적인 구조조정정책을 착수하게 되었다. 이집트정부는 1993년과 1996년 IMF와 두 차례 더 협정을 갱신하면서 1998년까지 구조조정정책을 수행하였다. 그리고 과거와 달리 이 과정은 IMF와 세계은행의 감독하에 8년 동안 비교적 충실히 이행되었다.

1970년대와 1980년대에 IMF의 정책을 도입하려다 실패를 경험한 이집트가 1990년대에는 장기간에 걸쳐 국내외의 큰 반발 없이 개혁을 수행한 과정이 본 연구의 주제로 분석되고 있다. 이러한 변화가 발생한 이유로는 무바라크 대통령의 신중한 통치 스타일로 개혁의 부작용을 최대한 피할 수 있는 정책 수행 방법이 실행되었으며, 서방 국가들 및 아랍 산유국들의 막대한 외채 탕감과 원조 제공 등으로 경제위기가 호전되었다는 점 등을 들 수 있다.

구조조정의 성과, 그리고 승자와 패자

본 연구는 장기간에 걸쳐 수행된 이집트의 구조조정정책이 어떠한 경제적 성과를 가져왔는가를 먼저 분석하고, 여러 정치.사회집단들(Political Actors 또는 Stakeholders)이 이 과정에 어떻게 관여하면서 어떤 이해를 추구했는가를 살펴보고 있다. 정치세력들을 유형화할 수 있는 방법은 다양하나, 본 연구는 영국의 중동전문가인 힌네부쉬(Raymond Hinnebusch) 교수의 논문에서 착상하여 다섯 개의 큰 집단으로 분류하였음을 밝히고 있다. 이러한 집단은 집권세력(The State), 국제원조 제공 그룹(International Donor Group), 부르주아(Bourgeoisie), 저항세력(Opposition Forces), 그리고 일반 대중(Mass Public)이다. 본문 2-2-2절은 이러한 집단의 개념적 틀과 구성인자에 대한 설명을 하고 있다.

구조조정정책이 수행된 1990년대 중 이집트의 경제 사정이 전반적으로 호전된 점은 분명하다. 개혁 기간 동안 경제성장률은 초기 1%대에서 마지막 3년 동안은 계속 5%를 넘어섰고, 재정적자는 GDP의 18%에서 1.0%로 줄어들었다. 1990년 GDP의 107%에 달했던 외채 규모도 1998년에는 34%로 줄어들었다. 이와 함께 제도적 개혁도 진행되어 무역과 투자 및 외환거래의 자유화 등이 상당 부분 실행되었다. 정치적

난제였던 공기업의 민영화도 상당한 실적을 거두었다. 이집트 정부는 1999년 시점에서 이러한 실적을 개혁의 성과로 자평하면서 이집트 경제가 이제 확실한 시장주도 체제로 자리 잡았고, 성장을 가속화해나갈 것이라고 예견하였다. 그러나 2000년대 초반에 들어오면서 이집트경제는 돌발적인 금융위기의 영향으로 다시 심각한 침체상황에 빠지게 되었다.

본 연구자는 1974년 사다트 대통령의 개방정책(Open Door: Infitah) 선언 이후 1980년대 초반까지 이집트 경제가 누렸던 호황과 1990년대 구조조정 시기의 호황을 비교하면서 그 유사성을 강조하는 결론으로 구조조정의 성과를 평가하고 있다. 1970년대의 호황은 제1차 오일쇼크로 인한 석유 달러의 증가에 힘입었으며, 이때 유입된 자본이 생산부문과 수출산업에 투자되지 않고 주로 소비적인 건설사업과 수입확대에 투입되었다. 이때의 개혁과 개방은 결국 수입과 금융의 자유화를 이용해 축재한 일부 부르주아적 계층의 생성만을 가져왔을 뿐, 이집트 경제의 지속적인 성장기반 구축에 기여하지 못했고, 이러한 결과가 1980년대 후반의 경제위기로 이어졌다는 것이다.

1990년대의 이집트 경제도 1970년대 개방정책 시기와 놀라울 정도로 유사성을 보인다는 점에 대해 본 연구자는 브롬리와 부쉬 (Bromley and Bush) 교수의 공동의견에 공감하고 있다. 즉 1990년대의 호황은 막대한 원조와 외채탕감이라는 외부로부터의 불로소득에 힘입었으며, 이 시기의 개혁과 개방정책도 결국은 수입업과 금융을 위주로 한 일부 부르주아적 계층의 축재에 기여하였을 뿐이라는 점이다. 일반 대중은 구조조정정책의 전형적 특징인 보조금 삭감, 복지 혜택 축소, 물가 상승, 경쟁과 고용불안 심화 등으로 피해를 입었으며, 이들이야말로 개혁의 피해자라는 것이다.

정치세력별로 개혁의 승자와 패자를 따져본다면 결국 최대의 승자는 축재와 함께 정치권력에 대한 접근까지 확대된 부르주아들이라는 것이 본 연구의 또 다른 결론이다. 가장 심각한 패자는 위에서 말한 일반 국민들이다. 한편 집권세력은 일시적으로 경제위기를 모면하게 되어 자신들의 최대 관심사항인 정권 안정과 그에 따른 각종 혜택을 입었다. 미국과 IMF, 세계은행 등의 국제원조 그룹은 이집트 경제를 세계시장에 한층 깊숙이 편입시키고, 중동지역에서 서방의 이해를 확보하는 전초기지로 이집트 정부를 굳건한 우방의 지위에 묶어두는 데 성공하였으므로 역시 자신들의 이해를 성취했다고 할 수 있다. 유명무실한 저항세력들은 개혁기간 중 별다른 반대의 소리를 내지 못했으며, 가장 치열한 반정부 세력인 이슬람 근본주의 세력은 철저하게 탄압되고 분쇄되었다. 이 과정이 본 연구의 각 장에서 주제별로 설명되고 있다.

마무리 말

본서는 2005년 필자의 지인이 경영하는 도서출판 시나리오 친구들에 의해 이미 영문으로 출판되었다. 그런데 이번에 한국학술정보(주)에서 새롭게 출판을 제의해 와 필자로서는 계면쩍지만 그대로 승인하였다. 한국에서 중동을 연구하는 연구자는 많지 않고, 특히 이집트 경제를 주제로 한 학술논문을 구해 볼 사람들이 얼마나 될지 의아스러운데 출판을 하겠다고 제의해 준 한국학술정보(주)의 관계자들께 우선 감사하다는 말씀을 드린다. 부족한 책이지만, 관심 있는 분들께 도움이 된다면 더없이 행복하게 생각하겠다. 지난번에 출판을 맡아 주었고, 이번 출판에도 양해를 해 준 시나리오 친구들의 윤태현 사장께도 감사드린다.

CONTENTS

CONTENTS

CONTENTS

CONTENTS

Preface

This book is a publication of my Ph. D. thesis of similar title, which was submitted to the University of Manchester in October 2003. The original thesis was slightly modified here to transform it into a general publication.

Completing this study would have been an impossible task without the advice and assistance I received from many sources. The kind comments and instruction of Dr. Paul Cook, my supervisor at the University of Manchester, has been the most invaluable guidance. The intellectual and humane encouragement of Dr. Kathy Powell and Dr. Tej Purewal, who instructed me during my Master's course at the University of Manchester, are also unforgettable. Dr. Pandeli Glavanis, who was originally my supervisor but moved to other place later, introduced me to the Development Studies course of the University of Manchester, and I appreciate him for that. I further appreciate the staff of the Institute for Development Policy and Management (IDPM) at the University of Manchester, especially Debra Whitehead and Fiona Wilson, for all their assistance with administrative arrangements.

I am especially grateful to my friends whom I met in Manchester. My life as a single parent with a son, and a self-financing student in a foreign country has been one that required extremely hard efforts and patience. Without the material and mental assistance from these friends, my survival itself would have been doubtful. Ryu Ho-Kyung (Bae Gyung-Jin), Jin Sung-Ho, Lee Chan-Goo (Kim Pal-Nam), Ko-Young-Joo (Park Sun-Min), Son San (Lyu Hyun-Sook), Eom Tae-Joon, Yeo Sam-Yul, Lee Nam-Kyoo, Park Tae-Joo (Kim In-Sook), Jung Bum-Jin, Jun Jong-

Chul, Sung Soo-Hwan, Jung Hyung-Jin, Kim Jong-Yul, Lee Won-Sam and Rev. Kim are among the numerous names I will not forget.

I am also grateful for the help from those whom I met in Cairo. Dr. Mohammad Selim and Dr. Alia El-Mahdi of Cairo University helped me to carry out my fieldwork. Dr. Heba Handoussa provided me with invaluable sources of information. She also gave me the full scripts of her unpublished work, for which I am especially grateful. Mr. Park Han-Soo at the Korean Embassy in Cairo provided me with logistical assistance. Mr. Lee Gil-Jae and Mr. Oh Se-Jong also helped me greatly in Cairo.

I have also received kind and warm assistance from many people, especially after my return to Korea. Some of my seniors and colleagues of the Korea Institute for Industrial Economics and Trade kindly (KIET) took care of me so that I could spare the time and energy for this hard work, while working at the job place. Dr. Pai Kwang-Sun and Dr. Oh Sang-Bong, the former and present Presidents of the KIET, warmly encouraged me to carry out this work. Dr. Sim Young-Sup, Dr. Kim Hwa-Sup, Dr. Lee Moon-Hyung, Dr. Lee Suk-Ki, Mr. Kim Hak-Ki, and Ms. Oh Mi-Sook also gave me warm assistance. Dr. Han Duck-Soo, formerly President of the KIET and the incumbent Prime Minister of Korea also kindly encouraged me.

I feel also indebted to those with whom I spent a short period of happy time working together in the Office of the Prime Minister of Korea. Dr. Park Gi-Jong, Dr. Kim Dong-Soo, Mr. Jung Hyun-Yong, Ms. Jung Eun-Young, Ms. Koo Moon-Im, and Ms. Lee Hwa-Sun kindly helped me to finish the degree course. To think, I feel I was lucky to get help and encouragement from so many people. Without them, it might have been much more difficult for me to finish this tedious and hard work.

Finally, my brothers and sisters in Korea are almost the co-authors of this work. They have always stood with me during the hard days of my life. My son, Yong-Hyun, who has endured all those hard days, is literally the greatest source of 'my pride and joy'. I ascribe all my achievement, if any, to them. Also, I think I will have to express gratitude for my friends Ryu Ho-Young and Yoon Tae-Hyun for their friendship and especially for their help for this publication.

Chapter 1

Introduction

1-1. Structural Adjustment Programme in Egypt

The objective of this study is to undertake research into the process and the results of the economic reforms that had been implemented in Egypt during the 1990s. Egypt faced a serious economic crisis in the late 1980s and early 1990s, and undertook far-reaching economic reforms with the financial assistance and policy supervision of the two Bretton Woods International Financial Institutions (IFIs), the International Monetary Fund (IMF) and the World Bank. This reform, which was named officially as "The Economic Reform and Structural Adjustment Programme" (ERSAP), had been guided by the strict conditionality of the IFIs. In fact, it was just another case of the Structural Adjustment Programme (SAP), which the IFIs had sponsored in many developing countries during the last two decades.

Since the early 1980s, the IMF and the World Bank have broadly and deeply intervened in the macro-economic policies of developing countries. After the rise of the debt crisis in the Third World during the 1980s, the IFIs have served as the "lender of last resort" (Pastor, 1996: 248) by providing financial assistance to developing countries with balance of payments deficits. Such assistance has been "conditional" upon the recipient countries agreeing to a set of macro-economic reform policies. These reform policies are called the "SAP", and they are often quite detailed, specifying both general policy measures and certain quantitative targets for various macro-economic variables. To promote compliance, credit is provided in instalments as successive short-term quantitative targets are met.

The SAP has been formulated around guidelines, which were frequently referred to as "The Washington Consensus" (Williamson, 1994: 26-28). This is not an official document, but points to certain implicit principles that underlay the distinctively common features of the SAPs implemented in many developing countries. Undoubtedly, the specific policy sets of SAP have been designed to promote the neo-liberal tenets of the IFIs, which advocate "A return to Laissez-Faire, Free Trade" (Weaver, 1995: 5). As such, the SAP has sought minimal state intervention in economy, and has promoted restructuring of developing economies into private-sector based, open market economy.

There is a typical division of roles between the IFIs in promoting the SAP. The IMF supervises macro-economic stabilisation, while the World Bank intervenes in more institutional reforms. Stabilisation is deemed as a prerequisite for structural adjustment, and is generally sequenced in the first place of all SAP processes (Ibid.: 8-14). Overall, the SAP prescribes typical sets of policy packages such as reduction of government spending and inflation, financial and trade liberalisation, and privatisation.

Egypt is one of those many developing countries that resorted to the financial assistance of the IFIs in response to its problems in balance of payments and overall economic conditions. Before the 1990s, Egypt had attempted economic reforms several times. In 1987, Egypt concluded a Standby Agreement with the IMF, and undertook a set of macro-economic reform programme. However, this programme was short-lived due to the Egyptian government's lack of commitment and the discontent of the IMF on its performance. Before that, in 1977, Egypt also started an IMF-sponsored adjustment programme, which caused a severe mass riot and was aborted immediately.

These painful experiences of failures have made the Egyptian government hesitate to undertake any orthodoxy-type reform seriously afterwards. However, the worsening of economic conditions necessitated the IFI's financial help and the acceptance of the need to implement reform in its economic policies. As a result, in May 1991, the Egyptian government concluded another Standby Agreement with the IMF, which was followed by an additional loan agreement with the World Bank next month. These two agreements with the IFIs signified the start of the reform, or the ERSAP. Unlike the past cases, this time, the reform had been implemented continuously until 1998, when it was officially terminated.

The IMF agreement was renewed two times in 1993 and 1996, as preceding agreements expired. These successive renewals of the IMF agreements were the precondition of a very important debt reduction scheme for Egypt. The Western donor countries grouped in the name of the Paris Club committed themselves to reduce the debt of Egypt owed to them by half, on the condition that Egypt would carry out the IMF-sponsored reform successfully. This fact that the debt reduction scheme was tied to the performance of the reform was one of the most important factors that made the Egyptian government continue the ERSAP to the expected end time.

The ERSAP had been implemented officially in three stages over the period 1991-98, according to the loan agreements between the Egyptian government and the IMF. However, before officially starting the programme, the Egyptian government had a long process of negotiation with the IMF over the conditionality of the loan, and during that period had undertaken much of the proposed reform measures. As such, this negotiation period that had lasted almost three years can be considered part of the ERSAP period, adding one preliminary stage to the official three stages.

The policy measures of the ERSAP were composed of the two typical structural adjustment packages, macro-economic stabilisation and institutional reform, including liberalisation and privatisation. As a comprehensive economic policy that aimed to change the economic structure from a formerly socialist-tainted to a market-oriented one, it has brought serious consequences for the development of the Egyptian economy.

The purpose of this study is to understand the overall development of the ERSAP in its economic and socio-political aspects. Since the ERSAP is a quite recent event, academic researches from a broad perspective has been rare, and most existing research approaches the subject from a much narrow perspective focusing on specific issues. This study, on the contrary, has attempted to adopt a wider approach by examining the background to the reform, its causes, and its various economic and socio-political impacts. In this context, the specific research targets of this study are grouped into following areas:

- The background and causes of the reform efforts
- The main contents of the policy measures
- The implementation process
- The economic performance following the reforms
- The social impact and the political implications of the reforms

Throughout the entire study, a particular focus has been put on the analysis of the influences and interactions of major political actors. The Egyptian state, the donor group, the bourgeoisie, the opposition forces, and the mass public are classified broadly as the major political actors that have affected the process of the reform. This study analyses how their influences affected the course of the reform, and which groups won and lost during the process of the reform. This analysis is based on the approach of political economy, of which the basic assumption is that economic reform is motivated and developed by political conditions. This assumption will be discussed more in detail in the next chapter.

To conclude, this study aims to present how the economic reforms in Egypt during the 1990s had developed using a political economy perspective. In so doing, this study will help to understand, from a comprehensive view, the economic and socio-political development of Egypt during the 1990s, the time in which far-reaching economic reforms had been promoted.

1-2. Political Economy of Reform: Some Topics

This research is based on an approach of political economy, which assumes that economic reform is motivated and developed by political conditions, especially by the interests and influences of major socio-political groups. This assumption has been widely discussed in the literature on political economy. It is the assumption of the "new political economy" (alias "public choice theory") that policymakers behave to maximise their 'personal' economic well-being rather than to follow normative economic analysis (Williamson, 1994; Streeten, 1995). It is one of the most important premises of the political economy that the political and economic domains cannot be separated in any meaningful sense (Underhill, 2000). About these assumptions, more detailed explanation will be given in the next chapter.

More specifically, in recent times, the politics of economic reform or structural adjustment has been ardently researched by many authors. According to Stephen Haggard et al. (1995: 11), there is now a growing consensus that stabilisation and structural adjustment can no longer be regarded as purely technical economic problems. One reason is that different adjustment paths have different distributional consequences. A second reason is that purely economic analyses fail to explain why certain adjustment policies are chosen in the first place. In the view of Haggard et al. (1995: 11-12), politics can affect the process of adjustment in a number of ways. They present this point clearly by following statement:

"Socio-economic groups seek to influence policy choices in order to maximise their incomes; politicians respond to such pressures in order to enhance their prospects for winning and holding office. Once policies are chosen, social groups react in their turn. Thus we can expect not only that politics will shape policy choices, but that economic policy and performance will have profound effects on political life. As these effects feed back into the policy process, initial choices may be either sustained and consolidated or reversed. The programmes that have been most successful economically are those which have succeeded politically by building bases of support and managing political resistance."

The debates on the political economy of reform, especially the SAP, have dealt with many topics. According to Anne Krueger (1995), there are three major themes in the emerging views on the political economy of economic policies in developing countries. The first is that politically determined policies have economic consequences that change the political equilibrium that generated those policies. The second is that analyses of the political economy of economic policy determination in developing countries can only be undertaken on the basis of assumptions about the nature of governments. The third is that it is often unsatisfactory to discuss either economic policies or governments as one-shot, enduring phenomena, since particular economic policies set in motion political and economic responses that are likely to change both the nature of the government and the economic policies.

However, even this broad categorisation by Krueger does not encompass all theoretical perspectives. As Joan Nelson (1990: 17) put it, there is no general theory of the politics of adjustment. A number of different theories and bodies of research are relevant to one aspect or another of the topic, but fall well short of an overarching conceptual scheme or theory. Different theories and hypotheses on specific topics are either backed up or refuted by conflicting evidence.

To deal with all topics on the political economy of economic reform here is out of the range of concern of this study. Here, some topics that have more direct relevance to the subject of this study will be discussed. A review of these will help to illuminate the Egyptian case in a global context.

1-2-1. The Crisis Hypothesis

This terminology, as dubbed by Williamson and Haggard (1994: 562), refers to the theory that attempts to explain the causes of economic reforms in developing countries. According to Sturzenegger and Tommasi (1998: 9), the claim that economic crises seem either to facilitate economic reforms or cause them outright is part of the new conventional wisdom on reform. This claim has been supported by many case studies. Thus, Bates and Krueger (1993: 454), concluding their case studies, state:

> "In all cases, of course, reforms have been undertaken in circumstances in which economic conditions were deteriorating. There is no recorded instance of the beginning of a reform program at a time when economic growth was satisfactory and when the price level and balance of payments situation were stable. Conditions of economic stagnation (and the recognition that it is likely to continue) or continued deterioration are evidently prerequisite for reform efforts."

However, according to Williamson and Haggard (1994: 564-565), crisis is clearly neither a necessary nor a sufficient condition to initiate reform. They present that, in three cases among the thirteen of their study, crisis appeared to play no role in stimulating the reform effort. In those cases, the changes of government provided the impetus to reform. As for the Egyptian case, this study found that economic crisis was one of the most important factors that set the environment for the reform in the 1990s.

1-2-2. Types of Government and the Implementation of Reform

As to the determinants of the likely success of reform, several hypotheses have been put forth (Bates and Krueger: 1993). One is that "strong" or authoritarian governments have more capacity to change economic policy than do democratic ones. According to Nelson (1990: 22), at least since the 1970s, the assumption has been widespread that authoritarian governments are more likely than democracies to decide upon and enforce unpopular economic stabilization and adjustment measures. Authoritarian governments, it was hypothesized, are better able to make long-run plans than are governments tied to electoral cycles. The former also can quash opposition to occasional economic retrenchment, with its inevitable squeeze on some segments of society.

According to Williamson and Haggard (1994: 568), this hypothesis appears to have been prompted by the record of military regimes installed in Argentina (1966 and 1976), Brazil (1964), Chile (1973), and Uruguay (1976). The experience of the East Asian newly industrialising countries, which pursued successful export-led growth under military (Korea), or one-party (Taiwan and Singapore) auspices, has also been widely cited in support of the hypothesis.

However, more recent studies find that there is no significant relationship one way or the other; neither democracy nor dictatorship is systematically related to economic performance (Haggard, et al., 1995; Nelson, 1990; Williamson, 1994; Little, et al., 1993). According to Williamson and Haggard (1994: 568-9), only four of the eleven successful reformers in their study could be generally classified as authoritarian. Six cases of successful reform were undertaken by governments that were unambiguously democratic at the time of the reform episode under consideration.

The study by Little et al. (1993) of the cases of eighteen countries show that neither the form of government nor the degree of political freedom seems to have had a significant bearing on the performance of the reforms. The study by Nelson (1998) on the cases of thirteen developing countries also shows the gamut of regime types and casts doubt on the concerned assumption.

Conclusively, there is no general theory on the determinants of the success of reform, especially on the relationship between the regime type and the economic performance. The Egyptian case in the 1990s, which is the subject of this study, will help to add one exemplary case to the discussions on this topic.

1-2-3. The Role of Interest Groups

As Little et al. (1993: 381) stated, the working assumption of political economists is that various elements of society will press the government for policies and actions favourable to their economic interests, and prospective losers from a given line of policy action will try to block its adoption, or undermine its implementation. Accordingly, as Haggard et al. (1995: 21) pointed out, popular analyses of the politics of economic reform typically begin with the power of entrenched interests, and a bias towards interest-group analysis is visible in the academic literature as well.

A number of researchers have attempted to theorise the relevance of the influence of interest groups to economic reforms. According to Nelson (1990: 25), the balance of interests among the government's supporters obviously is likely to influence its adjustment choice. Nelson summarised the findings of many researches and claimed that governments depending mainly on labour and popular support are more likely to adopt heterodox programs, while those relying on business and financial support to favour neoorthodox prescriptions.

However, interest group analysis is not at all straightforward, and some important limitations have been noted (Haggard, et al.: Ibid.). Such analysis on the advanced industrial states assumes a dense network of social organisations: the major actors, such as business, labour and agriculture, are well organised. In the developing countries, those assumptions are often misguided: interest groups in most developing countries are not so well organised, so they are less able to translate their interests into political action. To verify this point, Little et al.'s study (1993) showed that "surprisingly little" could be said about the interest group politics with respect to macroeconomic management in developing countries.

It is possible, however, that the assumption that only well-organised interest groups can exert political powers itself is also misguided. As this thesis will relate later through the case of Egypt, private networking of influential individuals or social groups in developing countries can affect the course of policy actions more effectively than official organisations. And, when people are under-represented by the official organisations participating in the political process, their discontents on certain economic policies can frequently lead to political upheavals such as mass riot. In this respect, it should be borne in mind that even under-organised social groups can affect the course of economic policy actions through forms of political actions.

1-2-4. The Role of External Agencies

Obviously, the SAPs start from the lending agreements between developing countries and the Bretton Woods IFIs. The conditonalities presented by the IMF and the World Bank stipulate the basic framework of the reforms, and they monitor the recipient countries' implementation processes. Subsequently, many researches have attempted to find a general theoretical scheme for the behaviour and roles of external agencies in the economic reform process.

According to Nelson (1990: 26), a good deal of past research focused on factors that determine the relative bargaining strength of debtor governments and external creditors as reflected in the amount, terms, and conditions of financing. Nelson presents that the evidence through the mid-1980s supported the generalization that the largest debtors, broadly speaking, received more favorable terms and conditions than smaller debtors. This argument has been challenged by Williamson and Feinberg (1987), who have argued that the main source of bargaining power for both debtors and creditors is not the size of the debt and the financing offered, but creditors' apparent willingness to provide positive flows. This contrary view is also recognised by Nelson (1990: 27).

More recently, it is widely assumed that the respective bargaining power of the IMF and governments is a function of the availability of alternative funding. If foreign exchange reserves are exhausted and no credit is available, government must negotiate with the Fund, which imposes relatively strong conditions (Haggard et al. 1995: 16).

As to the reasons why governments turn to the IFIs, the following statement of Haggard et al. (Ibid.: 28) provides a plausible explanation:

"Not only did the multilateral agencies grant direct loans at favourable conditions, but their support also allowed developing countries to obtain additional commercial financing from lenders who were reassured by the signature of an IMF standby agreement. According to one estimate, one dollar of IMF or World Bank money brings in four more."

The variety of views that have been reviewed so far provide some guidance for the approach adopted in the present study. However, as mentioned earlier, the unsettled nature of the academic issues and the lack of general theories make it difficult to apply them to this study. As the objective of this study is not to verify the authenticity of certain hypotheses and theories, this thesis will remain faithful to the analysis of the Egyptian case in its own context. In so doing, this study, will endeavour to contribute to understanding of another case of economic reform in developing countries.

Chapter 2

Definitions and Conceptual Boundaries of the Political Economy Approach

As mentioned in the first chapter, this thesis applies the approach of political economy to the economic and political implications of the structural adjustment process in Egypt. Given the varied perspectives of political economy and different usages of terminology, this chapter will present a more detailed explanation of the approach taken by this research, and more specifically delineate the concepts of the terminology used. Also, this chapter will define the conceptual boundaries of the complex research questions presented in the introduction.

2-1. Perspectives of Political Economy and the Approach of this Research

As mentioned by Little et. al (1993: 38) as cited in the previous chapter, it is the working assumption of political economists that various elements of society will either press or block the introduction of government policies according to their specific interests. However, different perspectives of political economy show discrepancies in identification of interest elements in society. In this section, these differing perspectives, and how they each see economic policy changes in society, will be briefly overviewed. Then, the perspective of the public choice theory is presented in more detail, as it is the most relevant perspective to the approach of this research.

2-1-1. Perspectives of Political Economy on Economic Policy Reform

Political economy is the study of how politics and economics are interrelated. There are a variety of approaches to the study of politico-economic interaction which are all labelled 'modern political economy': Marxist or neo-Marxist approaches, systems theory approaches, traditional or institutional approaches as well as the public choice approach (Lane and Ersson, 1990). No single interpretation of the history of political economy commands universal agreement among modern historians of ideas (Clark: 1991: 21).

Barry Clark (1991) classified the major schools of modern political economy into the following four groups: conservative, classical liberal, modern liberal, and radical. According to this classification, public choice theory belongs to the classical liberal perspective, and Marxist theory belongs to the radical perspective.

Lane and Ersson (1990: 3-4) further simplified the dominant perspectives of modern political economy, especially since the mid-sixties. On the one hand, there is the public choice school, which is actor oriented, and proceeds from a basic assumption about methodological individualism as well as utility-maximising selfish individuals. On the other hand, there is a set of Marxist or neo-Marxist models, which are holistic and emphasise macro aspects of political and economic systems: the dependency school, the world systems model and various state models. The distinction between a public choice or rational choice approach and a neo-Marxist or radical political economy bears on the separation between micro and macro theory, between a focus on microscopic entities and macroscopic units.

The Marxist tradition explains society with the conceptual tool of class struggle. In this view, the primary function of the state is to ensure the legal, institutional, and ideological hegemony of the dominant class over the subordinate class. Under normal conditions, the state is an instrument of domination that reflects the structure of class relationships, and the purpose of policy is to advance and protect the interests of exploiting classes over those of the exploited. In consequence, policy elites are best understood as tools of the dominant class to accomplish this end. According to the *Manifesto of the Communist Party* by Marx and Engels (1991: 37), "The executive of the modern State is but a committee for managing the common affairs of the whole bourgeoisie". In this view, policy change is explained by changes in the composition of the dominant class or class alliances (Grindle and Thomas, 1991: 21).

Public choice perspective assumes the existence of multiple interest groups in a society who seek their own economic well-being. In this view, the state apparatus exists to serve and protect the well-being of the whole society rather than to serve the interests of the dominant class. The policy elite is chosen by the majority through democratic processes, and policies are affected by the stronger interest groups. According to Buchanan (1972: 14), the public choice theory is the political economy of democratic society, where the rulers are also ruled. It can be said that this perspective on social composition is related to the view of Max Weber, who claimed the existence of multiple social stratifications rather than the two simplified classes of the ruling and the ruled.

Basically, as this researcher believes the multiple social stratification model of Max Weber to be more adaptable than the proletariat – bourgeoisie dichotomy of the Marxist theory in analysing complex modern society, the approach of this research sided with the perspective of the public choice theory, notwithstanding its limitations, especially with regard to its application to developing countries.[1]

In the following, the public choice theory is presented, especially with regard to the adaptations and limitations of its assumptions in this research.

---

[1] A comparison of the class and stratification theories of Karl Marx and Max Weber is compactly illustrated in Anthony Giddens (2001: 282-305)

2-1-2. Public Choice Theory and the Approach of this Research

Public choice theory developed from the study of taxation and public spending, and its assumptions have been applied to a wide range of studies of political economy. It emerged in the fifties, and received widespread public attention in 1986, when one of its leading proponents, James Buchanan, was awarded the Nobel Prize in economics. Other major figures in this theory are Gordon Tullock, Robert Tollison, and Anthony Downs (Shaw, 2003; Clark, 1991: 105-128).

Public choice theory is directed at the study of the political behaviours of people based on economic principles. It takes the same principles that economists use to analyse people's actions in the marketplace and applies them to people's actions in collective decision-making. According to Buchanan (1972: 12), the theory of public choice can be interpreted as the construction of a bridge between the behaviour of persons who act in the marketplace and the behaviour of persons who act in the political process. Jane Shaw (2002:http://www.econlib.org/library/-Enc/PublicChoiceTheory.html) summarised the basic assumptions of the public choice theory as follows:

> "Economists who study behavior in the private marketplace assume that people are motivated mainly by self-interest. Although most people base some of their actions on their concern for others, the dominant motive in people's actions in the marketplace —whether they are employers, employees, or consumers — is a concern for themselves. Public choice economists make the same assumption — that although people acting in the political marketplace have some concern for others, their main motive, whether they are voters, politicians, lobbyists, or bureaucrats, is self-interest."

From this assumption of self-interest, the public choice theorists coined the term "rent-seeking" to describe efforts to use the government's regulatory power for the purpose of advancing the interests of a particular group (Clark, 1991: 108). Businesses and individuals seek rent when they attempt to use the power of government to artificially restrict the supply or increase the demand for the resources they choose. According to public choice theorists, bureaucrats in government can be "captured" by special interests. They rely on Congress for their budgets, and often the people who will benefit from their mission can influence Congress to provide more funds. Thus interests groups become important to them. Such interrelationships can lead to bureaucrats being captured by interest groups (Shaw: Op.cit.).

From this point of view, government policies turn into political processes, as indicated in Haggard et al. (1995:11-12), quoted in the previous chapter. The approach of this research started from this point of view. It assumed that certain political groups might have affected the process of the structural adjustment in Egypt, and tries to reveal which groups have played what kind of roles and who gained and lost in the process. In this regard, it can be said that this research is deeply affected by the assumptions of public choice theory.

However, the argument of this research does not follow all of the prevailing doctrines of public choice theory. Due to the liberal ideas of the public choice school, which argue for "small government", or "state-minimalism", public choice theory has been associated with the neo-classical or neo-liberal counter-revolution of the 1980s, and is frequently called the New Political Economy (NPE), which substituted the "market failure" argument of the Keynesian school with a new "government failure" argument (Toye, 1991). Because of its scepticism about the supposedly benign nature of government, public choice theorists cast doubts on the Keynesian assumption that government can effectively correct market failures.

Although the public choice theory developed in the context of American society, its argument with regard to government failure has deeply affected development ideas in the international arena. According to Glavanis (2002: 452), prior to the 1980s, mainstream economic development theory had accepted as a matter of faith that the state would be the modernizer and initiate development. By the end of the 1970s, however, state-led developments in the Third World, based on the ideology of state capitalism, reached the limit of financial solvency. Chronic external imbalances in the balance of payments of numerous developing countries, as well as challenging internal budget deficits, called for the introduction of a new development paradigm.

A multiplicity of factors came to be identified as the indicators of failure of government intervention in the economic sphere. Important among such factors were loss-making public enterprises, wasteful subsidy programmes which favoured influential elites linked to Import Substitution Initiative (ISI) industries, overvalued currencies, anti-rural strategies and inappropriate educational policies. Against this background, from 1980 on, structural adjustment and stabilisation emerged as the new paradigm – as a development counter-revolution (Mehmet, 1995: 118). This situation will be presented more in detail in the next chapter, which will specialise in a review of the SAP.

Although this research uses the assumptions of public choice theory on self-interest and rent-seeking interest groups, it does not side with the New Political Economy as the neo-liberal ideology that has propped up the structural adjustment processes in developing countries. The following comments of John Toye (1991: 322) on the implications of the NPE in economic development was kept in mind in the process of this research:

> "The NPE is characterised first of all by a profoundly cynical view of the state in developing countries. To say, as exponents of the NPE do, that people in political positions are typically motivated *only* by individual self-interest is, and should be shocking. .. However one defines the public interest, and however

> much scope one grants to the protection of private interests as part of the definition of the public interest, the unbridled pursuit of self-interest by rulers belong to the pathology of politics – to tyranny or dictatorship or, ultimately, to anarchy. .. The NPE is not merely saying unflattering things about Third World politicians – that they are misguided, myopic, or cowardly. Its claims are much more extreme: that their unbridled egoism makes them constitutionally unfit for any political role whatsoever."

According to Glavanis (2002: 457-8), the NPE is primarily a political counteroffensive directed at developing societies in general and operating under the guise of SAPs. In particular it aims its cynicism and pessimism at the various nationalist regimes that emerged in the global arena during the post-colonial period and especially during the late 1960s and the 1970s. Furthermore, to attribute self-interested economic calculation as the sole explanation of nationalist politics is to ignore the hegemonic and predatory intentions of global capital.

Notwithstanding the fact that public choice or rational choice theory originated in the process of analysing the political and economic behaviours of people in advanced countries, its development as the NPE, which has had the aforementioned implications with regard to developing economies, was inevitable considering its methodological individualism and the argument of government failure.

Regarding in particular the SAPs implemented in developing countries in the meantime, this researcher has tried to maintain a critical stance on their ideological orientation, which has prescribed structural adjustment of the international and national economies only at the expenses of poor classes and poor countries. In this regard, it should be mentioned that this research has tried to be free from the ideological implications of the government failure argument of the public choice school.

2-2. Stakeholders in the Reform Process

As mentioned in the introduction, this thesis intends to analyse the interaction of five socio-political groups on the process of the economic reform in Egypt in the 1990s. Those five groups are: the Egyptian state, the international donor group, the bourgeoisie, the opposition forces, and the mass public. This actor oriented approach was motivated by the public choice theory assumption of "interest groups", but the terminology and concept have been somewhat modified to "stakeholders" or "political actors". This is because this research assumed the roles of groups for which the conceptual boundaries are larger than the normal definition of interest groups. This section will present the logical framework for the identification of these five groups of stakeholders, and the conceptual boundaries will be described for each group.

2-2-1. Identification of the Stakeholders

The socio-political actors in the reform process could be grouped in a variety of ways according to how one conceptualised them. Because the SAP started from an agreement between the IMF and the Egyptian government, the donor group and the Egyptian state are easily identified as the most direct stakeholders in the process. However, as this research assumed that interest groups might have affected the process of the reform, those groups had to be identified. There were some reservations in this work. To function as a unit of analysis, the groups had to be conceptualised in macro-entities, so that the multiplicity of micro-entities might not compound the analysis. Also, as this research intended to understand the development of the Egyptian society as a whole through the analytical tool of the interaction of those groups, the groups had to be conceptualised in a way that could encompass major parts of existing socio-political forces in Egypt.

In this way, various business entities and relevant social forces were grouped into the category of the 'bourgeoisie'. Likewise, the various socio-political organisations acting generally as opposition forces against the government were grouped into the single category of 'opposition forces'. Included in this category were the legal opposition parties, labour unions, and the Islamists. The last group, the mass public, was considered to be another major political actor, because, despite its unorganised nature, the Egyptian government had always been apprehensive of street responses to the reform, and such sensitivity had certainly affected the speed and range of the reform measures.

Before and after conceptualising these stakeholders, the researcher tried to establish a theoretical background for these groupings. However, through the literature study on this subject, not many articles were found, especially in the context of structural adjustment in Egypt. Dieter Weiss and Ulrich Wurzel (1998) described the responses of various political groups, both internal and external, to the structural adjustment process. However, their identification of these groups was on an ad hoc basis rather than following well-defined and fixed conceptualisation. Ibrahim Awad (1991) analysed the influence of eight Egyptian socio-political groups on the process of the 1987 IMF agreement. However, his analysis, focusing only on the activities of formal and legal organisations such as political parties, labour unions, and business organisations, seemed to miss large parts of the socio-political forces in Egyptian society. Also, his approach, which explored each individual entity without synthesis, seemed inappropriate to the framework of this research.

Concerning the conventional class-struggle model held by the Marxist school, any specific article that approached the Egyptian structural adjustment case from this perspective was unavailable to the researcher. Mark Cooper (1983) presented the class structure of Egypt under state capitalism as follows: the indispensable private sector capitalists, the new upper class consisting of the elite and the technocracy, the state-centred middle class comprising public sector labour and bureaucracy, and finally the dependent underclass containing small peasants and the private sector proletariat. His article dealt with the changes of class structure under the state capitalism of Nasser and Sadat, but seemed to fail to provide enough insight into the interaction of socio-political forces in the structural adjustment course of the 1990s.

The article by Raymond Hinnebusch (1993) presented the interaction of four groups in the process of the structural adjustment in the 1990s, and it explored the subject in an approach closest to the intentions of this research. The four groups Hinnebusch chose were the international forces, the state, the bourgeoisie, and the mass public. However, he did not give any explanatory comments as to why he classified the actors in this way. Despite this lack of an explanation, the selection of five stakeholder groups in this thesis basically followed the line of Hinnebusch, adding the opposition forces to his four groups. Hinnebusch treated the responses of the organised opposition forces in the same category with the mass public, yet this approach seemed inappropriate to this researcher. Accordingly, this research separated the organised part of the opposition forces from the mass public, and added it as one more separate unit of the analysis.

In the view of this researcher, the identities of these groups as units of analysis are rather clear, and the selection of those groups as relevant stakeholders in the structural adjustment process also has ample justification. The international donor group and the Egyptian state have the positions of official sponsor and implementer of the reform. The commercial bourgeoisie has had a deep interest in the liberalisation policy and has tried to affect the course of the reform. The organised part of the opposition forces also tried in various ways to affect the process. The unorganised mass public had also affected the speed and range of the reform as mentioned above. All these facts will be presented in detail in later chapters, and they provide the justification for selecting those groups as the stakeholders in the structural adjustment process, regardless of the successes or failures of the activities of each group.

2-2-2. Conceptual Boundaries and Composition of the Stakeholders

Thus far, this research has presented the reasoning behind why certain socio-political groups were identified as the stakeholders in the structural adjustment process in Egypt. In the following, the researcher presents his conceptualisation of the boundaries and composition of each group.

The State

The definition of the term 'state' in the dictionary (http://yahoo.com) is "the supreme public power within a sovereign political entity". Anthony Giddens (2001: 421) explains the concept of the state as follows: A state exists where there is a political apparatus of government (institutions like a parliament or congress, plus civil service officials) ruling over a given territory, whose authority is backed by a legal system and by the capacity to use military force to implement its policies. Notwithstanding this classic concept of the term 'state', its usage has been widely adapted in modified forms in various social science writings. Frequently, it is identified as the same existence with 'government'. In certain cases, it is used to simply to refer to a 'regime', or a small group of ruling elite that governs a state. This is how Hinnebusch used the term in the article previously referred to. In this thesis, it will also be used in the same manner.

In the context of Egypt, the sate can be identified as the group of power elite in the government sector, who is represented by the president, and works closely in the clientelist system under the patronage of the president. (For more information about the clientelist and patrimonialism of the Egyptian state, see Chapter 4.) The normal state apparatus, including the bureaucracy and the military, serves the power elite and provides coercive forces for the regime. There can be internal conflicts and specific interests among the power elite. However, as they are officially commanded and controlled by the president, they do not stray far from the boundaries of the regime.

This cohesion reflects the fact that the Egyptian state is an authoritarian state where the president dominates all areas of politics. According to Giddens (2001: 424), authoritarian states are states in which popular participation in political affairs is denied or severely curtailed. In such societies, the needs and interests of the state are prioritised over those of average citizens, and no legal mechanisms have been established for opposing government or for removing a leader from power. Due to this authoritarian nature of the Egyptian state, Ayubi (1989: 2) called it a "presidential state". About these characteristics, more detailed explanation is given in Chapter 4, where the political structure of Egypt is explored.

The International Donor Group

The category of international donor group contains a number of international organisations and advanced countries that have provided financial assistance to help the process of the structural adjustment of Egypt. As the SAP began with the signing of loan agreements between the Egyptian government and the IMF, followed by the World Bank, it is obvious that the IMF and the World Bank are the first and most direct donors. However, several Western countries that have assisted the structural adjustment process by providing various types of financial assistance, including aids, loans, and debt reductions, are also considered to be important components of the donor group. Among these countries, the USA is the most important.

In fact, the relationship between the two Bretton Woods institutions and the advanced countries is inseparable. As international organisations, the ultimate owners, or shareholders of the IMF and the World Bank, are their member countries, and the voting power of each member is decided by the size of its contribution to those organisations' financial resources. In the case of the IMF, each member is assigned a quota, based broadly on its relative size in the world economy, and this quota determines the voting power of the member. As of 1999, the USA was the biggest shareholder of the IMF, holding 17.46% of the total quota. The other nations, in order of the size of the quota, are: Japan 6.26%, Germany 6.11%, United Kingdom 5.05%, and France 5.05%. Thus, the five countries alone take up a total of 39.93% of the whole quota (http://www.imf.org).

This implies that the USA and its major Western allies are in fact the most important components in the international donor group. Their special interests in the structural adjustment of Egypt are explored in Chapter 5.

The Bourgeoisie

The classic concept of bourgeoisie in the Marxist tradition refers to the class owning the means of production, as opposed to the proletariat – the class who does not own any means of production other than the selling of their labour. In normal usage, the bourgeoisie refers to industrialists or capitalists (Giddens, 2001: 284). In general communication, it seems that the bourgeoisie simply means the rich class. In this thesis, it indicates the group of entrepreneurs engaging in business activities in various fields. Nazih Ayubi (1991: 231), while stating the relationship between the state and the commercial bourgeoisie of Egypt under Mubarak, indicated the existence of three competing groups as fragments of the bourgeoisie: (a) a state bourgeoisie represented by public sector managers and technocrats, (b) an embryonic 'private' entrepreneurial class interested in all profitable investment opportunities, and (c) a parasitic 'economic mafia' of currency dealers and speculators, monopoly importers and smugglers, black marketeers, and so on.

To this researcher, the last two groups above seem to comprise the typical segments of the commercial bourgeoisie in Egypt. The first group of state bourgeoisie is in a complex position as an overlapping segment of both the state and the bourgeoisie. According to Ayubi (Ibid.: 221), while the state bourgeoisie of the 'socialist era' under Nasser still controls the State machine and a good proportion of the national economy, the commercial bourgeoisie of the Infitah (open door) era under Sadat is in control of the dynamic 'parallel economy' (of finance and trade). The relationship between the two elements is complex. Ayubi contends that although they have developed several symbiotic relationships, the two are by no means in full continuous alliance.

It has frequently been observed that since the 1980s the power of the commercial bourgeoisie has been on the rise. Taking advantage of the oil boom of the 1970s and the liberalisation policies begun with the Infitah in the Sadat era, the so-called Infitah bourgeoisie, or munfatihun (literally 'openers'), has emerged as a powerful social force. It has won a proliferation of tax exemptions and has affected changes of government policies in various ways. In fact, it had so successfully shaped the policy to favour its interests that Springborg (1989: 22) mentioned that it was more powerful than the president. About these influences of the bourgeoisie, more detailed explanation is given in Chapters 5 and 7. The point to mention in this section is that the commercial bourgeoisie has obviously held a big stake in the liberalisation policies of the SAP.

The Opposition Forces

In Egypt, there are many political and social formations that can represent anti-governmental voices. However, the political and social influences of these organisational forces, legal or illegal, are rather limited. The government strictly controls legal groups such as the formal opposition parties, labour unions, and professional syndicates, and many of the leaders in those organisations act as co-opted members of the establishment. Illegal groups such as Muslim fundamentalists have been severely repressed and marginalized. As such, the influence of opposition parties in the policy-making process is very limited, and considering this fact, it might easily be assumed that the role of the opposition forces in the structural adjustment process might not have been so great.

However, the government has worried that the opposition forces might spark public unrest. Especially, the rise in Islamic activities since the 1980s has added to the concerns of the government. And this kind of concern has prevented the Egyptian government and its donors from actively pursuing unpopular policies such as privatisation and subsidy cuts. In this regard, the opposition forces can also be regarded as one group of stakeholders in the reform.

The Mass Public

Even though the general public is unorganised and is subjected to severe constraints in participating in the policy-making processes due to the authoritarian nature of the Egyptian state, it has certainly had a hand in deciding the pace and range of the reforms. In many cases throughout the history of modern Egypt, the Egyptian public proved that, when in-system channels are closed, they could make their point outside in the streets (Ebeid, 1989: 22). Even in recent times, the massive food riot in 1977 and the para-military mutiny in 1986 illustrated this power (About these incidents, see Chapter 5).

Due to the concerns of the Egyptian government on these 'street reactions', it had hesitated to introduce orthodox-type reforms for a long time. In this regard, the mass public could be also regarded as one of the political actors in the reform process.

2-3. Supplementary Notes to the Research Questions

As stated in the first chapter, the purpose of this research is to understand the overall process and impacts of the structural adjustment programme of Egypt implemented in the 1990s from economic and socio-political perspectives. However, considering the broad subject of the research and the complex nature of the research questions presented above, extensive conceptual boundaries must be set.

Basically, the questions in this research run in parallel in the two areas of economy and politics. The focus in the economic area is to evaluate the performance of the reform as a programme aiming at the stabilisation of the macro-economy and the liberalisation of economic institutions. The approach here is to analyse the economic performance of the programme as a given policy, without judging such issues as whether such a programme was necessary or not. The evaluation of the performance will be made basically through an analysis of the changes of economic conditions before and after the reforms. Fieldwork experience and interviews complement a survey of the literature.

On the political side, the researcher confined the questions to identifying the roles and shares of the stakeholders in the reform. Basically, as an economic policy, the reform did not expose any political contents officially or explicitly. As such, the research on the political side is intended to excavate the hidden and implicit aspects of the reform. The questions on the political side arose from the aforementioned assumption that self-interest seeking political groups might have affected the formulation as well as implementation of the economic reforms. As a result, the questions are confined to ascertain the actual manifestation of this assumption.

This means that this research does not intend to deal with all the varied political subjects such as democratisation or political development issues. Only as a synthesis of the paralleled questions in economic and political areas are some implications of the economic liberalisation with regard to political development presented in the concluding chapter. However, as subjects such as this are not the main concern of the research, it will be only briefly stated.

One limitation that should be acknowledged is that, mainly due to the severe constraints on access to informants, especially in the opposition forces, the researcher could not penetrate into them fully. With the status of a foreign student in an authoritarian state, it was difficult to contact significant figures in the opposition forces. For instance, in December 2002, when this researcher tried to visit the Ibn Khaldun Center for Development Studies in Cairo, which has issued publications critical of the government, its director Dr. Saad Eddin Ibrahim was in jail and the office was closed. Also, contacts with other parts of the opposition forces were almost impossible. In contrast, however, contacts with public officials and business interests as well as academic officials were comparatively easier.

Accordingly, the stakeholder analysis is expected to have particular shortcomings due to the lack of direct information on the opposition forces and the mass public as well. This researcher tried to complement these shortcomings as much as possible through literatures surveys and indirect information collected in the field.

Chapter 3

Structural Adjustment Programme in the Global Context

"Structural adjustment" in economic policies is a commonly used general term that refers to certain measures to redress the problematic sectors of an economy. Every country in the world, developing or developed, implements forms of structural adjustment whenever it finds that some parts of its economic structure are seriously malfunctioning. However, since the 1980s, this terminology has come to acquire rather distinct usage to refer to the specific sets of economic policies that have been implemented by most developing countries under the financial auspices of the two Bretton Woods institutions, the IMF and the World Bank. "Structural Adjustment Programme" (will be called SAP hereafter) as the subject of this writing refers to the economic policies that have the distinct characteristics formulated by these two institutions.

3-1. The Origins of the Structural Adjustment Programme

The inception of the SAP has a direct connection with the official names of the new lending facilities of the two institutions. At first, the World Bank named its new loan to assist the macro-economic adjustment of developing countries as "Structural Adjustment Lending" (SAL) in 1980. Then, in 1986, the IMF introduced the "Structural Adjustment Facility" (SAF) that had an objective and function similar to the SAL of the World Bank. Since then, the economic adjustment programmes of the developing countries sponsored by these financial resources came to be known as the SAP[1].

The introduction of the SAP by the World Bank and the IMF in the 1980s accompanied a dramatic expansion of their influence, especially on Third World development. Prior to the introduction of SAPs, the role of the IMF had been largely confined to the assistance of temporary balance of payments problems, while that of the World Bank had been to provide assistance to specific development projects. But, with the launch of SAPs, the two institutions demanded a full-scale macro-economic adjustment and reform in the borrowing countries. Against the backgrounds that will be described soon, most developing countries have had to accept those conditonalities and have implemented wide-ranging reform programmes.

As it persisted and dominated the economic policies of developing countries throughout the 1980s and 1990s, the SAP, which was originally introduced as a shock remedy to adverse external impacts, came to take the place of development plans. Pointing to the policy characteristics of the SAP, John Toye (1996) dubbed it as a 'scaled-down development plan' or a 'development mini-plan'. However, in view of its influence on the global scale, it may fairly be said that the SAP has been the single most important economic development paradigm in the Third World during the late 20th century.

In fact, the intervention of the World Bank and the IMF in the economic policies of developing countries through the arm of SAPs has been very extensive and in detail. So, when Ankie Hoogvelt (1997: 167) said that the

---

[1] Stanley Please (1994) says that the term 'structural adjustment' was coined by the World Bank in 1980, but then it has since been 'hijacked' by the IMF to cover its own programmes. This statement from the former Vice-President of the World Bank connotes a deep dissatisfaction on the Bank's relation with the IMF.

intervention of those two institutions became matched and perhaps exceeded the direct administration of bygone colonial governments, it was not just an exaggeration or abuse of words.

Then, what factors can account for the development of this process? For what reasons, did the two Bretton Woods institutions invent the SAP and use it to intervene in the domestic policies of developing countries? Why have the developing countries had to accept the strict conditionalities suggested by the two institutions? The answers to these questions have emerged from a variety of perspectives.

3-1-1. Donors' Perspective

In the first place, there are explanations from the donors' perspective, which have been presented by the staff of the IMF and World Bank and other relevant practitioners. This stream tries to explain the development as an autonomous response from the donors to the changes of the environment in the international financial market and development finance, especially after the two oil shocks of the 1970s. It tends to emphasise the technical aspects of the introduction of SAPs, and shows some dissatisfaction with such arguments that attempt to see it in an ideological or political context.

Paul Mosley, Jane Harrigan and John Toye (1995) discussed this perspective, especially from the World Bank point of view. According to these authors, economic and political changes may have strengthened the move towards SALs, but they did not create it in the first instance. The original pressures came from inside the Bank itself, as it reassessed its own effectiveness. They described in detail how traditional project lending became increasingly problematic after the first oil shock and became even harder to pursue after the second oil shock of 1979. They identified factors such as shortfalls in the general economic framework under which every project has to operate, problems concerning project identification and appraisal, and shortages of complementary domestic resources as accounting for much of the difficulties.

Robert Cassen (1994) rather simply summarised the same reasons. According to Cassen, there was widespread dissatisfaction with the results of past aid to developing countries. A large share of projects had not performed well, and technical assistance was not producing positive results. Regarding this, many donors believed that a major part of the problem lay in the policy environment in which the projects were operating. As a result, structural adjustment was embraced by the donors as a more powerful instrument with which to promote development.

This view was similarly felt in the IMF, and the World Bank initiative with the structural adjustment influenced the IMF. According to Tony Killick (1995: 6-7), the World Bank's initiative called for a Fund response, to ensure that it was not overshadowed by the Bank and that it retained its leading role in macro-economic policy matters. Besides, the emergence of the debt problem in the early 1980s was a traumatic development that exerted a decisive influence on the policies of the IMF. The effects of the large debt-servicing burdens of the heavily indebted countries, and their greatly reduced access to world capital markets, shifted the adjustment - financing balance sharply towards adjustment

3-1-2. The Impacts of the Global Recession and the Debt Crisis

Even though the views from the donors' perspective provide many useful insights into the real facts behind the process, their indulgence in the rather minute details of the events may not provide a comprehensive picture on such a wide global phenomenon. Most importantly, their description lacks the perspective from borrowing countries' points of view, and those of other influence groups surrounding the donors. So, what factors influenced borrowing countries' perspectives?

To answer this question, the impact of the two oil shocks of the 1970s and the successive global recession into the early 1980s needs to be considered. The steep rise of oil prices aggravated the chronic balance of payment deficit problems in most developing countries, and raised the issue of macro-economic adjustment. Furthermore, successive economic crises in developing countries brought in a reflective atmosphere in development policies. As Biersteker (1995: 186-7) pointed out, by the early 1980s, there was already a growing sense of failure in many developing countries, a belief that the policies of the past had not worked and something new should be considered. In this atmosphere, the economic success of some Asian Newly Industrializing Countries (NICs) came to be illuminated as the success of a trade-oriented, open economy model.[2]

Furthermore, the traumatic experiences of the debt crisis in the Third World, during the early 1980s, decisively set the environment for the introduction of the SAP. By the early 1980s, the debt problems of developing countries were very serious due to their worsening balance of payments deficits and the increase in interest rates in developed countries to cope with inflation. When Mexico declared a moratorium on its debts in 1982, the global debt problems arose onto the surface. Now, all private lenders terminated lending to risky countries and as such, the international financial market tightened. Moreover, donor countries, now working through a lender cartel called as the Paris Club, called for the debtor countries to reach an agreement with the IMF on macro-economic reform as a precondition for the rescheduling of existing debts (UNRISD, 1994: 10).

---

[2]   As Robert Cassen (1994) indicates, the Lagos Plan of Action taken by the states of the Organization of African Unity (OAU) in April 1980 was just a manifestation of the recognition by African countries that things could not go on as before. But the development strategies suggested by the Plan were quite different from the SAP later.

3-1-3. The Rise of the New Right Neoliberalism

In developed countries, the complex stagflation since the 1970s seriously damaged the post-Second World War social compromise of the Keynesian welfare state model, and reinvigorated the New Right neoliberal economic ideas. State intervention in the economy was to be denounced, and the market was hailed again as the invisible hand of God that could guarantee the maximization of social welfare. This rise of the New Right was politically consolidated when the conservative political parties won the electoral victories in the very centre of the capitalist world, represented by Thatcher in the United Kingdom (1979) and Reagan in the United States (1980).

Paul Mosley et al.'s (1995:38) description shows how the SAP was related to the rise of the New Right: "Although the SAL was devised before the electoral successes of conservative parties in Europe and the United States, it quickly began to be seen as the instrument which could exert pressure on developing countries to follow orthodox liberal economic prescriptions of price reform and privatisation". Biersteker (1995:186) pointed out the direct connection between the SAP and the New Right, when he mentioned the willingness on the part of the U.S. government to use the Fund and the World Bank to force changes in developing-country economic policy during the early 1980s.

Thus, despite the practitioners' complaints about such claims, the ideological aspects of the SAP are clearly seen. In this respect, Adrian Leftwich's claim that the aim of adjustment was to shatter the dominant postwar, state-led development paradigm, by promoting open and competitive free market economies can get its justification (cited from Hoogvelt, 1997: 167-8). And considering the Cold War rivalry of the 1980s, one important implication of this ideological orientation of the SAP is easily reminded: that is, to incorporate the developing economies into the system of the Western Capitalism.

3-2. Main Features in the Policy Measures of the SAP

During the past two decades, the SAP has been implemented very extensively throughout most developing countries. Even though it has been diversely expressed in different official versions in each country, containing varying policy targets in detail, the SAP as a whole has had distinctively common policy guidelines and instruments. John Toye (1996: 102) dubbed this phenomenon as a "family resemblance", although his context was to defend the different characteristics of each SAP package.

The policy instruments of SAP have been deliberately designed to accomplish the commitments to a free market economy, setting its principal goal on the abolition of major barriers and distortions in market functioning. Even though the very purpose of the IMF and the World Bank was to serve the expansion of free trade and the development of the capitalist world, the distinct ideological tints and strict conditionalities of the SAP have been unarguably reinforced by the rise of New Right neoliberalism since the 1980s.

Preston (1996: 255) presented the series of New Right principles in five points. It is useful to address these five points in identifying the guiding principles of SAPs. These are: 1) any regulation of the market is to be avoided, save for crises and the removal of malfunctions and inhibitions to full functioning; 2) any intervention in the market is to be avoided, save to remove causes of price distortions, so subsidies should be abolished, tax rates adjusted to encourage enterprise, tariff barriers removed along with other non-tariff barriers or disguised restrictions; 3) any government role in the economy should be avoided, as private enterprise can usually do the job better; 4) any collective intervention in the market should be avoided, so labour unions must be curbed; 5) international trade should be free trade with goods and currency freely traded.

3-2-1. The Berg Report and the early SAP formulation

The characteristic features of the SAP were presented in their prototype form in the famous "Berg Report" of the World Bank, *Accelerated Development in Sub-Saharan Africa*, written by a team led by an American expert Elliot Berg in 1981. Analysing the economic crisis of Sub-Saharan Africa, the report explained how the political and social interests at work had produced perverse outcomes in policy-making. It then suggested the retreat of the state from economic activity as the best remedy for the economic crisis. A wide range of market fostering policy measures and a new export-oriented development strategy, especially in agriculture, were recommended as necessary options. The measures prescribed in this report, such as the deregulation of foreign exchange and trade, currency devaluation, reduction of budget deficit and public sector reform, soon became the basic components in the typical SAP formulation.

As Mosley et al (1995: 24) put it, the naivety of political analysis in this report and the sweeping nature of the liberalisation proposals was startling, and as such signalled a major change of course in the following years. During the World Bank Presidency of Clausen (1981-6), the Bank moved its focus rather dramatically from the poverty alleviation of the former Presidency under Robert McNamara (1968-81) towards neoliberal structural adjustment. Mosley et al. indicates that it would be wrong to suggest that the Bank was united during the Clausen period behind the brash doctrines of the Berg Report. However, the publications of the Bank in this period deliberately focused on the affirmation of neoliberal values. For example, one of the prominent authors, Bela Balassa (1981), asserted that the developing countries applying an outward-oriented development strategy were better able to cope with the external shocks of the 1970s than the countries following an inward-oriented strategy.

3-2-2. Stabilisation and Institutional Reform

As the World Bank intervened in the macro-economic adjustment of developing countries, its relation with the IMF was raised as a new issue. As was stated earlier, the IMF felt that the World Bank's initiative in structural adjustment lending carried the Bank into IMF territory, and it needed to work out new modalities of cooperation with the Bank.

According to Finn Tarp (1993: 59), the original dividing line in the roles of the two institutions implied that the IMF received guidance from the World Bank on development issues. In turn, the World Bank followed IMF advice on macro-economic and exchange rate policies, adjustment of temporary balance of payments disequilibria and stabilisation programmes. This original line reconciled the two institutions on their roles in the SAP. The IMF was supposed to have a lead role in macro-economic management, and the Bank was to concentrate on long-term structural matters.

As a result, the SAP in practice has been typically composed of two large parts. The first part was the macro-economic stabilization programme, based on the IMF philosophy. This programme called for strict austerity measures, such as the reduction of budget and current account deficits, control of the money supply and interest rates, and the devaluation of currencies. The other part was the structural reform programme propelled by the World Bank. This programme aimed at the abolition of major market barriers and called for various institutional reforms such as the deregulation of trade and foreign exchange, revision of the customs tariff, privatisation of public enterprises, and the control of labor unions.

If the characteristics of the two parts are examined, it can be seen that the latter part undertaken by the World Bank needed a longer-term perspective, and was a more difficult task that required a systemic change of institutions. And as such, that part was closer to the original ideas of the SAP as a presentation of the neoliberal ideologies. But the strict monetarist approach of the IMF programme was also an inevitable part of the ideas, and it went side by side with the World Bank programme complementing each other.

3-2-3. The Washington Consensus

The IMF (1985) contended that the SAP had been designed in accordance with the specific conditions of specific countries, and as such there had been no such thing as the 'typical' SAP. But, it also admitted that the policy objectives and instruments of the SAP had been limited, and as a result they had shown distinctively common features. It is apparent that this is just a play on words expressing the same thing differently, since it is clear that the SAP had been designed around the typical pattern of policy sets. These policy sets have often been referred to as the "Washington Consensus" presented by John Williamson (1994: 26-28). In fact, this consensus is basically a confirmation and concretisation of the neoliberal principles and the policy prescriptions of the Berg Report. The Washington Consensus as presented by Williamson calls for:

• **Fiscal Discipline**: reduction of budget deficits and the roles of state enterprises and the central bank

• **Public Expenditure Priorities**: redirection of expenditures from politically sensitive, but economically improper areas (administration, defence, subsidies)

• **Tax Reform**: broadening the tax base and cutting marginal tax rates

• **Financial Liberalization**: introduction of market-determined interest rates

• **Exchange Rates**: introduction of unified exchange rates set at a market-determined level

• **Trade Liberalization**: replacement of quantitative traderestrictions by tariffs and reduction of tariffs

• **Foreign Direct Investment**: abolition of barriers impeding the entry and activities of foreign firms

• **Privatization**

• **Deregulation**

3-3. The Lending Facilities and Process

In this part, the technical parts of the SAP will be presented to explain the real processes which underline the design and implementation of SAPs.

3-3-1. The IMF Lending Facilities

The types of credit arrangements ("facilities") the IMF extends to its member countries include regular facilities, concessional facilities for low-income countries, and various special facilities. Regular facilities include the traditional Stand-By Arrangement (SBA) and the Extended Fund Facility (EFF). The concessional facilities include the Structural Adjustment Facility (SAF) and the Poverty Reduction and Growth Facility (PRGF). The PRGF was newly created in September 1999, replacing the previous Enhanced Structural Adjustment Facility (ESAF). These facilities accompany the conditionalities that characterise the typical SAP.

In fact, most of the IMF programmes supported even by the traditional Stand-by arrangements (SBA) include some policies to address structural matters, and the EFF programmes since the 1970s have strengthened this tendency. However, due to the highly concessional terms of the lending, the SAF and ESAF have demanded the most strict policy guidelines, which have provoked the debates on the SAP.

The two types of regular facilities have different terms and conditions, but both provide credit on market-related terms. Stand-by arrangements typically cover periods of one to two years. Borrowing (Purchase) is made in instalments and repayments (Repurchase) are made in 3 to 5 years. Extended Fund Facilities generally run for three years and repayments are made in 4.5 to 10 years. These regular facilities also carry with them conditionalities focusing on macro-economic policies, such as fiscal, monetary, and exchange rate policies, aimed at overcoming balance of payments difficulties. The SBA programmes generally do not have a strong focus due to the short duration of the arrangements, but the EFF programs frequently have entailed strong structural adjustment measures.

The SAF and ESAF were set up in March 1986 and December 1987 respectively. With the launch of these facilities programmes, the IMF has explicitly expressed its intervention in structural adjustment. These facilities have been offered to low-income countries with highly concessionary terms. The PRGF that replaced the ESAF applies even more concessionary terms to poor countries. The interest rate on loans is 0.5 percent and repayments are made in 5.5 to 10 years. Under these facilities, the borrowing countries set up structural and financial policies for a rolling three-year period in a Policy Framework Paper (PFP), which has been documented jointly by the IMF and the World Bank. In the case of the new PRGF, the PFP has been replaced with Poverty Reduction Strategy Paper (PRSP). Detailed annual programmes are formulated within this framework that include quarterly benchmarks to assess performance. The loan disbursements are made annually in accordance with this assessment.

Besides these, there are a number of special facilities, which are additionally available in contingent situations. The Compensatory and Contingency Financing Facility (CCFF), set up in August 1988 replacing the previous Compensatory Financing Facility (CFF), is one of these special facilities.

3-3-2. The World Bank Facilities

The World Bank lending facilities are grouped into two categories: Investment lending and Adjustment lending. The former is the traditional project lending, while the latter is the policy-based SAP lending. In the latter group, the facilities are again divided into the Structural Adjustment Lending (SAL) and Sector-Adjust Lending (SECAL), both of which were set up in 1980. The SAL resources are provided across three years and accompany macro-economic adjustment programmes for the recipient countries. The SECAL resources are usually provided over four years, and require adjustment of specific sectors of the economy in the recipient country.

The World Bank also creates various special facilities that are used on a temporary and contingent basis. In 1985, it created the Special Facility for Sub-Saharan Africa to help the adjustment of the poorest countries in Africa. More recently in 1998, it created two new kinds of adjustment loans in a response to the financial crisis of East Asia and the successive global impact. The two facilities are the Programmatic Structural Adjustment Loan and Special Structural Adjustment Loan.

The facilities of the World Bank are provided through the two subsidiaries of the World Bank as a group: International Bank for Reconstruction and Development (IBRD) and the International Development Association (IDA). Each country in the world has a limitation on its eligibility for borrowing from each of these two institutions. Generally, the IDA provides funding for the poorest countries, while the IBRD takes charge in middle income countries. However, income is not necessarily the only standard, as some policy considerations also affect eligibility. Some countries under specific conditions are eligible for a blend of IBRD and IDA funding.

3-3-3. The Negotiation Process

As mentioned previously, the division of roles between the IMF and the World Bank became an issue and reached a compromise. According to Mosley et al. (1995: 102-3), the soon established convention was that any developing country in balance-of-payments difficulties should approach the Fund first for a stand-by credit, and that requests for Bank programme finance would be considered only after an agreement had been reached with the Fund. This convention had been strictly applied throughout the 1980s and is still effective even though the World Bank sometimes grants sectoral adjustment loans in the absence of any IMF stabilisation agreement. Table 3-1 shows how the Fund and Bank operations were sequenced in the 1980s in nine developing countries.

Table 3-1 Sequencing of Fund and Bank Operations

	1980	1981	1982	1983	1984	1985	1986	1987	1988
Turkey	`	B1	F/B1	F/B1	B1	B2	B2	B2	
Philippines	F/B1	F		F/B1	F	B2	F	B2	B2
Thailand		F	B1	B1					
Kenya	F/B1		F/B1	F		F	B2		F/B2
Ghana				F/B2	F/B2	F/B2	B2	F/B1	F/B2
Malawi	F	B1		F/B1		B1	F	F/B2	B2
Guyana	F	B1							
Jamaica		F	B1	F/B1	B1			F/B2	
Ecuador					F	B2	F		B2

Key: F   = IMF stand-by or Extended Facility credit

B1 = World Bank Structural Adjustment Loan

B2 = Other World Bank policy-based loan

Source: Mosley, Harrigan and Toye (1995: 103)

Once a country requests a loan with the submission of a Letter of Intent, the IMF and World Bank identify the problems of the country and negotiate the terms of borrowing. In the case of the SBA or EFF arrangements, a policy programme is prescribed typically stating the general objectives for the first year; policies for subsequent years are spelled out in programme reviews. In the case of the SAF and ESAF arrangements, this is presented in Policy Framework Papers (PFPs), which are drafted jointly by the borrowing government, the IMF and the World Bank. However, as Killick describes (1993:27), the role of the borrowing government in the process was often minimal, and the PFPs were written in Washington by Fund and Bank staff, with the Fund generally having the final say. Even though this situation has gradually changed to incorporate more government views, many governments still see the PFP as essentially a 'Washington document' in which their views and priorities are inadequately reflected.

The IMF and the World Bank have generally cooperated closely in the process so as to abide by the division of roles between them and to evade unnecessary cross-conditionality. However, despite their official announcements of the satisfactory level of cooperation, there are several accounts indicating that there are conflicts among them. Thus, Cassen (1994: 12) indicated that existing conflicts between the two organizations over issues in (African) adjustment would not stand up to public scrutiny. Partly due to these conflicts, and also due to the characteristics of the prescribed policies, cross-conditionality on specific countries occasionally has become a point of criticism.

3-3-4. The Lending Status: Aggregate Data

As shown by the IMF, as of the end of July 1999, it was financing 56 countries with 10 Stand-by Arrangements, 12 Extended Arrangements and 35 Extended Structural Adjustment arrangements. Only one country on the list, Azerbaijan, had two arrangements at the same time. The total lending commitment amounted to

SDR 54.9 billion (about 75 billion US dollars) of which SDR 32.1 billion (about 44 billion dollars) had been disbursed. The shares of the three arrangements in total commitments accounted for 71.1, 21.4 and 7.5 percent respectively.

One thing worth special note regarding these statistics is that only two countries, Korea and Brazil, took up 51.9% of the total agreed amount, each receiving SDR 15.5 and 13.0 billion respectively. Due to the financial crises of these two big economies, Korea in 1997 and Brazil in 1998, the Fund loan had to be increased by more than three times in two years, from SDR 17.9 billion in the middle of 1997 to the above-mentioned amount.

These crises also affected The World Bank loans. The World Bank data show that during its Fiscal Year 1999, new lending commitments recorded $29.2 billion, rising from $21.6 billion of the previous year and marking a new high record. What is especially worth mentioning in this context is that adjustment lending exceeded investment lending for the first time, reaching 15.3 billion dollars and taking up 52.4 percent of the total. Previously, the share of adjustment lending used to fluctuate between 20-30 percent of the total commitments. It increased markedly to 39 percent in FY 1998 and then again soared in FY 1999. This sudden increase in adjustment lending is largely attributed to the crisis in East Asia and the subsequent adverse impacts on international finance.

Due to the time series limit of the available data, it was difficult to derive statistics showing the accumulated lending performance of the two institutions. According to Killick (1995), the IMF approved a total of 353 arrangements during the period April 1979 - April 1993. Of these, 251 were Stand-bys, 33 were EFFs, and 21 were SAFs. Table 3-2 is cited from Mosley (2000) and it summarises the IMF lending performance during the 1990s. With regard to the World Bank statistics, Reed (1996: 10) shows that it had financed 267 macro-economic and sectoral adjustment programmes in 75 countries by 1992. Table 3-2 shows the trend of the IMF facilities during the 1990s.

3-4. Performance and Criticism

During the last two decades since the launch of the SAP, there have been heated debates over the impacts of the SAP on developing economies. A host of articles has been published over this issue, defending or criticising the performance of the SAP. So varied were the views that, as late as 1995, James Weaver (1995: 15) stated, "One must remain agnostic concerning the impact of structural adjustment. The evidence is not yet available to be able to judge the strategy's effect".

However, not withstanding the defences, the criticism especially on the adverse effects of the contractionary stabilisation programme and improper liberalisation programmes especially on the weaker side of social strata, has been very strong. This 'social impact' of the SAP became an acute issue for the IFIs, and it increasingly led to the pressure that something should be changed about the SAP itself. In the following part, an evaluation of the SAP will be presented based on a literature review, and some issues leading to the adjustment of the SAP will be discussed.

Table 3-2 IMF Disbursements to Developing Countries

(Billions of SDRs)

	1990	1991	1992	1993	1994	1995	1996	1997	1998	1999
Number of agreements in force	51	45	53	45	47	56	57	60	60	56
Lending from General Resources Account	29.0	31.8	23.4	24.6	25.5	32.1	36.2	34.5	49.7	60.6
Stand-by	6.0	7.0	9.4	10.5	9.4	15.1	20.7	18.0	25.5	25.2
(long-term)				(1.0)			(1.5)	7.0	13.0	4.0
Compensatory Facility			5.3	4.2	3.7	3.0	1.6	1.3	0.6	2.8
EFF	7.0	7.8	8.6	9.8	9.5	10.1	9.9	1.1	12.5	16.5
Trust Fund	0.3	0.2	0.2	0.1	0.2	0.2	0.1	0.1	0.1	0.1
SAF/ESAF	3.3	4.4	3.1	3.6	4.2	4.5	5.6	5.8	6.2	6.4
Total Disbursement	32.3	36.4	26.7	28.3	29.9	36.8	41.9	40.4	56.0	67.1
Total 'long-term finance'	10.6	12.0	17.2	15.0	17.6	17.8	18.7	25.3	19.4	29.8
Percentage of 'long-term finance'	32.8	32.9	64.4	53.0	58.8	48.3	44.6	62.6	34.6	44.4

Source: Paul Mosley (2000)

3-4-1. Difficulties of the Evaluation

The SAP in the meantime has been implemented very widely on a global scale in most developing countries. As such, its impacts on specific economies have been quite varied, making it very difficult to present a standard evaluation of the performance of the SAP. Difficulties in evaluating SAPs arise not only from the multiplicity of the countries that have implemented SAPs, but also from the complexity of the assessment itself. There are some distinct methodologies that have been used to evaluate SAP performance. Each method has its own merits and weaknesses. Some typical methods are as follows:

① Before versus After method: This method tries to compare the economic indicators of target countries during the periods before and after the SAP implementation. It is useful to know how the economic situation of those countries changed during the periods, but does not show what were the specific effects of the SAP in the changes. As Goldstein said 'it is useful to show what happened in programme countries, but not why it happened'. (re-cited from Mosley et al., 1995: 190)

② With versus Without method: This is a method that compares the economic performance of specific countries that have implemented the SAP with that of those countries that have not. Through this method, the performance of the SAP may be easily inferred if the research shows some distinct differences in the performance of the two groups. However, the main problem of this method is how to assure the comparability of the selected country groups. Besides, it cannot be simply concluded that all the differences relate to the results of the SAP itself.

③ Plan versus Actual method: This method compares the original targets of the SAP with the real performance. This may be useful in evaluating the extent to which the SAP achieved its planned targets. But it does not give any information on whether the original targets were realistic enough, nor what the costs of achieving the results were.

In addition to these simple tabular methods, other methodologies employing sophisticated regression and simulation techniques are also used. One attempt in these non-tabular methods is to analyse the 'counterfactual' effect of the SAP, trying to see what would have happened if the SAP had not been implemented. All the methodologies described so far can present some useful information on the performance of the SAP. But basically, they do not show the whole shape, and should be used complementarily.

3-4-2. Some Early Assessment

Not withstanding the difficulties of the evaluation, much research has been carried out to assess the performance of the SAP. One of the earliest studies on the overall performance of the SAP was published by the World Bank in 1988. The *Report on Structural Adjustment Lending* (commonly known as RAL I) evaluated the effects of the SAP focusing on Sub-Saharan Africa (SSA) and presented some negative evidence of the SAP performance: the SSA countries studied in the report experienced a fall in GDP growth to 1.8 percent growth after the adoption of adjustment programmes, compared to 2.8 percent growth prior to adoption. Also, investment ratios fell and budget deficits rose after the implementation of adjustment programmes (Berg, 1995: 95).

However, after that, the World Bank published reports showing a different evaluation. In 1989, the World Bank published a report titled *Adjustment Lending: An Evaluation of the Ten Years of Experience*. In this report, it adopted the 'with - without' method and compared the economic performance of 30 adjusting countries with that of 63 non-adjusting countries. Its conclusion was that, despite some problems, the SAP in general worked positively, as proved by the improvement of major macro-economic indicators in the former group (World Bank, 1989: 79-85). Another World Bank report published in the same year, *Adjustment and Growth in Africa in the 1980s*, came out with an even more positive assessment. It said that since the mid-1980s there had been signs of faster growth, and that this was the evidence that adjustment programmes were working: Economic performance of nineteen African countries with "strong reform programs" was better than other countries in the region, the report claimed (Berg, 1995: 95).

Strong criticism followed these reports of the World Bank. One of the most comprehensive analyses that showed the negative performance of the SAP was a report published in 1989 by the United Nations Economic Commission on Africa (UNECA). In this report, the UNECA contended that the economies of strongly adjusting countries in Africa had shown negative growth during the years 1981-87, while those of weakly adjusting or non-adjusting countries had grown positively. The UNECA especially criticised the devastating social impacts of the SAP, and called for a change of the SAP focus from contractionary macro-economic adjustment to the Socio-Economic Recovery and Transformation that would give more attention to employment and income distribution. This aspect of the UNECA report was presented as the African Alternative Framework to Structural Adjustment Programmes (AAF-SAP).

Another UN branch, UNICEF, also strongly criticised the devastating social impacts of the SAP especially on the poor people, women and children. It pointed to the aggravation of social welfare indicators such as nutrition, education and health as the serious failures of the SAP. These claims of UNICEF were presented in *Structural Adjustment with a Human Face*, co-edited by Cornea, Jolly and Stewart in 1987. Cornea showed how the SAP had negatively affected the growth and distributive equity aspects of the adjusting countries, leading to the expansion of poverty. He pointed out the improper policies of the SAP packages that led to the negative effects as follows:

① indiscriminate cuts in government health expenditure

② a radical reduction in real food subsidies

③ sharp increases in food prices

④ often regressive fiscal policies

Regarding this criticism, the IMF and the World Bank responded that the problems of the SAP would be short-term, temporary by-products of the adjustment process, and that those problems would be overcome as the adjustment process settled down (Riddel, 1992: 55).

3-4-3. Continued Debates and Criticism

Even in the 1990s, criticism of the SAP did not decrease. This was particularly evident in SSA, where the continued deterioration of economies had been accompanied by the implementation of SAPs. World Bank data (1999) shows the annual average growth rate of GDP in SSA during 1980-90 was a mere 1.8 percent, much lower than the World average of 3.2 percent. Considering the high population increase rate of over 2 percent annually, this meant that the per capita income of SSA had declined continuously. The situation in Latin America was not much better during the 1980s, but it improved in the 1990s. So, the SSA problem remained as the most controversial issue in the 1990s, and articles with such conclusive titles as "Why Structural Adjustment Failed in Africa" (Ayittey, 1995) were published. In this context, Elliot Berg (1995: 89), the author of the 1981 Berg Report, said that "The ghost of Raúl Prebisch may no longer roam in

Santiago, but it is alive in Addis Ababa".

A report presented by a UN agency, UNRISD, in 1994, showed aspects of the social impacts of the SAP, claiming that the combined impact of economic crisis and free-market reforms in Africa seemed to be reversing the process of modernization, by seriously damaging the capacities of societies to provide a minimal framework of stability and justice. The report showed how people in those societies attempted to find survival strategies as follows:

> "Furthermore the coping strategies adopted by many different kinds of people, as they confront severe challenges to livelihood, reverse earlier trends toward occupational specialization. Workers and civil servants in Africa, for example, are increasingly devoting a part of their time to farming on the outskirts of their towns, or in the countryside. Teachers and nurses in many countries now opt to supplement miserable salaries by opening small shops, selling street foods, and so forth. Professionals may drive taxis." (UNRISD: 1994)

According to the report, these responses of people to crises have caused the fragmentation of modern interest groups such as trade unions, professional associations and so forth, eventually leading to the erosion of the capacities of societies to provide stability to their populace. Thus, more underrepresented and unsecured people are likely to depend on traditional ties and more easily join violent and unorganised protests. It seems that this process can account for the growth of many religious fundamentalist movements in the Third World.

Killick (1995: 156-166) introduced some interesting streams of criticism on the SAP from both the political Left and Right. According to Killick, at the time of the fiftieth anniversary of the IMF and World Bank in 1994, a group of non-governmental organisations (NGOs) formed a campaign called 'Fifty Years is Enough'. The essence of their criticism was that the IMF and World Bank programmes were causing deflation in borrowing countries, widening income inequalities and worsening the welfare of the poor, jeopardising prospects for sustainable recovery and poverty reduction. Accordingly, they called for a change of the defective and discredited adjustment policies especially in Africa with policies that do work. Some radicals asserted that the IMF and World Bank should be wound up (hence '50 years is enough'), or called for the phasing out of the ESAF.

According to Killick, critics on the political Right were scarcely less sweeping. Milton Friedman put it, "With the collapse of the Bretton Woods in 1971, the original function for which the IMF was established simply disappeared. But instead of closing down, the IMF turned itself into a junior World Bank". For some of these critics too, abolition of the Fund and the Bank was the answer (Ibid.: 157)

Now, facing this criticism, the IMF and World Bank could not present positive affirmation of their lending activities. Although the World Bank's Report on Adjustment Lending II(1990) contended that the adjusting economies performed better than the others, subsequent reports have presented contradictory results (Weaver, 1995: 10). In a report published in 1992, the World Bank (1992: 10) concluded the overall evaluation of the SAP performance as follows:[1] "After several years of adjustment operations, countries seem to fall into two broad categories: those that have emerged from severe disequilibria into sustainable

---

[1] Regarding the World Bank's evaluation of the SAP performance, Ankie Hoogvelt (1997: 170) introduced an interesting behind-the-scenes story based on a report in *The Economist*, 5 March 1994. According to Hoogvelt, it was "so disappointing that a World Bank-sponsored report in 1992, given the frank title 'Why Structural Adjustment has not Succeeded in subSaharan Africa', was retrieved from the publisher, re-issued with a less controversial title ... Since then the World Bank has issued a more upbeat report on the lessons of structural adjustment in subSaharan Africa."

growth, and those that are trapped in a cycle of low saving, low investment, and low growth."

The IMF's appraisal of its own activities was not much different from this. In a report of 1995 that examined the performance of 36 adjusting countries, the IMF presented a conclusion almost similar to that of the World Bank: the performance of the fund programme was mixed, showing some positive signs in overall macro-economic indicators with some disappointments in some sectors and regions.

In fact, this kind of conclusion nowadays seems to have become a standard evaluation of the SAP performance: the results have been mixed at best, and something should be changed about the SAP.

3-4-4. Some Defences

Some authors have tried to mitigate the harsh criticism on the IMF and the World Bank. Michael Chege (1995)'s following statement seems to show this line of argument: "If the World Bank and the IMF have earned themselves undue criticism and resentment in Africa over the past decade, it is primarily because they have taken initiatives in the formulation, financing, and implementation of socially painful economic liberalization programs in a frontal effort to meet the onerous development problems". Stanley Please (1994), formerly Vice President of the World Bank, expressed the feelings of the concerned staff when he wrote that structural adjustment "almost became a term of abuse by those wishing to be indiscriminately critical of the IMF and World Bank".

Berg (1995: 90) refuted the critics outright. He claimed that the criticisms were not well-founded because better strategies for adjustment and growth did not exist. He contended that the growth record did not permit the conclusion that the orthodox adjustment programmes had failed, and that there was little evidence to support the charge that the adjustment programmes of the 1980s hurt Africa's poor.

Killick (1995: 122) is also in this stream, and he is more positive in defending the IMF. He refuted the criticism from both the Left and Right, and based on the results of research undertaken by the Overseas Development Institute (ODI) in London, presented this conclusion:

> "Perhaps the most central conclusion emerging from the evidence ... is that it is difficult to understand the fierce controversies which have surrounded IMF programmes in developing countries, and the dramatically opposed positions that are sometimes taken up. Although, for different reasons, it suits both the Fund and its critics to assert that its programmes have large effects, for good or ill, the evidence presented here suggests otherwise. ..... Overall, then, the message is that the Fund has limited ability to achieve its objective and to assist deficit governments".

Killick's conclusion can be expressed more succinctly in his following statement in the same book, of which the context was to summarise the conclusion of his previous publication: "Overall, to mix our Shakespeare, the sound and fury of the controversies about Fund programmes seemed much ado about nothing". (Ibid.: 2)

However, considering the volume of studies that show the impacts of the SAP, be they negative or positive, it is rather doubtful whether Killick's discounting of the influence of the SAP itself could be fully justified.

3-5. Adjustment of the SAP

Certainly, it would be too much to say that the overall performance of the SAP is a failure. However, the failures of the SAP have been serious enough to shade its successes. Cassen (1994) indicated the failures of the SAP as errors of estimation, errors of judgement, and errors of strategy. His point is that the World Bank and IMF estimated or judged the policy targets wrongly, based on excessive optimism especially about the speed of the reform. He seems to indicate that the SAP has had from its design stage the defects that might lead to the performance failure.

Responding to the criticism discussed so far, the IMF and World Bank have tried to adjust the SAP to the desired direction. Even though there are still many debates over the desirable way of structural adjustment and over whether the two Bretton Woods institutions are working in such a direction, it might be useful to examine how the Fund and the Bank have tried to correct the defects of the SAP.

3-5-1. Reinvigorating Growth and Alleviation of Poverty

Killick (1995) presented how the IMF has changed its policy approaches responding to the criticism of the SAP. According to Killick, the IMF has modified the program objectives considerably to incorporate economic growth enhancing measures and to reduce the adverse social impacts. Being conscious of the criticism that its hard stance on demand control has led to the protracted recession and the expansion of poverty, the IMF has tried to be more flexible in setting its guidelines. Furthermore, an increasing number of programmes have contained some safety-net provisions to help socially weaker groups that are more vulnerable to the shocks of the adjustment. In addition, the creation of the PRGF replacing the ESAF in 1999 was clearly one of the most distinct responses of the

IMF to the criticism.

The changes of the IMF's approach are also visible in the recent issue of the "Country Ownership of Programs". According to the IMF (2001), it has recently engaged in a comprehensive analysis of the conditionality and ownership issue, and has solicited the views of the public on this matter. The ownership issue arose from a concept that policy content of the program should be similar to what the recipient country itself would have chosen in the absence of IMF involvement. According to the IMF, it has tried to foster the ownership through some measures so that the country is committed to the spirit of the program, rather than just to complying with its letter. The introduction of the aforementioned PRSP is said to be based on this very concept of country ownership of the programme.

The same mood of changes in the IMF position can be seen in the phrases in another report (1997) such as "From Conditional Financing to Financed Conditionality". A report from the IMF(2001) titled "Economic Growth and Poverty Reduction in Sub-Saharan Africa" also shows its increased concern on the social impacts of the SAP. However, as will be discussed in the next section, many critics still contend that there have been no significant changes in the practices and basic position of the IMF.

The World Bank has also tried to show its adjustment efforts. According to Mosley et al. (1995: 134-135), the Bank's then latest assessments of policy-based lending stressed the need for shorter lists of conditions, more tightly policed, with 'key conditions' identified and a higher down-payment. According to the writers, the shift from the SAL to the SECAL mode of financing is itself a response to the problem of overload.

The Bank's changes in the SAP policies seem to be more distinct in its recent emphasis on poverty alleviation The recent *Annual Report* of the World Bank (1999) stresses the serious expansion of poverty as its main focus of concern. Emphasis on the adjustment and reform looks rather scarce. Furthermore, its new strategy of Comprehensive Development Framework (CDF) launched in FY1999, stresses flexibility and partnership with relevant authorities, which is certainly a response to the criticism on its rigidity in policy design.

Coming to more recent times, the World Bank under the Presidency of James Wolfenson, seems to be more determined to focus its activities on poverty alleviation. *The World Development Report of 2000/2001* is subtitled "Attacking Poverty" and states in the Foreward as follows: "Poverty amid plenty is the world's greatest challenge. We at the Bank have made it our mission to fight poverty with passion and professionalism, putting it at the center of all the work we do." A recent World Bank report (2000), written by Dollar and Kraay and titled "Growth Is Good for the Poor", shows how the World Bank is approaching the issue of growth and poverty alleviation now.

3-5-2. Limitation of the Changes

Despite the efforts to adjust the SAP, critics have contended that the core elements of the SAP have been kept rather intact. With regard to the IMF programmes, Killick (1995: 22) said that "important changes … have not incorporated fundamental movement on the provisions that have traditionally formed the bedrock of Fund programmes: restriction of domestic credit creation and budget deficits, and currency devaluation". He expressed this in another way as follows: there has been no retreat on the eternal verities of fund conditionality. This expression might be fairly applied to the World Bank position. According to Mosley et al (1995: 135), "there is no sign of lists of conditions shrinking or the level of implementation improving".

Even as late as 2000, Joseph Stiglitz furiously criticised the IMF's inertia and its sticking to conventional, contractionary policy prescriptions especially for the recent financial crises in East Asia and Russia. He said, "The IMF inertia was so hard to stop but because, with everything going on behind closed-doors, it was impossible to know who was the real obstacle to change". The harsh criticism from the winner of the 2001 Nobel Prize for Economics vividly describes the practices of the IMF from an insider's view, and his narration of an episode raises a sense of frustration for the people who have to accept the policies presented by the staff of the IMF, completely irresponsible for the fortunes of the former. The episode reads:

> "I heard stories of one unfortunate incident when team members copied large parts of the text for one country's report and transferred them wholesale to another. They might have gotten away with it, except the "search and replace" function on the word processor didn't work properly, leaving the original country's name in a few places. Oops."

To conclude, the two Bretton Woods institutions, designed and set up as financial bumper stock for the capitalist world order, have certainly their own raison d'être and purposes of activities. 'Free market and free trade' is inseparably associated with these purposes. However, the SAP as a development paradigm with the distinct ideological tints of the New Rights is irrevocably linked with the politics of the international economy. It has been designed and implemented in the structure of power relations between the developed and developing countries, and as such, it is not easy for the SAP to change in its basic tenets unless such structure dramatically changes.

The political aspect of the SAP is briefly but vividly illustrated by an episode presented by Paul Nelson (1995: 136-7). When NGO members complained in the 1989 NGO-World Bank Committee meeting that the Bank had unfairly placed the entire burden of global adjustment on the poor countries that could afford it the least, one World Bank representative advanced the response: "The Bank cannot be expected to criticize too sharply the countries that guarantee or provide the lion's share of its funding. 'These are our bosses,' ho noted, and there are limits to what the Bank can do."

This episode illustrates, as Nelson indicated, that the Bank is powerless to implement the portions of its advice that apply to the national economic policies of the North. And it then shows the basic limitations of the SAP, which should consider the interests of the major shareholders.

Chapter 4

The Structure of Political Economy in Egypt

Strategically located at the nexus between Asia and Africa, while confronting Europe right across the Mediterranean, Egypt has been always one of the most important countries in the Middle East. Let alone the glorious history as one of the world's earliest civilisations, Egypt even in modern times has played an unusually important role in the region and in world politics. It has always been a leading power among the some 20 Arab states, and was also in the forefront of the Non-Align Movement. Egypt's strategic position was even more strengthened with the opening of the Suez Canal, which is one of the most critical points in world maritime transportation. Due to the control of this Canal, Egypt has occasionally been entangled in serious international conflicts, and even became involved in a war with concerned powers.

However, despite these strategic positions and critical roles, the present political and economic situation of Egypt is much less bright. Politically, Egypt's domestic conditions do not allow for a positive affirmation of democracy, the participation process and social stability. Economically, despite the reform and improved performance of recent years, Egypt is still suffering from a per capita income as low as 1,200 US dollars, and high unemployment. The high rates of population increase and the massive urban concentration of people continue to compound this situation.

The purpose of this chapter is to present some background knowledge on the political and economic structure of Egypt. After a brief description of the present situation, the chapter explores the historical context of economic development and in particular focuses on the changes in economic policies.

4-1. The Land and People

Egypt has a comparatively vast land territory of 1,001 thousand square kilometres, which is approximately double the size of France, and nearly five times larger than Great Britain. However, the problem with this vast land is that most of it is barren desert, with only 4 percent of it arable. As Herodotus called Egypt "the gift of Nile", the Nile River is almost the sole source of life in Egypt, where rainfall averages only an inch or two a year. Almost all food crops in Egypt come from the acreage within reach of irrigation from the Nile River and 99 percent of the people live along the Nile Valley that is never wider than just a few miles from the river. So, the populated area in Egypt is not larger than the total land area of Holland, and the population density of this area surpasses that of Holland, which is already one of the most densely populated countries. (Congressional Quarterly Inc., 1991)

Table 4-1 Key Facts for Egypt 1998

Area	1,001 thousand km^2 (386,661 square miles)
Population	61 million
Growth	2.65 % (1991-98 annual average)
GNP	79.2 billion dollars
GNP Per capita	1,290 dollars
GNP Increase Rate	4.6 % (1991-98)
Structure of Output	Value Added as % of GDP
Agriculture	17
Industry (Manufacturing)	33 (26)
Service	50
Exports	3,908 million dollars
Imports	13,600 million dollars
Total External Debt	29,849 million dollars
Debt Service Ratio	20.3 % of Exports
Exchange Rate	3.39 £E/US$

Source: The World Bank (1999)

Divided by the Nile Valley, in the western part of Egypt lies the Western (Libyan) Desert and in the eastern part the Eastern (Arabian) Desert. The former comprises about two-thirds of the whole country. It is a low plateau punctuated by depressions and basins, some of which form oases, and the great Sand Sea. The latter is a sloping plateau that develops into dry, barren hills until it reaches the Red Sea. There, and in the mountainous Sinai Peninsula across the Red Sea, the habitation is confined to a few seaside villages and some nomadic Bedouin groups herding their flocks.

Cairo, the capital, is the dividing point between Upper and Lower Egypt. The former is the region to the south of Cairo. It is a thread of villages and towns about 650 miles long that clusters on the banks of the river and terminates in Aswan.

Here the people have been more isolated from the outside world and thus are still traditional today. Lower Egypt is the triangular region on the estuary of the river. There, the Nile River is divided into many branches flowing into the Mediterranean, creating a fertile "Delta". The major cities of Cairo, Alexandria and Port Side are the three points of the triangular shaped region that compasses within about 100 miles from each of them.

The overwhelming majority of the population and their activities are centered in Lower Egypt. About a quarter of the 61 million population of Egypt lives in and around Cairo, making it the biggest metropolis in Africa and the Middle East. In this capital city are concentrated all the major social institutions of public and private sectors. However, the massive concentration of people there has overwhelmed its basic municipal service capacities, causing serious traffic congestion, housing shortages and other social problems. Due to the continuous inflow of people, the city is still stretching outward into the desert.

Alexandria, the second largest city with some 3 million population, is a thin strip of land on the seashores of Mediterranean. Since ancient times, this city has maintained more Mediterranean ties than any other city in Egypt. The three cities of Port Said, Ismailiya and Suez, in the Suez Canal area, all with population of about half a million or less, are modern cities living on the international traffic that plies the canal. So, all these cities tend to be more oriented to the outside world than the rest of the country.

The population of Egypt has been growing very fast. Within three decades, the population has almost doubled from 33 million in 1970 to 61 million in 1998. This rapid population increase brings with it serious economic and social problems. As the economic growth in the meantime has been very sluggish, the per capita income of Egyptian people has grown very little, from 205 dollars in 1970 to a mere 1,290 dollars in 1998. Considering the high inflation rate, this low increase of income implies that the standard of living for the average Egyptian has been seriously aggravated. As the economy could not provide enough jobs for the growing population, unemployment and underemployment have become a widespread social phenomenon.

However, Egypt's population is relatively homogeneous in ethnic and religious terms, and this gives the people a strong national identity. Descended from ancient Nile Valley inhabitants, Egyptians have somewhat intermixed with Mediterranean and Asiatic peoples in the north and with black Africans in the south. Since the Arab conquest of the seventh century, these people became Arabised and Islamised. As a result, 98 percent of the Egyptian people nowadays speak the Arabic language as their mother tongue and almost 90 percent of them believe in the Sunni sect of the Islamic religion. Minorities include Bedouins (Arabic speaking desert nomads), Nubians (black descendants of the migrants from Sudan), and the Copts (a Christian group).

4-2. The Political Structure

Egypt became a republic after the three years of military rule headed by Gamal Abdel Nasser, who led a successful coup d'etat against the monarchy of King Farouq in July 1952. Since then, Egypt has seen three presidents: Gamal Abdel Nasser (1956-70), Anwar Sadat (1970-81), and Hosni Mubarak (1981-present). All three presidents came from a military background. This was itself a part of the broad legacy of the coup d'etat or revolution, which has greatly affected the political culture and structure of present day Egypt. In addition, the distinct personalities and policies of the two predecessors have also bequeathed deeply influencing political legacies to the incumbent reign of Mubarak.

4-2-1. Constitutional Framework

Since the revolution of 1952, Egypt has been ruled under six constitutions. Among them, the Constitution of 1971 is the most recent one, which is still in effect. According to the constitution, the President is the most important office as the Head of the Republic, the head of the government, and the supreme commander of the armed forces. His power is vastly endowed by the constitution, but in reality even transcends all the legal regulations.

According to Article 77 of the Constitution, the President is nominated by a two-thirds majority of the People's Assembly. Then the Assembly's decision must be ratified by a popular plebiscite. Once ratified by the plebiscite, the President serves a six-year term, but can be re-elected indefinitely, as there are no limits on the number of terms. Mubarak was re-elected in October 1999 by a 95% vote of the people for his fourth consecutive term.

The president can appoint and dismiss all major officials, including one or some vice presidents, the prime minister, all the members of the Cabinet, military officers and the governors of the twenty six administrative subdivisions known as governorates (muhafazat). In the absence of the president, a vice president can succeed the presidency; this was seen in the cases of Sadat and Mubarak as they succeeded their predecessors. But until now, Mubarak himself has not appointed any vice president.

The legislative body of Egypt is composed of two chambers. The lower People's Assembly (Majlis al-Shaab) has 454 seats, of which 444 are elected by a direct vote of the people. The remaining 10 are appointed by the president. The members of the Assembly serve a five-year term. In the latest election, held in November 2000, the ruling National Democratic Party (NDP) took an overwhelming 88% of the total elected seats. The upper legislative body, or the Consultative Council (Majlis al-Shura), has 264 seats and functions only in an advisory role for the president.

4-2-2. The Presidential State: Clientelist and Patronage

As Ayubi (1989: 2) put it, Egypt is a presidential state. As seen in many developing countries, the Egyptian president holds extensive powers and dominates all areas of Egyptian politics. Any important policy or project must normally have the 'blessing' of the president before it can proceed. The president controls all the legislative processes, and he can issue decrees that have the force of law. All the members of the parliament, especially from the ruling party, are selected by the president for their candidacy, and in fact the parliament has never checked the will of the president.

As Kassem (1999:32) indicates, this dominant position of the president is the most salient aspect of the legacies of the revolution. It was institutionalised as early as 1953, when the provisional constitution formally accorded the "leader of the Revolution" the power to take any steps deemed necessary to protect it. Then, the personal charisma of Nasser added unusual power to the legal authority of the president. Sadat, who inherited this powerful position, even expanded the power by eliminating the two-term regulation of the constitution in 1980.

Mubarak succeeded the presidency after the assassination of Sadat by a member of the militant Islamic group, Jihad, in 1981. Though he was the then vice-president, Mubarak was deemed a junior member in the political ranks. However, once he took the position of the president, Mubarak swiftly eliminated possible competitors and consolidated his power base. He took advantage of the strength of the official power of the president in this process.

Now, it is widely indicated that Egyptian politics is a process of elite recruitment into the Establishment under a system of clientelist and presidential patronage. With so much power concentrated in the presidency, the political influence of specific individuals is decided by their closeness to the president. Thus, his confidants, whether they have held high office or not, are usually counted among the core elite. For example, a multimillionaire capitalist, Osman Ahmad Osman, who had a marital linkage with Sadat, was long regarded as the second most powerful man in Sadat's Egypt (Metz, 1991: 238).

The party system and the election process are also nothing more than an instrument for this process of elite recruitment under the clientelist system. Since the Revolutionary Command Council (RCC) banned all existing political parties in 1953, there have always been severe restrictions on political parties. Until Sadat instated the multi-party system in 1977, Egypt had long been ruled under a mono-party system. Even the ruling parties of the time had been dismissed and reorganised at the president's will: they were transformed into the National Union (1957), the Arab Socialist Union (1962), and the present National Democratic Party (1977). They have been simply an instrument of mass mobilisation and control, and recruitment of the new elite (Borthwick, 1980).

Even the multi-party system is far from a real participatory democracy. Although there are six opposition parties in parliament, they are severely controlled by the regime. As a result, the general elections have always resulted in a sweeping majority for the ruling party. Kassem (1999) analysed the function of the non-competitive multi-party election in Egypt as a process of co-option and control to incorporate opposition powers into the Establishment by giving them the chances to share national resources, so that otherwise underground resistance forces could be easily controlled.

Another major aspect of this multi-party system is its external utility. As Kassem (1999: 6) described, one of the main reasons why Sadat authorised the multi-party system was to appeal to the Western sources of support. It was believed that the political reform would make it "easier for the president and the US congress to provide aid, while very much reducing the possibility that Egypt will be criticised for human right abuses". And this intention is still in effect in Mubarak's reign.

4-2-3. Civil Unrest and the Mass Participation

In a country where the president and his entourage monopolise national resources, and where formal opposition parties do not represent any public base, the masses often express their discontent with demonstrations on the streets. Starting from the anti-imperialism riots in the early twentieth century, many occurrences of mass riots in Egypt led to significant changes in government policies or to the downfall of a regime. So, as Borthwick (1980:172) indicated, these demonstrations have become an established, but not legitimate, part of the political process.

Ayubi (1989:1) has analysed that, as complex legacies of the Nasser and Sadat eras, the dominance of presidential power in Egyptian politics is not simply a pure blessing for the president. It burdens him with the responsibility of satisfying the needs of the growing population, as well as of keeping secure the patronage system. However, in recent decades, this job has become harder, as the Egyptian economy has performed very poorly for a long time. As the economy fails, the once inflated hope of national independence and modernisation has waned, and as poverty and unemployment prevails, the frustrated masses have come to discredit the leadership, turning to alternative source of authority. This is why Islamic fundamentalism is regaining a social base.

Even inside the elite groups who are under presidential patronage, some serious signs of discontent have been amply manifested. As Ebeid (1989: 48) has indicated, if political opposition has to be destroyed, co-opted, or cajoled, the leaders should be able to resort to a number of economic policy instruments to do what is necessary: new investment or credit cut-offs, higher salaries or lower ones, price freezes or increases. Ever since the establishment of a state-controlled economy in the 1950s, Egyptian presidents and their close entourage have been able to use these economic levers for political purposes. However, with the economy stagnating or dwindling for a long time, the availability of these levers has seriously decreased until recently.

In this context, Cassandra warned in 1995 of an impending crisis facing Egypt, which meant that the political and economic system could potentially collapse. As will be discussed in the following chapters, this situation was the most important factor that drove Sadat to implement the Infitah (Open-Door) policy, and again for Mubarak to introduce the Structural Adjustment Programme. The key consideration was that they badly needed external sources of financial resources to help break through the dilemmas they faced.

4-2-4. Islamic Fundamentalism

In the past 20 years or so, Islamic fundamentalism has drawn a new attention to the politics of the Middle East and Egypt. In the regional context, as Hoogvelt (1997: 182) has indicated, the defining moment in this trend was no doubt the overthrow of the Shah's pro-western monarchy in Iran in 1979, and the establishment there of the modern world's first theocratic state. In the Egyptian context, it was dramatically expressed to the outside world by the assassination of President Sadat in 1981 by a fundamentalist Islamic group, Jihad.

The concept of Islamic fundamentalism can vary according to how it is defined. As is the same in most Middle Eastern countries, most of the Egyptian people believe in the Islamic religion, and in fact, the Egyptian state itself officially announces through its constitution, that "Islam is the religion of the state". However, there are varied tendencies in the religious movement, and among them, a certain tendency is associated with the concerned Islamic fundamentalism. According to Ibrahim (1988: 632), the tendencies in Islam in Egypt can be labelled as "establishment Islam", "Sufi Islam", and "activist Islam". Among these, the last one contains the fundamentalist factors that raise political issues these days.

Establishment Islam is symbolised by Al-Azhar, the Muslim world's oldest university. It is the centre of Islamic teaching and spiritual guidance. Previously, it had been an important lobbying institution for the powerless Egyptian masses vis-à-vis their despotic rulers. However, since the time of Muhammed Ali (1805-48), the founder of the modern Egyptian state, it has been incorporated into the state system. Nowadays, the Ministry of Religious Endowments (Awkaf) controls Al-Azhar and all the mosques in the nation (Ibrahim, 1988).

Establishment Islam is now an easily manipulated tool of the Egyptian state. It can be counted on to issue pronouncements (fatwa) to legitimise government policies. This situation has led to an erosion in the credibility of establishment Islam. However, it still commands considerable respect and prestige with common Egyptians. It controls some 10,000 mosques, hundreds of secondary educational institutions and several provincial branches of Al-Azhar university. It has monopoly access to the state-controlled media, especially radio and television.

Sufi Islam is known for its puritanical spiritualism and retreat from worldly concerns. It seeks human salvation and eternal peace through minimum involvement in societal affairs. There is little information available on the membership of Egypt's Sufi orders (ibid.).

Activist Islam is the tendency that is more politically and socially oriented, and this tendency is more often dubbed as Islamic fundamentalism. It defies the Western-influenced, secular-tainted socio-political systems in present Muslim societies, and advocates restoring the pure form of Islamic governance and ethics. The activists criticize their ruling elites as deviants from the pure paths of Islam, and claim that a 'holy war' (jihad) against these infidels is needed to restore Islamic governance.

Most authors agree that contemporary Islamic activism in Egypt has its roots in the Muslim Brotherhood (MB), which was established by Hassan al-Banna in

1928. According to Ibrahim (1988: 640), the MB has politicised Islam as no other indigenous popular movement has ever done in Egypt's history. Ayubi (1989: 72-73) contends that mainstream Islamic 'salafism' (fundamentalism) is best represented by the MB, and that it could be regarded as the oldest and most established movement of 'political Islam'.

Throughout its seventy years of history, the MB has had ups and downs in its membership and activities. After its attempt on Nasser's life in 1954, it had been severely cracked down upon by the Egyptian state and had been marginalized. Thousands of its members were jailed and several prominent leaders were executed, including top theoreticians such as Abdel Qader in 1955 and Sayyed Qutb in 1965.

Then, its remaining leaders made a conscious decision to give up violence and to carry out its opposition to the regime peacefully. It was this decision that caused several splits in the MB, and splinter groups continued their confrontation with the state (Ibrahim, 1996: 63). Among the splinter groups, three major groups, the Jihad, the Takfir wa al-Hijra, and the Gamaat al-Islamiya have had violent confrontations with the Egyptian state since the 1970s (Ibrahim, 1996: 72).[1] In 1974, another autonomous group, the Islamic Liberation Party – also known as Muhammad's Youths – attempted to take over the Technical College near Cairo to seize the weapons there and to capture or kill the President and declare the establishment of an Islamic state. In October 1981, the Jihad group succeeded in assassinating the President Sadat during a military parade commemorating the October 1973 war (Sagiv, 1995: 48-61).

After the assassination of Sadat, the Emergency was proclaimed and a severe crackdown upon the Islamists was launched by the government, which led to a temporary lull of their activities. However, the militant groups launched a new

---

[1]   About the details of the births of these splinter groups, see David Sagiv (1995)

wave of violent attacks in the early 1990s, and had violent clashes with the Egyptian state throughout the 1990s, which was the period when the reform, ERSAP, had been promoted. However, after an incident by a Gamaat cell in Luxor in November 1997 that killed 68 foreign and Egyptian tourists, the militants' movement has apparently waned due to the severe crackdowns by the state and the indifference of the general public toward their activities (Gerges, 2000).

In the meantime, the MB has kept its promise of non-violence and has taken a gradualist approach in seeking its objective, which is to change Egypt into a pure Islamic state. But during the Mubarak reign, this gradual approach has reaped considerable success and the MB has evolved into a viable and effective opposition force. Its multi-pronged strategies by far have proved to be very successful. Some of these strategies are parliamentary participation through alliances with opposition parties, the penetration into civil society by way of professional associations and various service institutions in such fields as health and education, and the running of Islamic business and financial companies. The MB took considerable seats in the parliament through coalitions with existing parties – the Wafd in 1984 and the Labour since 1987 (see Table 7-1) – and it took a controlling majority in the boards of the many professional syndicates (Fahmy, 1998).

4-3. The Economic Structure

Egypt has a relatively diversified economy among the countries in the Middle East and Africa. Plentiful domestic resources and the large population could be used as a source for diversified industrial bases. However, the inconsistent economic policies of the successive regimes and the poor management of the economy have prevented the development of competent industries. Until the early 1970s, the Egyptian economy had heavily relied on the export of raw cotton. After the oil shocks of the 1970s, petroleum and the remittance of the workers employed in oil rich Arab States have taken up more importance. The Suez Canal and tourism have also been major sources of national income, especially valuable hard currency.

During the 1990s, the overall macroeconomic situation of Egypt had remarkably improved, raising hope that the country was escaping from the chronic imbalances and poor performance. This can be fairly ascribed to the successful implementation of the Structural Adjustment Programme. However, it remains to be seen whether this momentum will be sustained in the future and whether the macroeconomic stabilisation will help to develop industrial competitiveness in microeconomic sectors.

4-3-1. Recent Economic Performance

During the late 1980s, the Egyptian economy had seriously suffered from low growth, high unemployment and inflation, as well as deficits in government finance and balance of payments, which led to the accumulation of enormous foreign debts. This situation finally compelled the Egyptian government to enter into an arrangement with the IMF in 1991, leading to the launch of the Structural Adjustment Programme. Since then, the overall macroeconomic situation of Egypt had largely improved throughout the 1990s.

As shown in Table 4-1, major macroeconomic indicators such as the GDP growth, inflation, and unemployment rate had generally shown an improving trend during the 1990s. This trend is shown more in detail in Table 8-1 in the eighth chapter of this thesis, while analysing the performance of the economic reform. Foreign debt and the debt service ratio had been also reduced to a manageable level, helped by the debt reduction of the Paris Club, of which the details are explained in the fifth chapter.

However, trade deficit began to increase rapidly in the late 1990s, mainly due to the rapid expansion of imports facilitated by the liberalisation measures of the reform. This accompanied the worsening of current account situation, and worries about the possible recurrence of balance of payment problems. Heading into the 2000s, the Egyptian economy rather abruptly fell into a liquidity problem caused by a shortage of the supply of local currency, and is currently known to be suffering from serious recession again.

Table 4-2 Selected Economic Indicators of Egypt

	Unit	1980	1985	1990	1995	1998
Real GDP Growth	%	..	..	3.7	5.0	6.1
Per Capita GDP	US Dollar	525	1,144	641	1,112	1,290
Annual Inflation	%	20.9	12.2	16.7	7.3	3.8
Unemployment	%	..	..	8.6	9.2	7.9
Trade Balance	US $ Million	-2,960	-5,215	-6,379	-7,597	-10,215
Current Account	US $ Million	-438	-2,166	185	-254	-2,552
Foreign Debt	US $ Billion	..	34.1	46.0	33.4	28.2
Debt Service Ratio	%	..	..	25.4	13.3	10.9
Total Reserves	US $ Million	709	734	1,385	7,380	9,202

Source: Ministry of Economy (1999), IMF (2000), etc.

4-3-2. The Industrial Structure and Activities

Regarding the economic structure of Egypt by industrial sectors, data from the World Bank (2000) and the Ministry of Economy (1999) show some differences mainly due to the classification of industries. According to the World Bank data, in 1998, the value added of industry was 33% of GDP among which 26%

belonged to manufacturing. In 1980, the share of industry was 37%, among which manufacturing took up a mere 12%. So, according to this data, it may be inferred that there has been considerable development in industrialisation during the last two decades. This is evidenced by the relatively high growth rate of industry in the same data, which shows that the industry sector, including manufacturing, grew annually by 5.2% during 1980-90 and by 4.2% during 1990-98. On the other hand, the share of agricultural value added changed little from 18% in 1980 to 17% in 1998, and that of the services sector from 45% to 50%.

Table 4-3 Industrial Structure and Growth

	Value added as a % of GDP		Average annual % Growth	
	1980	1998	1980-90	1990-98
Agriculture	18	17	2.7	2.9
Industry	37	33	5.2	4.2
(Manufacturing)	12	26	..	..
Services	45	50	6.6	4.1

Source: The World Bank (2000)

The data from the Ministry shows the structure based on a more detailed classification of industries. According to the data shown in Table 4-4, the output of industry and mining accounted for 18.5% of GDP in 1997/98, increasing from 16.6% in 1990/91. The share of agriculture changed a little, from 17.6% in 1990/91 to 17.5% in 1997/98. Trade, Finance & Insurance was the most important sector, taking up the largest portion, 21.5% in 1997/98, increased from 20.0% in 1990/91.

The same data also show the weights of each industry in employment. In this respect, agriculture is still very important, taking up nearly a third of the total workforce, even though its share decreased slightly from 33.9% in 1990/91 to 29.5% in 1997/98. Industry and mining employed 13.4% of total workers in 1997/98, while around one third of the total workers were employed in public sector services (signified as other services in the table).

Table 4-4 Industrial Structure by Output and Employment

	Output (% of GDP)		Employment (% of Total Workers)	
	1990/91	1997/98	1990/91	1997/98
Agriculture	17.6	17.5	33.9	29.5
Industry & Mining	16.6	18.5	12.7	13.4
Petroleum & Products	10.1	6.4	0.3	0.2
Electricity	1.4	1.7	0.8	0.8
Construction	5.2	5.5	6.1	7.4
Transportation & Suez Canal	10.4	9.3	3.5	4.5
Trade, Finance & Insurance	20.0	21.5	10.2	10.7
Tourism	0.8	1.2	1.0	0.9
Other Services	17.9	18.4	31.6	32.6

Source: Ministry of Economy (1999)

As in many industrialising countries, the decline of agriculture in the national economy has been a rather constant trend in Egypt. According to Mabro (1974:16), agriculture took up some 50 percent of national income and around 70 percent of total employment until the 1930s. With the continuous decline of agricultural significance, the gap in food self-sufficiency markedly increased. Egypt was self-sufficient in the supply of food until the 1960s, but after the 1970s, it transformed from being a net agricultural exporter to a net importer. By the end of the 1980s, the self-sufficiency ratio was only around 20 percent for wheat, lentils and edible oil. Egypt's main winter crops are wheat, barley and onions.

Main summer crops are cotton, rice and sugar cane.

Egypt's industrial base is comparatively diversified. Active sectors include the automotive, textiles, electronics, pharmaceuticals, cement, iron and steel, and aluminium industries. International involvement is present in many of these sectors. In recent years, export of textiles increased considerably. The Egyptian government is trying to expand the industrial base into non-traditional sectors including high technology sectors, by proving incentives and inducing foreign investment.

Petroleum and the downstream sector is another area of economic importance. The first oil well was drilled in 1886, but the output gained significantly only after the 1950s. About 80 percent of the output comes from the Gulf of Suez fields. Due to the limited volume of reserves, the output of crude oil has consistently decreased in recent years. In 1998, the crude oil production recorded 30.5 million tons, down by around 26.2 percent from the previous year. Around 80 percent of the petroleum production is consumed domestically, and only some marginal portions are exported. Since the 1980s, significant discoveries of natural gas have been made and are actively used now.

4-3-3. Fiscal Structure

Until the early 1990s, the Egyptian economy suffered from a huge fiscal deficit that reached as high as 17.6% of GDP in 1988. In 1988, government expenditure recorded 43.6% of GDP, whereas its revenue accounted for 25.9%. The huge fiscal deficits brought a heavy burden on the economy, and their reduction became one of the most urgent and important targets in the Structural Adjustment Program. Since the SAP was launched in 1991, it had targeted the correction of the fiscal structure, by means of reforms in taxes and reductions in expenditure. As a consequence of these measures, the fiscal deficit markedly declined, and in

1996, it recorded a mere 1.3% of GDP. Changes in the fiscal structure in the 1990s are shown in Table 4-5.

Table 4-5 Changes in the Fiscal Structure 1990-96

Unit: Million Egyptian Pound

	1990		1996	
	Value	% of GDP	Value	% of GDP
Total Revenue	21,876	22.8	60,893	26.4
Tax Revenue	11,743	12.2	38,249	16.6
Direct Tax	4,247	4.4	13,731	5.9
Indirect Tax	7,496	7.8	24,518	10.6
Sales	4,579	4.8	16,607	7.2
Customs	2,917	3.0	7,911	3.4
Capital Revenue	4,829	7.8	3,185	5.2
Total Expenditure	36,393	37,9	63,889	27.7
Current	22,446	23,4	51,967	22.5
External Debt Payment	687	0.7	3,796	1.6
Internal Debt Payment	2,969	3.1	12,231	5.3
Subsidies	2,971	3.1	11,548	5.0
Wages	6,064	6.3	14,045	6.1
Others	9,755	10.2	10,347	4.5
Investment	13,947	14.5	11,922	5.2
Fiscal Deficit	-14,517	-15.1	-2,996	-1.3

Source: The Overseas Economic Cooperation Fund (1999)

4-3-4. Trade and the External Sector

Egypt has been showing a chronic trade deficit for quite some time. Its export items are dominated by a few primary items, of which petroleum and cotton are the most important, and it imports most of the capital and intermediate goods, along with a large amount of foods. Since the 1970s, petroleum has taken the place of cotton as the leading export item, recording a dominant share of total exports. However, from the mid-1980s, some manufactured goods, of which textiles are the most important, found overseas markets especially in Europe, and their share in the nation's exports has increased considerably. As a result, the share of primary goods in total exports fell from 65.1% in 1990 to 48.1% in 1996, of which petroleum took up 55.8% and 35.2% respectively. The share of manufactured goods increased from 34.9% to 50.0% during the same period, of which textiles recorded 14.0% and 24.1% respectively (Ministry of Economy, 1999).

With respect to imports, intermediate and capital goods have always taken up a dominant portion. However, the shortage of foods became very significant from the 1970s, and food nowadays takes up around a quarter of total imports. The data in Table 4-6 show that the share of foods in total imports even increased from 21.9% to 24.2% of total imports during the years 1990-96.

Despite the chronic trade deficits, the current account and overall balance of payment of Egypt have fluctuated between modest surpluses and deficits. The other sources of foreign exchange, including the Suez Canal traffic fares, remittances from Egyptian workers abroad, and the tourism sector, have contributed to counteract the trade deficits. Besides, Egypt has received significant amounts of foreign aid from neighbouring Arab oil exporting countries and Western sources. However, Egypt has been suffering from huge foreign debts that reached as high as 206% of GDP in 1986/87.

With the help of the Structural Adjustment Programme and the subsequent debt reduction by Arab and Western countries, Egypt's foreign debt decreased significantly in the 1990s. The total foreign debt was reduced to a manageable 34.0% of GDP in 1997/98, and the debt service ratio, which once reached a record 91.7% in 1986/87, was also reduced markedly to 7.2% in 1997/98 (Ibid.).

Table 4-6 Changes in the Composition of Trade Commodities

	1990		1996	
	Value (billion dollars)	% of Total	Value (billion dollars)	% of Total
Exports	**4.3**	**100.0**	**5.4**	**100.0**
Primary Goods	2.8	65.1	2.6	48.1
Petroleum	2.4	55.8	1.9	35.2
Cotton	0.2	4.7	0.3	5.6
Manufactured Goods	1.5	34.9	2.7	50.0
Textiles	0.6	14.0	1.3	24.1
Other	0.8	18.6	1.4	25.9
Imports	**11.4**	**100.0**	**12.4**	**100.0**
Foods	2.5	21.9	3.0	24.2
Other Consumer Goods	0.8	7.0	0.5	4.0
Energy	0.4	3.5	0.8	6.5
Intermediate Goods	4.7	41.2	4.6	37.1
Capital Goods	2.9	25.4	3.4	27.4

Source: Ministry of Economy (1999)

4-4. History of Economic Policies 1952-91

Since the introduction of long staple cotton in the 1820s under the rule of Muhammed Ali (1805-48), Egypt's economy has turned to an export-oriented economy. The British occupation of Egypt in 1882 brought a full integration of the Egyptian economy into the world capitalist system. By the early twentieth century, it exhibited a classic Third World dependency, the essence of which was reliance on the exports of a single, primary commodity, or raw cotton in the case of Egypt (Metz, 1991: 157). As a result, the fluctuation of world price and consumption of cotton seriously affected the Egyptian economy.

Throughout the period of British control and the Farouq monarchy, industrial development had been confined to cotton export related fields, i.e., banking and finance, transport, cotton ginning and pressing. Most of these industries were owned by the foreign community until the revolutionary government nationalised them in the 1950s and 1960s. Following the revolution, a drive for rapid industrialisation was pursued. However, this drive generally failed due to the inconsistent economic policies and ineffective management of industries. In the following, the changes and development of economic policies from the Nasser era until the year 1991, which marked the beginning of the Structural Adjustment Programme, will be presented in an historical context.

4-4-1. The Nasser Era (1952-70): Statist Policies and Import Substitution

Nasser was a colonel in the Egyptian army, when he led a successful coup against the monarchy of King Farouq with a group of young army officers calling themselves the Free Officers. This coup d'etat took place on the night of July 23, 1952. King Farouq abdicated soon and on June 18 of the following year, Egypt proclaimed a republic. Nasser and the Free Officers led the country under the umbrella of the Revolutionary Command Council (RCC). After a three-year transition period, in June 1956, Nasser became the first President of the republic under a new constitution.

Following these events, Egypt in the 1950s and 1960s found itself among a handful of developing countries drawn into state-guided, state-dominated economic growth. These socialist economic policies, together with the Pan-Arabism and Non-Alignment in the politics and diplomacy arena, characterised the governing ideology of the Nasser era, which has been termed as Nasserism.

Many scholars these days believe that Nasserism was not introduced as a deliberately designed idea. Ismael (1991: 326) indicates that as the situation changed after 1956, there developed a more deliberate construction of ideological tenets and the application of these tenets. Waterbury (1983:63-64) contends that there is certainly a substantial element of truth in the judgement that Egypt backed or fell into socialism without really knowing where it was going. While there was a clear intent among RCC members to propel the state directly into the management of the economy, it was practical issues rather than ideological inclination that obliged the regime to adopt socialist policies. In this sense, Waterbury says that it was a question of ideology catching up with practice.

In early September 1952, the RCC launched a land reform programme that placed a ceiling on individual land ownership. But aside from this land reform, the new regime followed traditional patterns in its economic policy. Although the RCC put more emphasis on government investment in social overhead capital than the old regime had, no new principles of economic policy or social organisation were established at this time.

However, by 1957-58, government planning had become an economic reality in Egypt. When the West refused to finance the Aswan High Dam, to provide water for the large land reclamation projects in the desert in 1956, Nasser nationalised the Suez Canal as a profitable source of foreign exchange. This action was followed by the military intervention of Britain, France and Israel, and Egypt's subsequent orientation towards the Soviet Union and the Eastern bloc.

Once the hostilities were over, the Egyptian government seized all French and British assets in Egypt, apparently as a retaliatory measure for the Suez War. By Laws 22, 23, and 24 of January 1957, all commercial banks, insurance companies and commercial agencies for foreign trade were fully Egyptianised in management and capital. The Suez War was thus a major watershed. The state found itself the owner of considerable assets and from then on until 1967, there was no turning back in the systematic expansion of the public sector.

In July 1961, a series of nationalisation laws were promulgated. Laws 117, 118 and 119 put a considerable portion of the non-agricultural sector of the economy under public ownership or control. All remaining private banks and insurance companies, as well as shipping and firms in heavy or basic industries, were nationalised. All aspects of foreign trade were brought under the state monopoly.

And further land reform measures followed.

All these measures consolidated the statist control of the economy. According to Waterbury (1983: 81), by 1965, the public sector accounted for nearly 40% of total output, 45% of domestic savings, and 90% of gross domestic capital formation. Waterbury says that few developing countries other than those that are professedly Marxist ever cut so deeply into the private sector as Egypt (Ibid.: 76).

With this economic reorganisation, the strategy of Import Substitution Industrialisation (ISI) was pursued. In the late 1950s, Egypt had already taken a major stride toward heavy industrialisation with the launching of the Helwan Iron and Steel complex. However, during the First Five Year Plan (1960/61-64/65) which was designed under the initiative of the National Planning Committee (NPC) formed in 1957, the Egyptian government also tried to foster a wide range of industrial bases in consumer goods: from food processing, beverages, textiles, soaps, etc., to a full range of consumer durables such as automobiles, refrigerators, washers, radios and so forth. These projects had too often been inadequately studied and hastily pursued.

These hastily built industrial bases were to be protected from foreign competition through high tariff rates. In January 1962, a new system of tariffs was introduced. It grouped all imports into three categories of raw materials, semi-manufactured goods, and finished goods. Tariffs in each category were determined by the possibility or actuality of local production. Even though the levels varied widely, the effective rates of protection were as high as 305% for automobiles and 599% for iron and steel (Ibid.: 93).

The employment drive was another characteristic policy of the Nasser era. The regime guaranteed employment for all university graduates. The growing public sector supplied jobs to fulfil this commitment. It also provided remunerative management positions for former army officials. This kind of employment drive soon led to overstaffing and low productivity of the public sector. (Ibid.: 90-93)

4-4-2.   The Sadat Era (1970-80): Infitah and the Failure of Reform

Nasser died suddenly in September 1970, and his vice president Sadat succeeded the presidency. Even though Sadat was one of the original Free Officers of the 1952 revolution, his position was not confirmed until then. So, a search for legitimacy of the power characterised the early politics of the Sadat regime. In October 1973, Sadat launched a war against Israel and in this war, the Egyptian army reaped a limited victory. This gave Sadat sufficient legitimacy and popularity to pursue overtly the de-Nasserisation of the Egyptian state. Thus, the October 1973 war marked a radical redirection of Egypt's policies – both foreign and domestic.

Egypt had suffered from a state of increasing economic deterioration. As a result of the military defeat in June 1967 by Israel, Egypt had to suffer the great war damages, and bore further losses from the enforced closure of the Suez Canal, the loss of Sinai oil, a drastic drop in tourism revenues, and a great reduction in Western aid. Other losses followed during the Canal War of 1969-70, when Israeli bombardment caused widespread destruction in the cities of Port Said, Ismailia and Suez. Increased military expenditure also became a heavy burden for the Egyptian economy.

In this context, Sadat felt that a new approach in economic policy was badly needed. Already in the later days of the Nasser era, there had been criticism over the inefficient operation of the socialist economy, and in March 1968, Nasser announced a shift in his economic policy to improve the public sector economy. After succeeding Nasser, Sadat went a little further in this shift by passing Law 65 in 1971 establishing "free zones" in which new companies could be offered tax holidays and other privileges.

After the October 1973 War, Sadat took advantage of the prestige given to him to announce the introduction of a new economic policy. In April 1974, Sadat disclosed the outline of the new "Infitah" (Open-Door) policy in his "October Paper." The basic aim of this new policy was to overcome Egypt's economic stagnation by measures designed to encourage foreign investment, as well as to promote local private sector activity. The pretext was that Egypt needed external sources of finance, and had to improve the efficiency of the whole economic system by introducing more strongly market-oriented economic policies.

A series of laws were enacted to provide the legal framework for this Infitah policy, among which Law 43, passed in June 1974, was the basic and comprehensive reference. It set out the terms on which foreign capital could operate. The most important provision was that all companies founded under the law would now be considered private, whatever the source of their capital. Owen (1998: 135) finds the significance of this provision in that it placed Egyptian capital on much the same basis as foreign capital. Waterbury (1983: 135) pointed out that not all private companies would be subject to the strict regulations of labour laws applied to the public sector. Besides, Law 43 stipulated various incentives such as exemption from nationalisation and a five-year tax holiday, and created an Investment Authority to screen all investment applications.

Law 32 of 1977 provided more concessions to both local and foreign capital, including exemption from the strict foreign exchange regulations. Law 111 of 1975 was one that aimed at the reform of public sector enterprises. It was designed to improve the management system of the public enterprises by abolishing the control bodies, or General Organisations. In 1978, it was announced that some wholly-owned state enterprises would sell shares, and subsequent plans were announced that the government would reduce its share in public enterprises to 51 per cent.

Nowadays, it is widely believed that the real achievement of the Infitah policy was disappointing, and that it had brought seriously negative impacts on the Egyptian economy. Even though it was designed to encourage foreign investment, the only sectors in which foreigners proved to be interested were petroleum and to a lesser extent, tourism and consultancy. Meanwhile, as the private sector expanded, its activities mostly concentrated on speculative and non-productive commercial fields. The new private entrepreneurs took advantage of the trade liberalisation measures and mainly engaged in import trade, which led to their amassing spectacular profits (Richards and Waterbury, 1990: Ismael and Ismael, 1991).

Moreover, reform in the public sector proved to be just a verbal service. Steps towards profit-oriented management practices in the public sector did not go far enough, mainly because of the political risks of dismissing the excess employees in the overstaffed enterprises. Throughout the entire era of the Sadat regime, no public enterprises were sold to the private sector in reality. Posusney (1992: 81-105) describes how the Egyptian labour organisations resisted the privatisation attempts and turned the matter into a political problem, slowing down the whole reform process.

The fiscal reform programme, which was endorsed by an IMF loan and was supposed to cut subsidies on many basic consumer items, caused a skyrocketing price increase and a resultant mass riot in January 1977. It left 79 dead and 1,000 wounded and finally made the government rescind the programme and reinstate the subsidies.

The Egyptian economy had grown at considerably high rates during the years 1974-85 largely as a result of the increase in oil revenues and Arab aid. The oil boom of the Gulf countries and Libya brought Egypt a significant amount of remittances sent back by the growing numbers of Egyptian workers in these countries. However, the adverse impacts of the Infitah revealed themselves quite clearly. They were reflected in a huge deficit in the trade balance, brought about by the extravagant importation of consumer and intermediary goods. During the years 1974-80, the deficit in the trade balance grew from 505 million Egyptian pounds to 2,088 million pounds.

The impacts on the socio-economic structure of society were also disastrous. While the Infitah led to the emergence of a new upper class, mainly merchants and middlemen, it also aggravated inflation to an unprecedented scale and threw a greater burden on the middle and lower classes.

From 1977 on, the overall political economy of Egypt had been overshadowed by the peace treaty with Israel, which brought a furious reply from the entire Arab world. Egypt was expelled from the Arab League and had to rely more and more on the relationship with America. In this situation, Sadat was assassinated in October 1981 by a member of an Islamic fundamentalist group, Jihad, and the days of the Infitah finally ended.

4-4-3. The Mubarak Era (1981-91): Economic Decline and Crisis

After the assassination of Sadat, the then vice-president Mubarak succeeded the presidency. Being conscious of the criticism on the dictatorship of Sadat, Mubarak tried to introduce some democratic processes in the political arena as a means to enhance his legitimacy. Thus, the once banned opposition political groups such as the Wafd Party and the Muslim Brotherhood came back to the parliament by winning seats in successive general elections in 1984 and 1987. However, as Hopwood (1993: 186) indicated, once an opposition is legalised and open debate permitted, there is virtually no end to the demands for further freedoms. Mubarak has not been willing to contemplate this possibility and has always been ready to limit what he considered too outspoken criticism. As a result, in the following years, various measures to restrict the democratic process had been introduced, and according to Kienle (1998: 20), the process of deliberalisation came to mark Egyptian politics in the 1990s.

Mubarak's policy was one that had not such distinct colours as those of Nasser and Sadat, and his main concern was to ensure continuity and stability. But he reaped considerable success in the diplomacy arena. By correcting the one-sided diplomacy line of Sadat, Mubarak restored the relationship with Arab countries and the Soviet Union, while not undermining the relationship with America and Israel. The restoration of Egypt's Arab League membership in 1989 returned its traditional status and role as the leader of all Arab countries.

However, from the mid-1980s, Egypt came to face serious economic problems. This was the result of the faulty economic policies of the former regimes as well as the adverse impacts of external factors. In 1986, the international oil price collapsed, and the government oil revenue of Egypt in that year fell by 70%. With the oil price collapse, the economic boom of the Arab oil producing countries ended, which led to the reduction of remittances of Egyptian workers abroad. And by this time, the problems of the over-weighted public sector economy of Egypt revealed themselves too clearly.

As a result of these combined effects, the Egyptian economy fell into a deep depression. GNP growth fell from 7.5% in the 1975-82 period to 1.9% in the 1987-89 period. This drop and the continuing population growth of about 2.4% per annum led to a fall in per capita income. Meanwhile, government attempts to reduce expenditure led to a reduction of imports by an average of 4.7% a year and of gross investment by nearly 6% (Owen and Pamuk, 1998: 138). And due to the expansion policies of the Infitah era, Egypt's foreign debt had been accumulated enormously to reach almost 50 billion dollars by 1990. The debt servicing soon became an acute problem for the Mubarak regime.

It was this situation which finally forced the Mubarak regime to enter into new negotiations with the IMF, leading to the signing of an 18-month stand-by agreement in May 1987. Through this agreement, the Egyptian government promised to reduce public expenditure and to make a significant move towards unifying the system of multiple exchange rates introduced by the Nasser regime.

However, as early as the spring of 1988, the IMF decided that Egypt was not implementing the reforms as promised and refused to release the second tranche.

In the following years, Egypt fell further into economic crisis. Budget and current account deficits, along with increasing foreign debts, led to unsustainable macroeconomic imbalances. Egypt was no longer able to service its foreign debt. Capital inflows decreased, arrears piled up, and GDP growth dropped, while inflation accelerated to more than 20% and open unemployment rose to more than 10%. A number of social indicators showed the erosion of the standard of living of the majority of people. For example, real per capita consumption of the lower income strata during the 1980s decreased by 50%. Acute malnutrition rose from 2.3% to 7 %, and anaemia among pre-school children increased from 38% to 52% (Weiss and Wurzel, 1998:23).

Against this situation, the Egyptian government began a new series of negotiations with the IMF and the World Bank in 1989. These negotiations did not go easily and lasted for three years until separate, but tied agreements with the IMF and the World Bank were reached in 1991. The IMF and the World Bank widened their concerns from stabilisation to structural adjustment, in which the particular emphasis was the expansion of market economy through the rolling back of the state control. The Mubarak regime was extremely sensitive to the strong opposition within Egypt to the structural adjustment, and so did not come to terms with the proposed conditionalities easily.

A major breakthrough in the negotiations was made when Iraq invaded Kuwait in August 1990 and Egypt took part in the Anti-Iraq multi-national coalition force led by the US in the next year. In exchange for Egyptian support of American policy in the Gulf, the US government announced that it would cancel Egypt's 7.1 billion dollars of military debt. In addition, most of the Arab Gulf countries cancelled Egypt's debt to them, estimated to be another 7 billion dollars (Ismael and Ismael, 1991: 354).

This development provided a favourable environment for all counterparts of the negotiations. So finally in May 1991, the Egyptian government entered into an 18-month stand-by agreement amounting to 278 million SDR, and the World Bank approved a $300 million structural adjustment loan in June 1991. The IMF support was conditional on the World Bank's judgement that the structural adjustment programme was being implemented satisfactorily. Also tied to this agreement was the Paris Club plan that would grant debt relief of 50% for Egypt. This plan was supposed to be implemented in three phases according to the Egyptian government's reform performance (Weiss and Wurzel, 1998: 24-24). In this way, the Structural Adjustment Programme of Egypt came to be launched, and it lasted until 1998 through renewed agreements with the IMF in 1993 and 1996.

Chapter 5

Motives for Reform and the Interest Groups

By the early 1970s, the Egyptian economy suffered from several maladies. The growth rate was low and trade deficit was high. As McDermott (1988: 132) indicated, the ruling elite was dissatisfied with the poor performance of the public sector, and a need for reform in the statist economic policies was discussed. Finally, in 1974, Sadat announced the Infitah (Opening-Up), which attempted to liberalise the economy in full scale, to open it to foreign investment, and to encourage the private sector. Even though the Infitah was aborted with the death of Sadat in 1981, the succeeding Mubarak regime had never strayed far from the spirits of the Infitah. There had been attempts to regenerate the market-oriented reform in the 1980s, and finally in the 1990s, the Structural Adjustment Programme had been effectively implemented. As Hinnebusch (1993: 160) anticipated, the SAP in the 1990s carried the unfinished Infitah to its logical end.

In this chapter, the factors that affected the process of economic reforms since the Infitah era will be analysed. In the first part, the reform attempts of the 1970s and 1980s will be presented and an analysis of the causes of the failure of those attempts will follow. Then the focus will move to examine the factors that made the now cautious Egyptian state re-launch the reforms in the 1990s. Finally, the interests of major socio-political groups in the economic reform will be analysed.

5-1. Aborted Reforms in the 1970s and 1980s

Beginning from the Infitah, Sadat and Mubarak had tried to introduce types of reforms in their economic policies. However, their attempts of such reforms had mostly failed until the launch of the ERSAP in the 1990s. The Infitah brought unexpected negative impacts to the economy, which forced Sadat to introduce an IMF-sponsored stabilisation programme in 1977. But, this programme was aborted quickly after a mass riot. Mubarak also launched an IMF programme in 1987, which was also aborted shortly after its initiation. In this section, the process of these aborted reforms and the causes of their failures will be analysed.

5-1-1. The Political Economy of the Infitah

The Infitah was formally introduced in April 1974 with the announcement of the "October Paper". As indicated by Richards and Waterbury (1990: 240), it was a response to the internal problems faced by the Egyptian economy and to changes in the international environment. The malfunctioning of the public sector-dominated economy had already shown enough symptoms by the early 1970s to prove the inefficiency of the system. To the ruling elite, this situation raised the question of the resource gap: how could they maintain the 'social contract' of the Nasserist welfare state in the face of the dwindling economic resources and the rapid population growth? It felt rather obvious that without further resources from abroad, it would be difficult to maintain the system.

The October 1973 War and the consequent oil shock presented unusual chances to redress these problems. Sadat won the legitimacy and popularity to pursue his own policy vision. The oil price increase offered his regime the prospect of enhanced capital inflows from Arab oil-exporting countries, from workers' remittances, and from direct oil sales of Egypt. However, as Richards and Waterbury (1990: 240) pointed out, such opportunities required changes in the economic institutional environment. They needed to liberalise the tightly state-controlled economy to persuade the Gulf, and even the Western investors, to put money into Egypt. Also, they needed to modify the grossly overvalued exchange rate to induce the workers abroad to repatriate their savings. The Infitah was launched in this background.

However, the Infitah was not introduced as a shock therapy in a political vacuum. From the early 1970s, a number of different elite factions prescribed different solutions to the economic problems, and there had been debates over the issue of "Opening". Some Marxists favoured a deepening of the socialist experiment and another small group stood for a controlled role for private and foreign capital, compatible with the dominant public sector. The dominant thinking that emerged advocated the creation of a new foreign sector, restriction of the public sector to large industry and infrastructure, and the opening of all other sectors to private capital. Some of Sadat's closest confidants, major figures of the Egyptian bourgeoisie such as Osman Ahmad Osman and Sayyid Marii, played major roles in persuading the President to pursue this option (Metz, 1991: 248).

According to Derek Hopwood (1993: 131), the Infitah was clearly a political issue in which Sadat was opposed by the left who wanted more nationalisation, and pushed by the right who wanted more private enterprise. In the view of Hopwood, Sadat himself, who was faced with severe economic problems on taking power, believed that too much socialism killed initiative, and so as early as 1971, he adopted a new law (Law 65) to encourage foreign investment. However, this measure was not successful at the time because foreign businessmen were haunted by the fear of nationalisation and lacked confidence in the Egyptian economy.

After the announcement of the Infitah, various reform measures were introduced in the following years, focusing on liberalisation of trade and the capital market. Assurances were given that money invested would be safe from nationalisation or expropriation. Helped by these measures and the better prospect for peace and stability after the 1973 war, foreign investment increased considerably, although tentative for a while. Financial inflows from external sources including oil revenue, workers remittances, Suez Canal revenues, tourism, and Arab aid also increased rapidly. After the 1979 Peace Accords with Israel at Camp David, increased U.S. aid took the place of the ceased Arab aids.

In the following years till the early 1980s, all the financial inflows brought the Egyptian economy into an unusual boom. During the years 1973-81/82, the Gross Domestic Product of Egypt at factor cost grew annually by 8.1%, and per capita income grew by 5.5% (Owen and Pamuk, 1998: 252).

However, as McDermott (1988: 138-9) put it, this boom in the late 1970s and early 1980s signified a misleadingly golden period, and the seeds of economic predicaments in the late 1980s were sown during this period. As Richards and Waterbury (1990: 242) indicated, the improved growth performance was as much the results of windfalls as of domestic policy shifts. It had little to do with the improvement of productivity in the Egyptian economy, but had more to do with the fluctuating "foreign largesse". As such, it was vulnerable to the changes of external environment, and when the oil prices collapsed in 1986, serious economic crises materialised.

Rather than solving the balance of trade problem, the Infitah exacerbated it. With the rapid increase of imports, trade deficit grew four times in ten years from 1974. The balance of agricultural trade, negative since the early 1970s, continued to deteriorate. By 1985, 25% of Egypt's imports were foodstuffs. Industrial exports also failed to take off, and commodity exports were increasingly dominated by petroleum products (Ibid.: 242). The increased foreign investment did not help to boost the productive sector, but had mostly gone into tourist ventures, hotels, office and apartment buildings, and banking. Taking advantage of the trade liberalisation, new private entrepreneurs mostly engaged in import trade and financing. On the other hand, the public sector, previously protected under Nasser, came to suffer both from the lack of commitment on the part of the government and from competition from imports (Hopwood, 1993: 132).

The Infitah also caused a disruptive social effect. As Richards and Waterbury (1990: 244) indicated, the equity consequences of the Infitah are as hotly debated as they are unclear. However, there has arisen a widespread perception that the economic reforms have benefited a well-placed minority of the population but have left very large segments of the population behind. According to McDermott (1988: 133), the Infitah, which was started as a potentially profitable economic and financial policy ultimately divided Egyptian society and created more problems than it solved.

As the macroeconomic imbalance including the trade deficit became serious, Sadat turned to the IMF prescription. In January 1977, the government announced the ending of several subsidies – including those on flour, sugar, rice and cooking oil – as part of an IMF-sponsored stabilisation programme. The result was immediate and shocking. In the next two days, there was heavy rioting in towns of major cities nationwide, and the army had to be used to quell the disturbances. Sadat was stunned and immediately rescinded the stabilisation programme. Since then, the Egyptian government has not attempted such a radical reform (Hopwood, 1993: 109).

5-1-2. The Reform Attempts of the Mubarak Regime

Succeeding the presidency in 1981, Mubarak took charge of the task of managing the Infitah. Rather than producing a dynamic capitalist alternative to Nasserist statism, the Infitah had stimulated a consumption boom that put Egypt in debt and led to an economic crisis. The trade deficit had rapidly increased from

1.2 billion dollars in 1974 to 3.9 billion dollars in 1981, the year when Mubarak was inaugurated. It had grown to 6.6 billion dollars by 1988. External debt rose from approximately 3 billion dollars in 1974 to 24 billion dollars in 1985 and to 46 billion dollars in 1988.

In February 1982, Mubarak held a broad economic conference to discuss the difficulties facing the Egyptian economy. Some 35 leading economists in the country convened to discuss the economic problems. However, no consensus was reached and Mubarak could not find a proper alternative to the Infitah. Mubarak insisted that the Infitah would not be reversed, but would be pursued in modified form as a productive one. However, as Springborg (1989: 5) put it, the excesses of the Infitah served to discredit economic liberalization among broad sectors of the population, and "the bungled reform" had made the task of the Mubarak's generation of reformers more difficult.

Meanwhile, the economy was increasingly running into trouble. In late 1986, the US embassy in Cairo wrote (McDermott, 1988: 149):

"As Egypt enters 1987, the Egyptian economy has been stagnant for two years. It is suffering from economic distortions, and is not poised to resume growth without economic reforms … economic policies inherited from the past hinder investment, export growth, adequate new housing construction, development of the private sector, and long overdue structural adjustment. Farm policies aimed at self-sufficiency rather than comparative economic advantage increase the food deficit every year."

The World Bank presented a bleaker forecast of the Egyptian economy around the same time. It concluded as follows (Ibid.: 149):

"Even with drastic cuts in the volume of imports lasting the end of the decade, Egypt would be hard pressed to meet its external debt service obligations.

> Economic activity would fall resulting in severe declines in real levels of living for a prolonged period. Given the resource scarcities facing Egypt, some decline in real per capita income is inescapable."

With this bleak forecast of the economic conditions on the one side, and the reform-abhorring public on the other, Mubarak's attitude toward economic reform was reluctant and ambivalent. He weighed the benefits of reform and the status quo throughout the 1980s. According to Ibrahim (1994: 141), several renowned Egyptian economists sent loud warnings from the mid to the late 1980s that further delay in implementing economic reform would make things worse for the rulers and ruled alike. However, Mubarak was hesitant and the economic policies during the first term of his presidency (1981-87) remained essentially unchanged from those of the 1970s.

Due to the rapid deterioration of the economic situation during the late 1980s, Mubarak attempted some reform measures. But his concern about the social and political implications of adjustment made him extremely cautious. In late 1986, the Egyptian policy makers devised a program of orthodox adjustment containing such measures as reduction of fiscal deficit, exchange rate reform, and removal of price distortions. But these measures were not fully implemented since they were not backed up by commitment from the supreme leader. According to Abdallah and Brown (1988: 42), it is widely thought that Mubarak dismissed Prime Minister Lutfi and Central Bank Governor Negm in late 1986 because they accepted the IMF's prescribed austerity too readily.

This ambivalent attitude of Mubarak also affected the introduction and abortion of the 1987 standby agreement programme. Egypt signed an 18-month standby agreement with the IMF for a loan of SDR 250 million (approximately $325 million) in May 1987. However, six months later, the IMF cancelled the agreement because it felt that the performance was poor and the Egyptian government lacked sincere commitment to reform (Holt and Roe, 1993: 203).

The Egyptian government restarted a series of negotiation with the IMF from 1988, which took almost three years to reach a conclusion in 1991. Against the worsening economic situation, Mubarak felt that it would be difficult to maintain even the status quo without additional sources of financial support. By 1991, some changes of domestic and international environment eased the concern of the Mubarak regime regarding the social and political implications of the reform and this enabled the launch of the ERSAP.

5-1-3. Causes of the Failures of the Reforms

Regarding the reasons why the Infitah and the reform attempts thereafter had failed, various analyses have been made. In the first place, the lack of proper strategies to implement the reform is considered to be an important factor. Although the Infitah envisaged a dynamic inflow of foreign capital into the productive sectors, foreign investment in reality tended to cluster in service sectors, especially in the banking and finance, and tourism sectors. As Waterbury (1983: 154) indicated, all attempts to define and insist upon priorities in foreign investment had been pretty much abandoned. And this lack of strategy toward foreign investment merely reflected the lack of comprehensive planning for all sectors. The constant elaboration of plans since 1966 had gone hand in hand with their constant revision, postponement and non-implementation.

The corruption of bureaucrats and the merchants who had a connection with them hastened the derailment of the Infitah from the originally expected productive liberalisation to a consumptive and speculative "opening". The Infitah brought the rise of a new parasitic bourgeoisie called the "Munfatihun" (openers). They were the importers and the middlemen between foreign firms and the government, many of whom had a direct link to public sector officials and the political elite. As Waterbury (1983: 175) pointed out, they were the architects of the speculative, commercial open-door. Their influence on the policy changes was so strong that Springborg (1989: 22) even mentioned that they were more powerful than the president.

The last important factor that contributed to the abortion of the reforms was the domestic resistance and the resultant lack of will to reform from the leaders. As the author of a country study (Metz, 1991: 249) described, the interests created under Nasser remained obstacles to capitalize rationalization and belt-tightening. Hinnebusch (1993: 160) pointed out these crucial Nasserite constituencies were notably public sector managers and unionised workers, who seemed to defend Nasser's heritage, as well as a mass public which had been taught that it was entitled, as part of a social contract, to populist benefits.

The most illustrative case of the resistance by these Nasserite elements was the January 1977 riot. This riot was provoked by the government announcement to cut subsidies in basic commodities. It was initiated by workers and students and left 79 dead and 1,000 wounded with widespread destruction of property and about 1,500 arrests. It finally compelled Sadat to abandon the stabilisation programme and has haunted even the Mubarak regime as a warning against an orthodox reform.

Due to the concerns on this kind of mass resistance, as Springborg (1989: 6) put it, Egyptian decision-makers had remained surprisingly unwilling or unable to take the requisite steps to put the reform programme in place. According to Posusney (1992: 101), Egyptian policy makers were fearful of labour unrest, and both the Sadat and Mubarak governments had been ready to back off schemes for economic reform in order to prevent a unified political challenge from labour. Another document (Brumberg, 1995) indicated that the Egyptian government had put the Islamist opposition into consideration, and had sacrificed the reform for domestic stability.

It was not only the Nasserite heritages that blocked the reform, but Sadat's

Infitah also created interests resistant to reform. A larger and richer bourgeoisie was unprepared to give up opportunities for enrichment to trim its level of consumption. They were unwilling to accept the tax burden needed to correct the imbalances of the economy. As was described above, they had derailed the Infitah to a speculative liberalisation and in the Mubarak era, had vetoed several reform initiatives.

It should be noted that what has lain behind the lack of will from the leaders has been the lack of confidence in their legitimacy. Holt and Roe (1993: 221) indicated the lack of legitimacy, either moral or procedural, of the Mubarak regime, and described how this had caused the hesitancy of the regime toward reform as follows:

> "The government perceived that it would not survive the mass demonstration that would follow any significant changes. It did not have the legitimacy required to push through a policy that at least in the short run would require sacrifices by the urban population. This is clearly the case of a government that would not act."

All these factors described so far worked as causes of the failure of the reforms in the 1970s and 1980s. The analysis in the next section focuses on how this situation changed in the 1990s, and what the additional factors were that affected the introduction of the SAP.

5-2. Environments for the Reform in the 1990s

In May 1991, the Egyptian government concluded the long-protracted Standby Agreement negotiation with the IMF and launched the Structural Adjustment

Programme. It was a full-scale market-oriented reform programme, which the Egyptian government had been so hesitant to carry out during the past decade. However, this time, the scale and pace of the reforms were different from the preceding ones. Since 1991, the reforms developed on such a full scale that after two years since their inauguration, Hans Löfgren (1993: 410) stated, "Given the changes in economic policy in 1990 and 1991, it seems that the road to orthodox reform is now no longer blocked". And in the same year, Hinnebusch (1993: 159) also noted "The logjam which obstructed economic reform in Egypt in the 1980s appears to have been broken".

This observation of the two authors leads to an issue, which is raised in the following question of Matthew Gray (1998: 98): "How was it that Egypt agreed to the 1991 agreement with the IMF despite the forces and actors within Egypt which had opposed, and successfully delayed such reforms almost two decades?" Answering this question is the subject of this section. It will focus on the analysis of the factors that affected the full-scale development of the long-hesitated economic reform.

5-2-1. Changes of the Pro and Anti-Reform Power Balance

While analysing the same issue questioned by Gray, Löfgren presented six points as the factors that led to the implementation of the reform and the breakdown of the resistance. Hinnebusch tried to explain it in terms of the changes in power relations between the state and society. Their explanations vary in detailed descriptions, but seem to have reached similar conclusions, which can be synthesised by the following statement by Gray (1993: 98-99):

"The most likely explanation for the acceleration of liberalization in 1991 is that a combination of pro-liberalization forces and actors, internal and external to

Egypt, were in place by 1991 and for the first time were more powerful than those opposing economic liberalization."

This implies that significant changes in the political and economic conditions, internal or external to Egypt, had taken place by 1991, and that these changes worked in the direction that paved the way for the reform. According to Sturzenegger and Tommasi (1998: 10), a reform occurs when the payoffs associated with the policy change first exceeds that associated with the status quo. This was exactly the case of Egypt when it entered into the Standby Agreement with the IMF in 1991.

As stated in the previous chapter, the most important factor that led the Egyptian government to accept the Structural Adjustment Programme was the prolonged economic depression. With this, the enormous rents given after the Gulf War by the Western and Arab donors as a reward for Egypt's strategic service, which will be also examined in detail in the following section, also played an important role. These factors changed the payoffs counted by the Egyptian state and affected the changes of the power balance between the anti and pro-reform forces in Egyptian politics. For the regime, or the ruling elite, what was the most important calculation was the stability of the regime itself. The economic crisis had jeopardised that stability and the rents were needed to escape from the crisis. As a result, by 1991, the balance of intra-elite opinion had shifted in favour of the orthodox reforms. These motives are explored more in detail in the following stakeholders section.

By this time, the balance of power in the Egyptian socio-political groups had also turned in favour of orthodox reforms. Since the open-door policies of the 1970s, businessmen have emerged as a strong and unified force that could translate its newly enlarged wealth into political influence. The business community favoured most of the orthodox reform packages, and its members were able to apply direct pressure to government officials in favour of their positions. On the contrary, according to Löfgren (1993: 413-4), the trade unions, which were regarded as a "veto group" in the mid-1980s, had been seriously weakened by government control and their factionalism. So, this change of situation provided a favourable condition for the implementation of the reforms.

Externally, the decay of socialism in the international arena also helped to change the views of the Egyptian elite. The successive breakdown of the communist regimes in the Eastern Europe from the late 1980s, which culminated in the breakdown of the Soviet Union in early 1992, literally signified the collapse of socialism and the global triumph of capitalism. As a result, as Hinnebusch (1993: 164) indicated, the Egyptian elite now came to perceive a unipolar world and to be more sensitive to the intention of the American hegemon..

To sum up, by the early 1990s, the power balance inside the elite circle as well as between the socio-political groups had shifted to favour the pro-orthodox reform groups. In addition, the donors were ready to support the reform. This change of situation enabled the full-scale development of the Structural Adjustment Programme.

5-2-2. The Economic Crisis

As stated in the first chapter, the "Crisis Hypothesis" is one of the most distinct theories that explain the causes of economic reforms. Undoubtedly, the IMF intervenes in a country when the country is facing serious economic problems. In this context, most cases of the IMF-sponsored reform illustrate the role of economic crisis in initiating the reform. Thus, Sturzenegger and Tommasi (1998: 11) wrote, "Crises create a sense of urgency. Something needs to be done soon, because the crisis requires an urgent resolution. In the language of some analysts, this creates room for 'special politics' for a finite period of time."

Bates and Krueger (1993: 6) synthesised the cases of eight reforming countries, and presented the typical process as follows:

> "Frequently, although not always, serious consideration of a policy reform package begins when there are serious economic difficulties. These might be of a crisis nature, such as when a country is unable voluntarily to continue servicing its debts, or when a large fraction of the industrial production capacity of a country is operating at severely reduced capacity because of an inability to obtain imports because the authorities have no foreign exchange and hence issue no import licenses."

It can be fairly said that the Egyptian case of structural adjustment in the 1990s is just another exemplification of such a typical process of reform. It was the continued deterioration of economic conditions and the debt service crisis that pressed the Mubarak regime to deal with the IMF for a new loan. The following description of Owen and Pamuk (1998: 138) about the cause of the aborted 1987 standby agreement clearly emphasises this point.

> "Among the many short-term problems which confronted the Egyptian government, undoubtedly the most pressing was that of servicing its international debt at a time when repayments of principle and interest were costing the equivalent of 70 percent of the country's export earnings. It was this which finally forced it to enter into new negotiations with the IMF, leading to the signing of an 18 month stand-by agreement in May 1987 ..."

Since the 1987 agreement was cancelled soon and the economic problems had not improved, the Egyptian government started renegotiation with the IMF and finally launched the structural adjustment programme in 1991.

As mentioned earlier, the Egyptian economy since the 1960s had not performed well for a long period of time. The "misleadingly golden period" of the Infitah era from the mid-1970s to the early 1980s even widened imbalances in the macro-economy and left disruptive social impacts. Then, with the dramatic fall in oil prices in 1986, a sense of crisis concentrated the minds of Egypt's policy makers. In 1985, net oil revenues – exports minus imports – totalled just over $2,600 million. In 1986, these revenues fell by 70% to $686 million. The decline in oil receipts was accompanied by a sharp fall in workers' remittances, a consequence of recession and a shakeout of expatriate workers in the Gulf (Butter, 1989: 128; Abdallah and Brown, 1988: 38).

This rapid reduction of foreign exchange revenues seriously hampered the pursuing of economic policies for the Egyptian government and made the already pressing debt service problem even more worrisome. According to Abdallah and Brown (1988: 37), with the balance of payment deficits and very low foreign exchange reserves, which was equivalent to less than one month's imports at end-January 1987, Egypt could no longer service its debt. By late 1986, arrears had risen to $6 billion. The debt statistics vary according to sources. According to an OECD source (Weiss and Wurzel, 1998: 22), Egypt's foreign debt reached $50 billion in 1990 with an annual debt service of $6.6 billion and a debt service ratio of 56%.

As described in the previous chapter, aspects of the economic crisis of Egypt during the late 1980s were serious enough in all fronts of the economy. This implied for the ruling elite that their source of power was seriously endangered. As Ebeid (1989: 48) put it, co-optation, protection, subsidies, and public investment were no longer available as political tools – there were far fewer buttons to push.

In this situation, some development of the regional and international environment in the early 1990s inflated the crisis sense of the Egyptian elite. The eruption of the Gulf crisis following the Iraqi invasion of Kuwait in August 1990, caused the returning home of some 700,000 Egyptian workers from the Gulf countries, disrupting the already vulnerable Egyptian economy. In fact, the Gulf crisis later provided an unusual opportunity for Egypt to get a huge amount of windfall in return for its participation in the US-led anti-Iraq allied forces. This windfall, or the geostrategic rents of Egypt played a deciding role to spur the Egyptian regime to enter into the standby agreement with the IMF. However, during the Gulf crisis until the windfall materialised later, Egypt had seriously suffered from the loss of foreign exchange earnings from tourism and worker remittances, higher international transportation costs, and a generally uncertain economic climate (Löfgren, 1993: 411).

So, considering all these factors, by 1991, it was clear for the Egyptian elite that there was no other alternative than to accept and implement the structural adjustment. As a result, the balance of power in the intra elite politics turned in favour of the option supporting the orthodox reform.

5-2-3. The Geostrategic Rents

If the economic crisis was a stick to spur the Egyptian regime to go into the structural adjustment, the enormous rent paid by the Western and Arab Gulf countries in the form of grant and debt reduction was a carrot to allure the reluctant regime to hasten the reform. Egypt has traditionally received huge amounts of foreign assistance by selling its 'strategic services'. As David Butter (1989: 129) put it, the trick has been to emphasise the importance of Egypt remaining politically stable for the interest of a wide range of creditors – the US, West European states, the Soviet Union and the Arab Gulf states.

During the Nasser era, the Soviet Union provided financial and technical assistance to build the Aswan Dam, as well as enormous military assistance to build up the Egyptian army. Even in the Mubarak era, the Soviets still tried to hold Egypt on their side by offering generous financial treatment. In April 1987, they agreed to cancel interest owed on $3 billion of outstanding debt, to suspend repayment of principal for six years, and to allow Egypt to repay the balance over 25 years. But the Soviet assistance had been rather sporadic and small in size compared to the Western aid that flowed later (Springborg, 1989: 265).

From the Sadat to present Mubarak era on, Egypt has secured much greater financial sources from the Western donors through its shift in the foreign policy toward closer ties with the United States. According to the OECD (Weiss and Wurzel, 1998: 52) report cited above, Egypt received $32 billion in aid from 1975 to 1990. Major donors were the United States ($15 billion), the European Community and its member countries (8.3 billion), the Arab Gulf countries ($3.3 billion), the World Bank ($3.5 billion), and various international and regional organisations ($2 billion). And in 1991, by securing the reward for its role in the Gulf crisis, Egypt became the largest recipient of official development assistance, averaging $2.3 billion per year, which was greater than India ($1.8 billion) and Israel ($1.5 billion).

As regards the strategic services, Said (2000) properly described the contents as follows:

"Strategic services to the US, delivered by Egypt under Sadat and Mubarak, included blocking the export of Iranian revolution to the Arab World, aiding Iraq in the war against Iran 1980-1988, mobilizing against Soviet presence in Afghanistan. The most vital service was helping the US construct the Arab and international alliance against the Iraqi invasion of Kuwait. It also included aiding American policy objectives in the Third world at large and sub-Saharan Africa in particular. However, the most valuable strategic service to the US is maintaining peace with Israel in spite of the latter's failure to act in harmony with the UN resolutions and the principles of international law and international legitimacy".

This rent has always served various functions in the Egyptian political economy. It has supported the regime, and as Löfgren (1993: 410) put it, has made it possible to continue economic policies that otherwise would have collapsed. However, it has negative effects too. Said (2000) has argued that this rent has brought in the moral decay of the regime and the society and caused a rise in consumerism, which has seriously undermined the health of the economy.

Then, how has this rent set the course to the structural adjustment programme of 1991? During the Gulf crisis of 1990-91, the Mubarak regime firmly sided with the US-led anti-Saddam Hussein coalition. Some 30,000 Egyptian troops took part in the defence of Kuwait and demonstrated Egypt's position as a close Middle Eastern ally of the United States. This strategic service was immediately rewarded with the US cancellation of Egypt's $7.1 billion military debt in October 1990. In addition, the Arab Gulf states also cancelled Egypt's debt owed to them, estimated to be another $7 billion (Weiss and Wurzel, 1998: 44).

The Egyptian government took advantage of the crisis as much as possible and secured another big debt reduction. In November 1991, the Paris Club decided to cut Egypt's $50 billion debt by 50 percent on the condition that Egypt would carry out the reform demanded by the IMF. Egypt then secured another $613 million social fund from the World Bank, which was supposed to be used to cover the social impact of the reform.

Now, with all these rents, the Egyptian government was willing to reform. As Hinnebusch (1993: 163) has indicated, the rent now made the reform less risky politically and economically. Considering the conditional characteristics of the rents tied to the IMF's appraisal of the reform, it was too much to lose. So, all these considerations finally led the Egyptian regime to the Standby Agreement of May 1991.

5-3. The Stakeholders and Their Interests

Until now, this chapter has focused on the factors that had derailed the reform attempts in the 1970s and 1980s, and the factors that induced the launch of the SAP in the 1990s. In this section, the focus will move on to the analysis of the interests of the concerned stakeholders. As stated in Chapter 2, this research attempts to explore the interests of five stakeholder groups who are considered to have the most direct interests with the reform: they are the Egyptian state, the international donor group, the Egyptian bourgeoisie, the opposition forces, and the mass public. Their positions and interests are examined one by one in the following.

5-3-1. The State

As mentioned earlier, for the Egyptian ruling elite, what was the most important calculation in accepting the IMF-sponsored reform programme was the stability of the regime itself. The prolonged economic crisis had jeopardised that stability and the enormous rents accompanying the programme were needed to escape from the crisis.

According to Hinnebusch (1993: 164), the power elite now saw their own self-interest as compatible with the reforms. In the 1980s, they had feared the reaction on the streets to reform, but when Egypt accepted the reform package this was less salient in their calculations. The enormous rents, including the Social Fund, eased their concern over the street reaction. In the view of Hinnebusch, the failure to reform was now seen as more dangerous in the long run, since the stagnant public sector could no longer absorb job seekers and unemployment was climbing.

Löfgren (1993: 410) also indicated similar point. According to Löfgren, it has become clear beyond any doubt that the economic policy package of the 1980s is unsustainable in the long run. Falling real incomes and rising unemployment threatened to produce exactly what the ruling circle feared would be the result of orthodox economic reforms: riots and political instability.

Reform had been discussed for years in government circles, and there had been conflicts over the issue of the proper remedy for the economic crisis. In 1985, the then Minister of Economy Mustafa al-Said resigned in the wake of the elite politics over the issue of his attempted foreign exchange control. In 1986, the government of Prime Minister Ali Lutfi fell as a result of the elite conflicts over the issue of control of Islamic investment companies. These two issues have frequently been used to illustrate the cases proving the power of the new bourgeoisie class, which could affect the changes of the government policies (Springborg, 1989; Hinnebusch, 1993).

However, they are also used as an indicator to show how much the elite circle lacked a consensus on economic reform. According to Hinnebusch (1993: 163), this lack of consensus on economic reform left the door open to its obstruction by bureaucratic rivalries and inertia, and by the rent-seeking special interests. And as there was no clear signal from the president for reform, few ministers wanted to risk initiatives that could provoke popular reaction.

By 1991, this situation had changed and as Hinnebusch indicated, the balance of intra-elite opinion had shifted toward economic liberalism. Being aware that import substitution was exhausted and an export-oriented strategy necessary, the elite circle concluded that Egypt ought to fully integrate into the international market. According to Hinnebusch, this liberalisation of economic views was also associated with their increasing personal stake in business and the growing alliances with business families.

However, as the stability of the regime was the primary concern, the ruling elites were determined that the reforms would not jeopardise the stability. They had watched the East European experiences in the late 1980s and were concerned about the dangers of near collapse from shock reform. Thus, the Egyptian elite preferred a gradual approach to reform, and it had bargained hard with the donor group over the issue. Even though the IMF and the World Bank had frequently complained about the slow progress of the reforms, the Egyptian government managed to keep control over the degree and pace, if not the direction of the reform, and in this way it could avoid the East European shock therapy type of reform. Since the stability of the Egyptian regime was basically compatible with their interests in the Middle East, the donors, though not full-heartedly, approved the position of the Egyptian state. As a result, as Said (2000) has indicated, Egypt gained the most lenient programme.

While the adjustment programme carried the same economic medicine as is typical with IMF programmes, the implementation was gradual and was supported by enormous rents including unprecedented debt relief and a social fund. To reinforce the point, Hinnebusch (1993: 163) indicated that, "the reform agreements were negotiated, not simply imposed."

On the other hand, the concern over the stability of the regime prevented the ruling elite from undertaking political liberalisation alongside economic liberalisation. They thought that democratisation might permit the mobilisation of reform victims, and decided that this case should not be allowed. As a result, by 1990, democratisation had reached an impasse and the government was no longer under pressure to expand it (Hinnebusch, 1993: 168).

5-3-2. International Donor Group

There is a long history of international donor groups competing to secure the strategic importance of Egypt to their advantage. They have tried to use their loans and financial assistance as the leverage by which they can move the Egyptian government in the direction that they want. The most distinct among these donor groups were Great Britain and France during the colonial era, the Soviet Union and the Eastern Bloc in the Nasser era, and the United States and its Western allies from the Sadat era until the present. The role of the oil rich Arab Gulf states and the West-backed IFIs represented by the IMF and the World Bank have conspicuously increased during the recent period.

However, as Springborg (1989: 256) reported, the United States had since 1979 up to the late 1980s provided approximately two-thirds of all economic assistance to Egypt. And it has also played the leading role in the IMF and the World Bank. In this sense, it can be fairly said that the US is the principal force of the international donor groups today. The American interests in Egypt constitute an important part of American interests in the whole Middle East. Ever since the Second World War, American interests in the Middle East have typically evolved around the three issues of Israel, Oil, and Anti-Communism (see Hudson, 1996). But now, with the collapse of the Soviet Union and the communist powers, the last issue seems to have been replaced with Anti-Islamic Fundamentalism. The "Clash of Civilizations" theory of Huntington (1997) reflects this change of issues.

As a leading power among the Arab states, Egypt is an important partner for the United States to protect its three major interests in the region. Egypt's role is central in   Arab-Israeli peace, and it is also essential in protecting the oil rich, but militarily vulnerable pro-Western Arab Gulf states from the threats of radical regional powers such as Iraq and Iran. Egypt's secular government can also play an important role as a bulwark against the increasing threats of the militant Islamic fundamentalists.

Then how can these interests be related to the economic reform issues? The arguments of the so-called "Egyptian equivalents of Latin American dependistas", as is dubbed by Springborg (1989: 256), seem to provide a useful viewpoint to answer this question. According to their claims, the reform is a preliminary phase for the Western capitalists to subordinate the Egyptian political economy to their will and integrate it into the world capitalist order on favourable terms. For these capitalists to operate profitably, infrastructure must be put in place, consumerism stimulated, and most of all, appropriate policies implemented and supportive elites entrenched in the commanding heights.

In this respect, the dependistas argue that the purpose of the orthodox reform as demanded by the IMF, the World Bank and the USAID is to lever open the Egyptian political economy. Their strategy is to encourage the growth of indebtedness and then to make further economic assistance conditional upon policy reform, while simultaneously cultivating a constituency among the comprador bourgeoisie and, most importantly, within the state itself. In summary, the United States and Western capitalists have a direct interest in the economic reform of Egypt in that it is a necessary step to strengthen their foothold in the strategically important regional power.

Similar views could be heard frequently from many Egyptian intellectuals, even from those who may not like themselves to be classified as the dependista. The following comments of Dr. Mohammad Selim, professor at the Faculty of Politics and Economics at the Cairo University show the case:

> "In our judgement, the emphasis of the IMF on privatization and integration into world economy is a part of strategy to make sure that Arab world countries would be able to re-pay their debts, and their markets would be open to the manufactured goods of the capitalist countries." (Excerpts from his unpublished article "Models of Development in the Arab World", 2002)

Dr. Nader Fergany, formerly a professor of economics at the Cairo University, who is now leading an NGO, Al-Mishkat Center, presented the same perspective:

"Well, their motives are quite clear. They are putting the interests of global capitalism over the interests of Egyptians. They don't care for the welfare of Egyptians … Now, even within some of the international organisations, there is a realisation that they have made major mistakes. But, as long as the IMF and the World Bank are run by the American Treasury for the interests of global capital, especially financial capital, it will continue to be the case." (Interview on Dec. 16, 2002)

Another viewpoint is to relate the reform to the orthodox rationale for structural adjustment propagated by the donors and neo-liberal academics. In this view, the donors appear to be motivated by nothing more than altruistic considerations. According to Springborg, there has been a kind of missionary zeal among the experts and officials involved in the reform programmes in Egypt. The following statement by Springborg (1989: 257) shows how the donors perceived their missions in the reform.

"They believe that by forcing Egypt to accept the tenets of the new orthodoxy they will save it from itself. By encouraging the growth of the private at the expense of the public sector, by forcing relaxation of controls over producers, especially those in agriculture, by inducing economic decision makers to devalue the currency, raise the interest rates and rationalize consumer subsidies, they will help establish an economically viable, productive, and ultimately more independent Egypt. In their thinking MNCs can assist this process providing capital, technology, expertise, and access to international markets."

Though this view explains the necessity of reforms from an economic perspective, it does not sound plausible to explain the motives of foreign donors. It would not be reasonable to believe that foreign assistance has only to do with the humanistic and altruistic considerations of donors. As Streeten (1995: 194) indicated, it is more typical that aid policies, just like domestic policies, are motivated by political pressures, national interests, idealism and human solidarity. Military security, altruistic and Machiavellian motives or profit-seeking export interests can inspire foreign assistance policies.

To prove this in the Egyptian case, Springborg (1989: 257) commented that, while virtually all of those who were involved in channelling aid to Egypt disagreed with most contentions of Egyptian dependistas, they did not contest the claim that assistance had been utilised for policy leverage. In fact, these complex motives were so distinct in the case of Egypt that, in the late 1980s, Harris (1988: 111) advised that the donors needed to resist the temptation to take unfair advantage of the leverage over Egyptian economic and political life, which external patronage and financial dependence have provided.

According to Harris, because of the US' attitude to use the financial assistance as a policy leverage in Egypt, Egyptian people largely had the conviction that Washington's policies had been almost exclusively determined by Israeli interest, with little regard for Egypt. The following statement of an Egyptian official (Ibid.: 111) about the Egyptian-American-Israeli triangle expresses this conviction: "Egypt knows who is the wife and who the mistress is. But even the mistress has her right."

In summary, all the arguments discussed so far seem to lead to the conclusion that the US and the Western donors had distinct interest in the reform of Egypt. And it seems fair to believe that such interest was to, as argued by the dependistas and critical intellectuals, incorporate Egypt into the global capitalist system, and to increase their leverage in the political economy of Egypt. The usage of this leverage was to serve the strategic targets of the Western powers in the Middle East.

5-3-3. The Bourgeoisie

As mentioned in Chapter 2, the oil boom and the liberalisation policies begun with the Infitah in the Sadat era, has greatly widened the room for interest group politics in Egypt. Of all interests, business made the best use of the widened scope for interest-group activity. As Springborg (1989: 63-78) indicated, it has been widely observed that an Infitah bourgeoisie has emerged as the most powerful social force in domestic economy and political systems.

This Infitah bourgeoisie is fragmented into various categories according to religion, place of residence, type of economic activity, the period in which economic success was achieved, and so on. Springborg categorised them as the following three groups: the modern Islamic bourgeoisie, traditional Islamic bourgeoisie, and the secular bourgeoisie. As he indicated, the main academic issue about this social class is how cohesive that class is and whether it has succeeded in rendering the state subservient to it.

Regarding the first question, Springborg argues that, there are relatively few visible intraclass connections, be they intermarriages between families drawn from different sectors or the formation of formal or semiformal organisation of a political nature. The bourgeoisie is never a coherent group and as such, is far from united on many issues. Business people compete with each other to get lucrative privileged deals or to protect their own interests. Clashes frequently occurred between the interests of various business sectors, for example, importers and local industrialists, and between the secular 'haute bourgeoisie' and Islamic oriented bourgeoisie.

However, as another source (Metz, 1991: 264) observed, on the big issues such as Infitah, government regulation, taxation, prices and wages, business shared a common view. Thus, business groups were instrumental in pressurising for the widening of the Infitah under Sadat. They continually lobbied, with considerable success, for tax reductions and exemptions on the ground that the mobilisation of savings and investment required these concessions.

Regarding the power of the bourgeoisie versus the state, Hinnebusch claimed that "the bourgeoisie is yet nowhere capturing state power". As mentioned earlier, Egypt is a presidential state in which the state power is still strong and acts unilaterally, often at the expense of business. The state still can allow and prohibit specific business activities and it shows hostility to any force it cannot control.

However, as is widely observed, the power of the bourgeoisie has been on the rise since the 1980s. Business has won a proliferation of tax exemptions, had shifted in many cases the government policies, and has often directly affected the intra-elite politics. In 1985, the Minister of Economy Mustafa Said resigned when business blocked his attempt to extend governmental control over foreign exchange. In 1986, when the governor of the Central Bank attacked Islamic investment companies, he faced a backfire from business, which resulted in his resignation. This incident also contributed to the fall of the Prime Minister Ali Lutfi's government. So, observing this formidable power of the bourgeoisie, Hinnebusch (1993: 165) stated that, "when the bourgeoisie is united and the state not threatened by its demands, it is unstoppable in contests with other social forces."

The new power of this bourgeoisie has arisen from its ability to disrupt the economy, its payoffs to the press, and its connections to the political opposition and inside the elite itself. The 1985 incident around the issue of foreign currency and importation control explicitly manifested this power of the bourgeoisie. When the government announced a new measure prohibiting the dealings of foreign currency outside the banking system and forbidding the importation of over 300 items, the bourgeoisie used all the manner to resist that policy. They spread rumours that these measures were the work of the Minister of Economy alone and not of the whole government, and temporarily halted their importing activities in order to create an atmosphere of shortages and uncertainties.

Al-Wafd newspaper was especially vociferous in attacking both the new policy and the Minister of Economy. Business organisations such as the Federation of the Chamber of Commerce, the Federation of Industries, and the Egyptian Businessmen's Association concentrated stiff pressure on the government to revoke the measure. In just three months, the Minister of Economy Mustafa Said resigned and the 'January Decree' was replaced with the 'April Decrees', revoking the policies stipulated by the former (Ayubi, 1988: 59).

According to Hinnebusch (1993: 166), even Mubarak acknowledged that the citizens [i.e., the bourgeoisie] were richer than the government, and admitted that the regime was no longer able to carry the burden of economic development, and had to rely on investors.

It is observed that the basic interests of the bourgeoisie in the reforms lay in securing the legal framework that could guarantee a stable business environment and protect profit-making. In this context, such issues as the protection of property rights, the retreat of regulation, improved access to power, and a stable rule of law have remained the main concerns of the bourgeoisie (Hinnebusch, Ibid.; Metz, 1991).

However, as Hinnebusch has pointed out, the bourgeoisie power had not been uniformly translated into increased reform since the bourgeoisie was split or ambivalent over the diverse aspects of the reform. For example, business people who enjoyed privileged connections to get import monopolies or foreign exchange and credit at subsidised rates, opposed liberalisation. In this respect, it can be said that reform had been shaped in part by an intra-bourgeoisie struggle.

5-3-4. The Opposition Forces

As mentioned in Chapter 2, the explicit power of the opposition forces in the public political process is very weak. The Egyptian state strictly controls the legal groups and severely represses any illegal group by laws and forces. According to Kienle (1998: 220), this tendency became stronger during the 1990s. For instance, by the amendment of the party law in December 1992, the establishment of any new political party came to be subjected to the verdict of a state commission, judging whether the program of the new party is different from those of existing parties, and yet in line with the stringent requirements of the party law and the constitution.

As for the existing opposition parties, six among the then 13 parties won more than one seat in the 1995 parliament election. However, as shown in Table 7-1, their total seats reached only 14, representing a mere 3.2 percent of the 444 total elected seats. In the previous election in 1990, only one opposition party participated in the election and won 5 seats among the same total.

These parties are mainly dependent on the personalities of specific leaders, mostly very old and having reputation from their activities in the past. And, due to the lack of organisational and financial resources, they can hardly draw mass public support. The following passage from a report in *The Middle East* (April, 1996: 5) properly depicts the "personality cults"-like and co-opted nature of the opposition parties in Egypt:

> "The leftist Tagammu party's Khaled Mohieddin was one of the Free Officers who helped lead Egypt from its British-influenced monarchy to the Nasserite Republic; the Wafd's Fouad Serag Eddin, is a luminary from the pre-Revolutionary Wafd party which fought the British occupiers in 1919 and instituted constitutional democracy; the Labour Party's Ibrahim Shokri is a founding member of the Young Egypt Party whose chief claim to fame is that he helped step up the fight to rid the country of the British in the 1930s, and the Liberals' Mustapha Kamal Murad is a former Nasser and Sadat confidante.

Most of the parties were established with the blessing of the state which saw for
them a specific use and purpose when Sadat decided to make peace with Israel."

Anyway, major opposition parties were ideologically divided in their positions
toward the economic reform. The New Wafd Party (NWP) and the Liberal Party
(LP) were in general agreement with the government over the need for the reform.
However, they objected to its implementation in "a totally unhealthy political
situation, at the hands of an unqualified, inept, and corrupt ruling regime." The
following comments by the NWP chairman Fouad Serag Eddin represented the
position of these groups: "The prerequisite for successful economic, social, and
educational reform is political reform, which means constitutional change to
ensure fair and honest elections under judicial supervision and peaceful change of
government" (Ibrahim, 1996: 163).

Three other opposition parties, Tagammu (The Progressive Unionist Party), the
Amal (The Socialist Labour Party: SLP), and the Arab Democratic Nasserist
Party (ANDP), which are viewed as left of centre, were principally opposed to the
reform and criticised its foreign influence, showing concerns on social equity,
economic development, and preservation of Egyptian independence (Ibid.: 163-
166). However, as all these opposition parties lack the political infrastructure
needed to mobilise the mass public into the policy process (Ebeid, 1989:47), their
responses have been almost completely ignored by the government.

The co-opted nature and limited influence are not much different in the case of
labour unions. In Egypt, it is no secret that the present chairman of the GFELU
(General Federation of Egyptian Labour Unions), the umbrella organisation of all
labour unions, is most likely to be the next Minister of Manpower (Kassem,
2001). In fact, the present chairman of the GFELU, Al-Sayed Rashed is not
simply a minister in waiting, but also a veteran member of the ruling party (NDP),
a member of the People's Assembly and its deputy speaker. The deputy chairman

of the GFELU is also a veteran NDP member and an incumbent in the People's Assembly (Ibid.). In this context, as Kassem (Ibid: 4) indicated, the intertwined relationship between the government and organised labour has prevented autonomous representation of Egyptian workers.

As the reform progressed, even the limited influence of potential opposition forces have been fragmented along separate interests. The concerns of labour unions on job security and wages had been eased by improved treatment by the government like the Employee Shareholders Associations (ESAs) and lump-sum retirement fees. Public sector managers who once strongly opposed the privatisation came to accept the necessities and trends of the reform, and they could find new opportunities for their status in the expanding private sectors. The Islamists, the most credible opposition force, have also been divided and fragmented. The moderate, mainstream Islamists including the Al-Azhar and the Muslim Brotherhood have worked inside the system, and remained rather indifferent to the development of the reform. The radical, militant Islamist groups have launched a severe military campaign against the government, but they failed to draw public support and have finally waned.

To sum up, the influence of the opposition forces on the structural adjustment of the 1990s remained minimal. And this was one important factor of the smooth launching and successful implementation of the reform.

5-3-5. The Mass Public

As the opposition forces, including formal parties and labour unions, do not represent mass public properly, their discontent and frustration over government policies often erupts as a spontaneous civil unrest on the streets. The 1977 riot, which left 79 dead and more than 1,000 wounded, was the most distinct example of such a case in recent times. Prior to and throughout the reforms, what the government most feared was this kind of civil unrest. As Kassem (2001) has indicated, government policies continued to be influenced by the potential reaction of workers, both in the work place and on the streets, rather than by the organised constituency represented by labour unions. The Mubarak regime's careful approach to the reform and its sticking to gradualist approach was apparently due to its apprehension over potential for civil unrest. The co-option and control of opposition forces were to segregate those groups from the mass public and prevent them from inciting any civil unrest.

As the 1977 riot was directly caused by the announcement of the IMF programme, it was the most recent test case that revealed the perceptions and responses of the mass public to the economic reform. It presented complicated implications to the ruling elite. According to Ayubi (1988: 66), the 1977 riot was "the revolt of an urban dispossessed against the early bitter harvest of Infitah." In this sense, it was an explosion of class struggle that had been inflated through the Infitah. For thirty-six hours, the rioters unleashed their pent-up fury on targets that symbolised the gap between the haves and have-nots, and shouted slogans like, "Hero of the crossing, where is our breakfast?" and "Thieves of the Infitah, the people are famished." There were also shouts of "Nasser, Nasser." (Metz, 1991).

Also, to the Egyptian people, the IMF programme meant a symbolic event of national degradation against foreign influence. As Harris (1988: 105) indicated, the government's economic reliance on foreign countries and foreign organisations strengthened the Egyptian's widely held perception that their country remained a victim of outside forces which sought to keep it politically and economically weak and its government dependent. Widespread perception of governmental weakness aroused public anger, further impeding the government's ability to implement economic reforms.

In this situation, for the Egyptian rulers, introducing one more case of IMF packages was still a difficult task that had potentially hazardous political implications. It was not only the recent version of economic reforms, but the historical experiences of Egypt has also negatively affected the perceptions of the Egyptian public toward any foreign-sponsored economic reforms. As Butter (1989: 124) indicated, Egypt was the original Third World debtor, getting into trouble with its debt in the late 19th century that caused to cede much of its sovereignty to Britain and France. Against this backdrop, the Mubarak regime had to be careful not to create the impression that the economic reforms being carried out were being dictated by the IMF, so as to avoid the politically hazardous perception of spendthrift rulers once more pawning Egypt's hard won independence.

The upsurge of violent activities of militant Islamic groups from the late 1980s and a 'food riot' of the Central Security Forces, an ill-treated paramilitary force, in February 1986 added concerns of the government about the social stability effect of the orthodox reforms. However, helped by the factors explained in the previous section, the Egyptian government entered into the ERSAP and has successfully implemented it to the expected end. In this process, the mass public remained rather calm, and this phenomenon will be explained more in detail in Chapter 7.

Chapter 6

The Framework of the Reform

After the 1987 standby agreement was aborted, the Egyptian government began another series of talks with the IMF. The negotiation started in the mid-1988, but it took almost three years to reach a consensus. The IMF, being conscious of the Egyptian government's hesitancy toward reform, insisted on more strict conditionality. As described in the previous chapter, this situation changed after the Gulf Crisis of the early 1990s, and the Egyptian government and the IMF finally reached an 18-month standby agreement in May of 1991. The conclusion of these talks paved the way for another loan agreement with the World Bank in the following month.

These two agreements signified the launch of a full-scale structural adjustment programme in Egypt. The Egyptian government named this programme as "The Economic Reform and Structural Adjustment Programme" (ERSAP). This programme was a localised version of the typical SAP, with all the factors of the Washington Consensus as its basic elements. It was implemented in three stages until 1998 through renewed agreements with the IMF.

In this chapter, the framework and contents of the SAP agreements will be presented. Then, some detailed analysis of major issues will follow.

6-1. The SAP Agreement and the Framework of the Reform

The 1991 standby agreement with the IMF was renewed two times, first, in May 1993, and again in September 1996. These successive renewals meant that the reform of Egypt would be continued in the same manner as had been prescribed by the IMF. But these renewals were not made smoothly, as the IMF and the Egyptian government had frequent conflicts over the scope and pace of the reform.

6-1-1. An Overview of the SAP Agreements

After protracted negotiations, the standby agreement with the IMF was concluded in principle on April 4 and was ratified on May 17, 1991. Under the terms of this agreement, Egypt was enabled to draw SDR 278 million (then $372 million) during the following 18 months from the IMF. But the significance of this agreement lay not in the loan itself, but in the fact that it was a condition for the security of a massive debt reduction by the Paris Club and other subsequent financial assistance. With this agreement, Egypt was entitled to an unprecedented 50% reduction of its debt owed to the Paris Club. It also gained access to a total of $500 million of loans from the World Bank, the African Development Bank, and the European Investment Bank.

Soon after the signing of the IMF agreement, on May 25, 1991, the member states of the Paris Club signed an agreement to cut the foreign debt of Egypt owed to them by 50% and to reschedule the remainder. According to data from the Egyptian Ministry of Economy (1999), the final debt reduction based on this agreement reached a total of $14.2 billion, and an equivalent amount was rescheduled (see Table 6-2).

Then, in June 24, 1991, the World Bank approved a $300 million Structural Adjustment Loan (SAL) to Egypt. This agreement was signed on November 22, 1991. According to the agreement, repayment of the loan was to be made over 20 years, with a five-year grace period and a variable interest rate (then 7.73 percent). The World Bank also approved a plan to establish a Social Fund for Development of $613 million, to be financed by its affiliate, the International Development Agency (IDA), together with the European Union and other bilateral donors (Weiss and Wurzel, 1998:47-48).

However, all these funds were not to be automatically released. It was stipulated that the debt reduction would take place in three phases on the condition that the IMF approved the performance of Egypt's reform, and would sign follow-up agreements. Likewise, the World Bank loan was to be disbursed according to the appraisal of the reform.

According to the Paris Club agreement, the first 15% of the promised 50% debt reduction was immediately written off on July 1, 1991. The second 15% was originally due on December 31, 1992, on the occasion of the expiration of the first standby agreement and the signing of a follow-up agreement with the IMF. The last 20% was due in July 1994, on the same conditions that the IMF approved the reform efforts and would sign a new agreement. Finally, the rescheduling of the remaining 50% of the debt was to take place also depending on the IMF appraisal of the reform's performance (Ibid.: 47).

The utility of these loan conditions was in keeping the reform going in the long term. And in fact, they comprised the single most important factor compelling the hesitant Egyptian government to continue the reform process. However, the process did not move forward easily, and there was serious political and diplomatic manoeuvring over the issues of the IMF appraisal and the renewal of the follow-up agreements.

In the first place, a turnaround in the economic situation of Egypt subsequently eased the concern and loosened the attitude of the Egyptian government. According to an OECD source (Ibid.: 219), the first 15% debt reduction in 1991 alone helped Egypt to save some $1 billion annually. Egypt's total debt service amount was reduced from $3.4 billion in 1991 to $2.6 billion in the next year, and to $2.2 billion in 1993. As a result of this debt reduction and other windfall incomes after the Gulf Crisis, the balance of payment of Egypt improved considerably, and the total foreign reserve at the end of 1992 reached some $15 billion, which was equivalent to 18 months of imports.

As the foreign exchange situation improved, the Egyptian government did not want to pursue the reform actively. It tried to delay or evade especially the measures that could provoke unnecessary threats to the regime, such as privatisation. Then, wanting to reduce the leverage of the donors on its policies, the Egyptian government did not draw later portions of the agreed loans from the IMF and the World Bank. As shown in Table 6-1, it did not draw any amount from the second and third loans of the IMF, implying that it did not need those agreements in fact.

Similarly, the Egyptian government did not want the World Bank loan, and it drew the second tranche of $150 million from the $300 million SAL in March 1993, eight months later than was originally scheduled (Ibid.: 59-66). So, by the time the first standby agreement expired, the remaining function of the IMF agreement was not the provision of loans, but to open the way to the second and the third rounds of debt reduction by the Paris Club.

Since the IMF and the World Bank were not content with this development, it seemed that the follow-up agreement would not be easily concluded. However, through the intense diplomatic efforts of the Egyptian government and the understanding of the US government under Bill Clinton, the IMF finally evaluated the reform of Egypt favourably, and signed a new 3-year Extended Funding Facility loan agreement in September 1993. In the meantime, the validity of the first standby agreement, which was originally scheduled to expire in November 1991, was postponed two times. A similar situation persisted during the second agreement period, but again with the intermediation of the US government, the IMF finally signed another 24-month standby agreement in October 1996.

Table 6-1 The SAP Agreements of Egypt with the IMF

Unit: million SDRs

	Agreed Date	Expiration Date	Agreed Amount	Drawn Amount
SBA	May 17, 1991	May 31, 1993	278.0	278.0
EFF	Sep. 20, 1993	Sep. 19, 1996	400.0	-
SBA	Oct. 11, 1996	Sep. 30, 1998	271.4	-

Source: IMF (1992-99)

Table 6-2 The Debt Reduction Scheme by the Paris Club

Unit: Billion US Dollars

Stage	Date Implemented	Reduction in Outstanding Debt	Reduction in Debt Service	Total
1	Jul. 1, 1991	0.4	3.0	3.4
2	Sep. 20, 1993	0.4	4.0	4.4
3	Oct. 11, 1996	0.6	5.8	6.4
Total		1.4	12.8	14.2

Source: Ministry of Economy (1999)

These renewals of the IMF agreement allowed Egypt to secure the originally planned debt reduction completely. And, when the third agreement expired in September 1998, the Egyptian government announced that it did not need to continue the SAP any longer (Ministry of Economy Internet Homepage).

6-1-2. The Framework of the Policy Measures

The SAP of Egypt, or the ERSAP in local terms, was simply another case of the typical SAP propelled by the IMF and the World Bank, and as such there was also the typical division of roles between the two institutions in monitoring the programme. Whereas the IMF took care of the macro economic elements of monetary, foreign exchange, and fiscal policies, the World Bank supported and monitored investment and trade liberalisation, public enterprise reform and privatisation, regulatory reform, financial sector reform and the social safety net. The IFIs, together with the Egyptian government, set up the Structural Monitoring Programme and periodically evaluated the performance of the reform.

It should be noted here that the official documents of the SAP agreements have never been published, either by the IFIs or the Egyptian government, due to the political concerns of the Egyptian government. As a result, the full texts of the SAP agreements have been completely unavailable.[1] However, the essence of the agreement has been revealed through various sources, and later publications of the Egyptian government and the IFIs have generally introduced the contents.

According to the available information, the framework of the ERSAP was composed of the following policy guidelines, illustrated in Figure 6-1.

---

[1] I contacted the IMF, its office in Cairo, the Egyptian Ministry of Economy, and the US and Korean embassies in Cairo, but all of them said that the agreements texts are unavailable. The IMF replied to me that it could not publicise the documents because the Egyptian government had not joined the Article 4 Consultation Pilot Project, in which a number of countries have agreed to publish their reports. It added that a member country has the right to decide on whether to allow publication of their reports or not. Considering that even Egyptian Parliamentarians criticised the government for not presenting any details of the reform programme (see Elah, 1996: 245-248), it can be inferred that the agreements were a politically very sensitive issue and were kept strictly confidential.

- Overall Macroeconomic Stabilisation:
  - To redress the severe macro economic imbalances, some stabilisation measures were immediately required. Balancing public finances, lowering inflation and reducing the deficit in the current account were the main targets.
  - An immediate reduction in the government budget deficit was prescribed. This was to be achieved by reduction in public expenditure, mainly by cuts in subsidies and investment. On the revenue side, some measures to raise the efficiency of taxation were recommended. While abolishing various taxes and fees, the introduction of a new value added tax as a general sales tax was recommended. This new tax was immediately introduced in April 1991, one month before the signing of the standby agreement. In regards to deficit financing, a non-inflationary measure relying on the issue of Treasury Bills, instead of borrowing from the Central Bank, was recommended and was soon implemented.
  - To assess performance in this field, target levels for some indicators such as the fiscal deficit as a percentage of GDP, the percentage of public investment as a share of GDP, the rate of monetary expansion and inflation rate were presented as conditions by the IMF.

- Financial Sector Reform:
  - A range of banking sector reform and capital market enhancing measures were prescribed. In the banking sector, deregulation of credit and interest control was the primary concern, of which some measures were already introduced even before the SAP agreement. To enhance private sector financing through the capital market, deregulation of securities dealings was recommended. Participation of various types of brokerage companies and investment funds in stock market dealings was to be facilitated by the deregulation.

- Redressing the distortions in the foreign exchange market was another immediate concern of the reform. The unification of the multi-tiered exchange rates and subsequent devaluation of the Egyptian Pound were strongly recommended.

● Trade and Investment Liberalisation:
- Reform in trade policies has been pursued in two directions. One was to remove non-tariff barriers such as export and import bans, thus making tariffs the only trade policy instrument. Another was to reduce the tariff rates and rationalise the tariff structure. Several indicators, such as the amount of domestic production covered by import bans, levels of maximum and minimum import tariffs and the degree of various non-tariff barriers, were used in the World Bank monitoring.
- Main targets in the investment liberalisation were to remove the negative list, which prohibited foreign investment in certain economic sectors, and to expand guarantees and incentives for the investment of foreign capital. Simplifying the administrative procedures needed for foreign investment was another important concern.

● Privatisation of Public Companies
- Privatisation has been an enduring dilemma for the Egyptian economy, and was the major source of conflict between the donors and the Egyptian government. Restructuring demanded by the donors included such measures as the selling off of public companies, the reform of the financial relationships between the government, banking sector and public enterprises, full managerial autonomy and the liquidation of nonviable public enterprises.
- Indicators needed to assess the performance in this area included the share of production and investment of the public sector in the national economy,

the amount of asset value brought to the point of sale and actually complete sales, etc.

- Market Deregulation
  - Promoting competition and easing market entry and exit for private enterprises were the targets of this policy. Many investment and production controls were to be abolished, government monopolies were to be dismantled, and the discrimination of private sector from public enterprises in the market was to be phased out.

Figure 6-1 The Basic Framework of the Reform

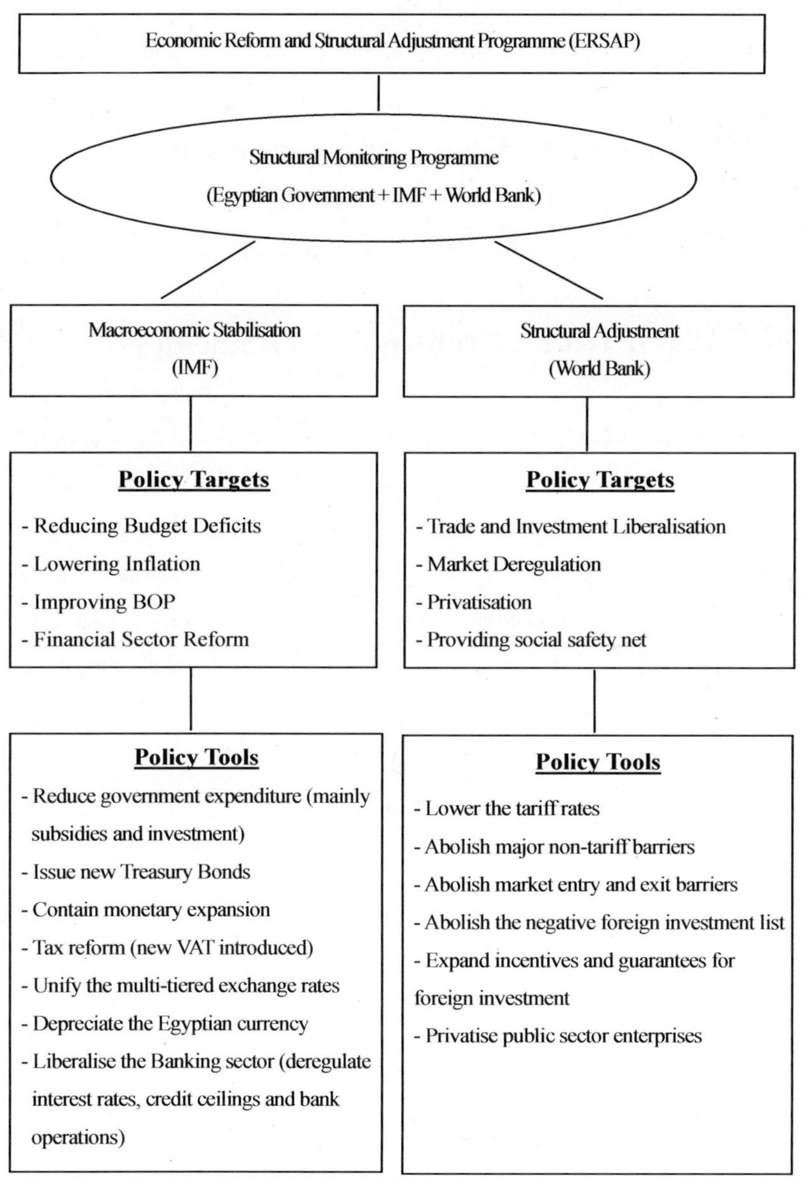

- Price liberalisation and the removal of distortions were also hailed as a prerequisite for a free market economy. The reduction of government subsidies and decontrol of prices were the focus of these policy measures. The prices of many subsidised items, such as oil, gasoline, kerosene and cotton were to be gradually increased to international levels, and transport and electricity tariffs to their long-term marginal costs.

6-2. Major Issues: Problems and Remedies

In this section, the aforementioned policy guidelines will be more closely examined. The focus is to examine the economic conditions in which such policy measures had to be prescribed. The issues will be presented generally along the lines of the aforementioned policy framework. However, certain issues such as the exchange rate system and privatisation will be separately analysed, as it seems necessary to deal with such topics in greater detail. Privatisation will be examined later in this chapter.

6-2-1. Macro Economic Stabilisation

The economic crisis of Egypt before the ERSAP has already been described in previous chapters. The IMF prescription for this crisis was the typical demand management policies, which were designed to achieve balance in public finance and external balances, and to contain inflation by means of tight fiscal and monetary policies, and devaluation. For this, an immediate reduction of the budget deficit was prescribed. The main target was the reduction of government expenditure especially in such items as wages, subsidies, and investment.

Specifically, the IMF recommended that the wage increase in 1991/92 should not exceed the 1990/91 level by more than 16.4%, while in 1992/93, the total wage bill should decrease by 15% in real terms. Subsidies were to decrease by £E 1 billion in 1991/92 from the 1990/91 level, to equal 1% of GDP. In 1991/92, subsidies represented 6.3% of GDP. But in 1992/93, they showed a significant reduction, falling by more than £E 3 billion to 2.6% of GDP, thus approaching the original target (Korayem, 1997: 16). According to Mahdi (1997: 28), as the subsidies were directed to essential commodities such as bread and wheat, and were "targeted to the poor", their reduction had significantly negative impacts on poor urban and rural households.

As for investment, in 1989/90, it reached 18.1% of GDP. With the ERSAP, it was to decrease to 11% of GDP in 1991/92. This target was more than achieved in 1991/92 when it declined to 10.4% of GDP, and continued to fall in the following four years. According to Korayem (1997: 17), since government investment fell annually by 20.9% in real terms during the period, the reduction had a contractionary impact on the economy.

On the revenue side, the IMF recommended measures to broaden various tax bases, such as widening the corporate tax base and the sales tax base, and increasing indirect taxes on items like cigarettes, etc. As mentioned earlier, the new value added tax was introduced even before the official launch of the ERSAP.

With all these measures, the goal of reducing the budget deficit was more than achieved in the reform period. Indeed, the overall budget deficit was reduced from 17.2% of GDP in 1990/91 to a mere 1.6% in 1994/96, surpassing the original targets by far (Ibid.: 17).

To contain inflation, tight monetary policies were undertaken. The growth of domestic credit fell from 25% in 1989/90 and 1990/91 to only 1.5% in 1991/92, later increasing to 11.7% in 1993/94. The budget deficits were financed by selling treasury bills to the public and banks, rather than by relying on borrowing from the Central Bank.

Finally, the devaluation of the Egyptian currency was strongly recommended as a means to improve the balance of payment. The IMF has put great emphasis on this issue and used it as a nominal anchor in stabilisation packages (IMF, 1998: 2). This issue will be examined in the following section.

6-2-2. Foreign Exchange Market Reform

Like many other developing countries, Egypt has been suffering from a chronic shortage in supply of hard currencies and this situation has led to resultant distortions in the foreign exchange market. The major problems in this market could be summarised as follows: an unrealistic official exchange rate and the resultant necessity of a parallel exchange market, the prevalence of black market dealing, and the preference to save in the US dollar (Central Bank of Egypt, 1993a).

Before the reform in 1991, the exchange rate of the Egyptian currency was tightly controlled by the government. It was deliberately kept lower than the market-evaluated rate mainly due to policy considerations. During the import substitution policy era of the Nasser regime, providing hard currencies for public companies at cheaper prices was the primary concern. After then, preventing inflation pressure in the heavily import-reliant economy became a major policy concern.

However, as the low exchange rate prevented foreign exchange transactions in the official banking sector and led to the prevalence of black market dealings instead, the Egyptian government introduced a multiple exchange rate system to give preferential treatment to specific sources of foreign exchanges. This policy persisted until 1987 when the three-tiered foreign exchange rates were unified according to the then IMF standby agreement. But again, as the newly introduced foreign exchange rate system did not catch up with the market-evaluated exchange rate, the strong demand for black market dealings did not perish. And as shall be seen, these distortions in the foreign exchange market have been a source of corruption surrounding the distribution of valuable hard currencies.

The historical context of this development needs to be examined more closely. The multiple exchange rate system dates back to June 1968, when a premium of 35.8 % was set on the official exchange rate of US$ 2.6=£E 1 or PT (Piasters; 100 PT= 1 Egyptian Pound) 39.1=1 US $ for the savings of Egyptians working abroad. In May 1972, this premium was increased to 50%.

In September 1973, the Egyptian government decided to institutionalise this premium rate system more officially and established the Parallel Foreign Exchange Market. The function of this market was to induce foreign investment as well as the workers' remittances. It was meant to absorb the in-flowing foreign exchanges through the banking sector by applying preferential exchange rates. The rates applied in this market included a premium of 50% for buying and 55% for selling, and they were increased several times responding to the inflation. However, as these premiums did not reflect the real market rates and inflation properly, a large portion of the foreign exchange dealings were still channelled through an informal market, or black market.

In January 1979, the government announced a new unified exchange rate of PT 70=US$ 1, replacing the previous official exchange rate of PT 39.1=US$ 1. This policy was meant to simplify the foreign exchange system by adopting the then parallel market rate as the new official exchange rate and abandoning the parallel market system. However, as this system still failed to absorb the foreign exchange dealings, in April 1982, a new secondary rate of PT 82.2=US $1 was introduced. In April 1983, a new preferential rate for workers' remittances, varying between PT 108 and 116 per US$ 1, was again announced.

From January 3, 1985, the preferential exchange rate was to be decided by a committee that would determine the size of the premium and the fields to which the premium would be applied. This system was expected to maintain the preferential rate flexibly so that it could compete with the black market rate and absorb hard currency resources through banks. However, dealings outside the banking sector still prevailed.

Fully understandably, the negative impacts of this black market economy were serious. Dealers in the black market accumulated wealth through illegal businesses, and after the Infitah of the Sadat era, they directed their hard currency resources to import extravagant consumer goods, taking advantage of the liberalisation. As Mourad Wahba (1996:78) put it, many of these individuals later became pillars of the economic order. They formed the group of "Munfatihun" (see Chapter 4), or the comprador bourgeoisie that derailed the Infitah to the course of speculative and consumptive open-door. There is little wonder that their advent was closely related to the corruption of administrative officials.

On May 11, 1987, the Egyptian government announced a new foreign exchange system based on a new and realistic unified rate. From then on, the exchange rate was to be determined daily by a committee in light of the supply and demand indicators of hard currencies and other economic indicators. This policy was based on the then standby agreement with the IMF, and it applied a highly depreciated starting exchange rate of PT 217=US $ 1. However, due to a lack of flexibility from the committee, this policy also largely failed to absorb hard currency resources in the banking sector.

Finally, another important aspect of the problems arising from the distorted exchange rate was the dollarisation of savings. With the issuance of the Foreign Exchange Law No.97 of 1976, it was allowed for any Egyptians to hold foreign exchange in three specific accounts without specifying their source. This tended to increase the preference of Egyptians to save the dollars they earned in these accounts. The high inflation and the low interest rate of the Egyptian currency, together with the expectation that their currency would depreciate continuously, led to this phenomenon. As a result, according to a report by the IMF (1997: 6), the dollarisation rate was as high as some 50% just before the 1991 reform.[2]

In light of this situation, the prescription of the IMF was the same as applied in many other countries: unification of the multiple exchange rates and the decontrol of the exchange rate decision mechanism. Liberalisation in the banking sector, especially the interest rate, was to take place complementarily. These policy measures were adopted and implemented at an earlier stage of the reform, thus in October 1991, the unified and free floating exchange rate system was established with the amendment of the relevant regulations. However, the IMF and Egyptian government had some serious conflicts over the speed of the depreciation thereafter.

6-2-3. Trade and Investment Liberalisation

Before the Nasser era, trade and investment activities in Egypt had been comparatively free. Since the British occupation in 1882, European capital and individuals dominated business in Egypt. As far back as in 1914, more than 90% of the paid-up capital of joint stock companies was held by French, British and Belgian interests (UNCTAD, 1991: 1). Under the influence of this foreign capital, the Egyptian market was incorporated into the world capitalist system.

After the revolution of Nasser and the Free Officers in 1952, this era of a free and open market economy under foreign domination ended. Foreign trade as well as all other economic activities came under direct government control gradually in the 1950s, and then decisively in 1961. From that year on until Sadat's Infitah in

---

[2] The term "dollarisation rate" in this report is defined as the foreign currency deposits as percentage of liquidity.

1974, almost all exports and imports were handled by public organisations and enterprises.

Central planning and budget allocations left little room for private initiative, and even the privately owned agricultural sector was subjected to controls on cropping, procurement and price setting. Foreign investment was largely regarded as hostile to national independence, and beginning with the nationalisation of the Suez Canal in 1956, a series of nationalisation measures followed. Finally, all joint stock companies were nationalised between 1960 and 1964.

This policy changed again after the adoption of the Infitah, or the Open-door policy by Sadat. The state monopoly was eased and foreign investment was welcomed again. Initially, private firms were permitted to import some commodities under particular conditions. Then, in 1976, the government holding company that had controlled foreign trade was abolished, and the private sector was allowed to trade in most goods, with a few exceptions such as petroleum and cotton. Foreign investment in Egypt was now encouraged and various incentives were granted. The Mubarak regime carried this process of liberalisation further. However, the period of State intervention left a legacy of institutional rigidity, centralisation and public sector domination which has proved difficult to shake-off.

Even though the private sector was allowed to trade in most goods in principle, in reality, trade was still largely dominated by the public sector and was under serious government control. For example, the export of petroleum, the most strategic export item, was monopolised by the Egyptian General Petroleum Company (EGPC). The export of cotton, traditionally the most important export item before the advent of petroleum, was carried out by seven public trading companies and ten private companies under the Federation of Cotton Exporters. There were other public sector monopolies as well, which were all discontinued in 1991 (WTO, 1999:52).

In the import area, formidable non-tariff barriers complemented the high tariff rates. In 1991, the applied average tariff rate was 42.2%, or 30.6% if alcoholic beverages were excluded. As a result of the tariff reform since then, tariffs have declined by more than half. However, according to a report published by the World Trade Organization (1999:33), Egyptian tariffs still remained still relatively high. Many non-tariff barriers including import bans, licenses, prior approval, foreign exchange quotas, and quality inspections made import activities more difficult. As of 1989, the items on the import ban list numbered 571. Still more items needed licenses or prior approval for import. For public sector companies, annual foreign exchange quotas were allocated according to the government budget (CBE, 1993b: 85).

As for foreign investment policy, a considerable number of business sectors were still on the negative list, which forbade foreign investment in the field completely. Even though a number of incentives had been introduced since the Infitah, significant regulations on foreign equity, capital and profit repatriation, real estate ownership, price controls, exchange controls, and employment still existed. Furthermore, inadequate administration rendered the incentives, such as tax holidays, meaningless as their benefits were outweighed by the tax uncertainty and other penalties (Giugale and Mobarak, 1996: 5).

This was the context in which the reform was prescribed. As stated earlier, the main purpose of the reform in the trade sector was to remove the non-tariff barriers and to reduce the tariff barriers. Most non-tariff barriers were either to be phased out or replaced with tariffs, thus making the tariff the only trade policy instrument. Appropriate reduction of the tariff rates was naturally prescribed. In the foreign investment policy area, the primary concern was to remove the negative list. Expansion of various incentives and guarantees was also required against confiscation, administrative sequestration, price control, import and export controls. Simplifying the administrative procedures was another important concern.

Along with the IMF and the World Bank prescriptions, it should be noted, Egypt's acquisition of WTO membership in June 1995 also required a liberalisation process in the trade and investment sectors.

6-2-4. Financial Sector Reform

In the financial sector, the reform in the banking sector and the capital market went hand in hand with the reform in government finances and the foreign exchange market. These reforms in the banking sector and the capital market were, by themselves, an important step toward a modern capitalist economy, but were also strategically positioned as a stepping stone to facilitate privatisation, the single most difficult task of the whole reform.

The banking sector and the capital market of Egypt had been severely repressed ever since the wave of nationalisation during the Nasser era. Following the confiscation and nationalisation of 27 commercial and specialised banks during the period 1959-61, Egypt's banking system was consolidated into four non-competing state banks, each focusing on separate economic sectors.

Under the Infitah of Sadat, Egypt authorised in 1974 the establishment of joint-venture banks with minority foreign participation. Foreign banks were also permitted to set up branches in Egypt. Owing to this policy, Egypt's banking system expanded to 28 commercial banks, 32 investment and merchant banks, and 7 specialised banks. However, the "big four" state banks continued to account for over three-fourths of commercial bank deposits based on their extensive branch networks, with a similar share of total lending (IMF, 1998: 56).

Before the reform in 1991, the Egyptian banking sector was still under serious government control. The central bank imposed interest rate limits on bank deposits and loans that were well below inflation. In particular, low preferential rates were mandated for loans to public enterprises and to certain private enterprises. As a result, banks could not provide incentives to draw savings and a large portion of the deposits shifted to foreign currency accounts allowed for every Egyptians since the Infitah era. For the most part, these deposits were used to finance overseas investment and imports, resulting in capital outflows. Credit ceilings and regulations on business areas still restricted free bank operations. For example, special banks and foreign branches were allowed to deal only in foreign currencies.

In the capital market, the situation was even worse. Although the Egyptian Stock Exchange (ESE) is one of the oldest in the world, it remained largely dormant until the 1990s. The ESE is comprised of two separate exchanges: the Alexandria Stock Exchange, officially established in 1888, and Cairo, established in 1903. The ESE was the fifth most active stock exchange worldwide before the nationalisation and central planning wave of the 1950s (IMF, 1999:3). These policies naturally led to the decay of the stock exchange and the function of the ESE was largely abandoned. As the public banks continued to dominate the financing of companies, the securities industry as well as all other types of financial intermediaries was hampered by the absence of governing regulations and the inadequate business infrastructure. Even the insurance sector was underdeveloped and largely state-owned.

The revitalisation of the ESE was designed as a channel to divest state-owned enterprises through public stock offerings, and as a venue to enable the private sector to raise capital. A new capital market law was key to this process, as it defined the regulatory framework for financial intermediaries. And a new independent agency was needed to supervise the functioning of this regulatory framework.

The conditions described so far were the targets of the reform in the financial sector, and some important steps in this regard were taken rather early. The restriction on the interest rate was abolished in January 1991, four months before the signing of the first IMF standby agreement. The suspension of credit ceilings on private companies followed in October 1992. Also, a series of amendments in relevant laws enabled the arrangement of new regulatory framework in the financial sector. The Banking Sector Law No.37 of 1992 and the Capital Market Law No.95 of 1992 provided the new framework (CBE, 1993c)

6-3. Privatisation

In the reform that aimed to rectify the overtly public sector-dominated structure of the economy and to expand the private sector-led market economy system, privatisation was naturally the focus of the whole reform programme. It had been an issue ever since the Infitah era, but had been a taboo as well, as the strong interests in the huge public sector opposed it. It was also the most significant issue during the structural adjustment of the 1990s, and was the major source of conflict between the Egyptian government and the international donor groups.

6-3-1. Rationale for Privatisation

Since the mid-1970s, privatisation has attracted much interest not only in Egypt but also in most developing countries. In fact, privatisation was one of the pivotal ideas of the new development orthodoxy, which has supported the Structural Adjustment Programmes. In this respect, the issue of privatisation in Egypt was just a reflection of this global phenomenon.

According to Cook and Kirkpatrick (1988: 3), the growing appeal of privatisation stems from the ideological desire for smaller government, as well as a belief in the superior economic performance of the private sector. It was a reflection of the disappointing results of the state intervention and development planning that prevailed in most developing countries during the 1950s and 1960s. The poor performance of public sector enterprises in economic, financial and distributional areas contributed to those disappointing results, and by themselves, proved the failure of the planning.

Privatisation became a significant issue in economic circles not only in developing countries, but also in developed countries. In Britain, for example, during the tenure of Prime Minister Margaret Thatcher (1979-90), a wide variety of public sector enterprises in major industrial and social services sectors including telecommunication, railway, gas, and so forth were privatised. In this case as well, the poor performance of public sector enterprises provided a rationale for privatisation. The following statement of John Moore (1986) shows the argument for privatisation quite clearly.

> "The message is clear. Public enterprises perform relatively poorly in terms of their competitive position, use labour and capital inefficiently, and are less profitable."

However, there are debates on this performance aspect, as an outright comparison of public and private enterprises is not that simple. According to Cook and Kirkpatrick (1988), a change of ownership itself does not have a significant impact on the economic and financial performance of public enterprises. They argue that an improvement in performance is more likely to result from an increase in market competition than from a change in ownership.

The term privatisation embraces broad concepts. Cook and Kirkpatrick (Ibid.: 3-4) distinguished three main approaches to privatisation: 1) change in the ownership of an enterprise from the public to the private sector, 2) liberalisation, or deregulation of entry into activities previously restricted to public sector enterprises, and 3) transferring the provision of a good or service from the public to the private sector, while the government still retains ultimate responsibility for supplying the services.

In most of the economic reforms, especially under the typical SAP, privatisation was developed using all of the above three approaches. In Egypt as well, the restructuring of the public sector embraced various aspects. However, the most significant issue was, of course, the selling off of public enterprises, or denationalisation.

As Iliya Harik (1992: 5) said, "the irony of modern times in postcolonial countries is that liberalization and privatization policies are now being advanced in order to correct the failure of the centrally controlled economy: inefficiency, huge financial deficits, low productivity, parasitic tendencies, waste, shortages, noncompetitive products, lower investment, low growth rates, and poverty."

During the 1950s and 1960s, "the state stepped in presumably to correct or make up for market failures: scarcity of capital, monopolies, sectoral imbalances, lack of economies of scale, small and timid entrepreneurial class, low investment, and distributional imbalances." (Ibid.: 5)

Despite the weakness and deficiencies of the market economy, particularly in developing countries, it seems that the proponents of privatisation may not encounter difficulties in justifying their arguments. Iliya Harik's (Ibid.: 5) following statement seems to explain why privatisation is so strongly advocated.

> "After more than three decades of state hegemony, it is clear that the state had extended itself and stretched the limits of its economic activities to the breaking point. …… The tragic part of the developmental experiences of LDCs is that the takeover of the entrepreneurial role by the state has made only minor corrections of the market deficiencies it had set out to eradicate, and it compounded the picture by adding new problems to the old ones."

6-3-2. The Egyptian Case

Ever since the Infitah era, privatisation has been advocated by many Egyptian elite as a remedy for the ailing economy. However, even stronger interests in the public sector have resisted such claims, and until very recently, privatisation has been practically a taboo. Despite all the government announcements of plans for privatisation, no public enterprise was sold during the Infitah era (1974-80), and even after then, only two hotels were sold up to 1989 (Aly, 1992: 47).

As Khattab (1998:5) expressed, there was a strong pro-state intervention trend among the Egyptian public including labour, students, intellectuals, and think-tanks in universities and media institutions. They believed in the state's role in fair distribution, protection of the poor, and hence social stability. In this situation, it was dangerous for any Egyptian leader to speak openly about privatisation.

Against such a backdrop, privatisation even in the reform process of the 1990s did not proceed easily. It was only from 1996 that privatisation was more aggressively promoted, after the president gave a clear signal for it and the administration of the new Prime Minister, Kamal Al-Ghanzouri actively stepped in. As will be shown in later chapters, several factors including mounting pressure from the donor groups contributed to this process. However, it should be noted that the proponents of privatisation had gradually gained momentum over the long years of reform attempts.

Even though the Infitah had not produced any visible achievements in privatisation, it sparked off public debates and repercussions. And in the following years of the reform attempts up to the 1990s, the untouchable nature of the issue was slowly dissolved through repeated debates and media announcements. The deteriorating performance of the public enterprises was rather clear, and by the mid-1990s, privatisation and private sector-led development became an irrefutable development strategy.

The following points presented by Giugale and Mobarak (1994), who summarised the proceedings of the country's first Private Sector Development Conference held on October 9-10, 1994, are an attempt to explain why private sector-led development is essential for the Egyptian economy.

1) Unemployment: without an accelerated economic growth, the country cannot provide enough jobs to new entries to the labour market. Halving Egypt's unemployment level by the year 2000 will require the creation of five million new jobs.

2) Poverty: the serious poverty situation also requires a rapid economic development. About six million Egyptians are ultra poor. In other words, they have an income lower than a third of the national average.

3) Investment: economic growth of the kind that will deliver a major alleviation of the unemployment and poverty situation will require a major investment effort. Given the reduction of public sector investment, private investment would have to more than double in real terms.

4) Exports: to achieve fast growth, Egypt will need a sustainable flow of foreign currency. Considering the insufficiency of the income from the traditional four major sources, private sector, non-oil merchandise exports would have to increase six fold.

Even though these points do not directly touch on the issue of privatisation, it seems rather clear that they take the retreat of the state and privatisation as a given. According to the publisher, this conference was a landmark event, organised by the Egyptian government in association with the largest local business associations and international donor community. Keeping this in mind, it seems clear that views on privatisation within the elite group have changed over time.

6-3-3. Status of the Public Sector

As was described in Chapter 4, the nationalisation and sequestration drive of 1956-61 under the Nasser regime created a massive public sector, and this sector even expanded in the following years through an extensive public investment programme. However, as the malfunctioning of this sector became felt rather seriously from as early as the late 1960s, the Egyptian government tried to solve the problems through various ways. The changes in the legislation on public enterprises, appearing in Table 6-3, detail how the Egyptian government perceived the situation.

Ever since the Law 32 of 1966 was passed to grant more flexibility to public sector managers, the direction of all following legislation was to raise the efficiency of malfunctioning public sector enterprises through the revision of their supervision systems and the introduction of profitability goals. To accomplish this, public enterprises have been repeatedly regrouped under supervisory bodies, which have been changed from the General Organisations to Higher Sectoral Councils, and again to the current 16 Holding Companies. Each change was meant to reduce the bureaucratic nature of the supervisory bodies and deregulate the operations of public enterprises. After the Infitah of 1974, privatisation and joint ventures with foreign capital have been sought as a major tool to redress the ailing public enterprises.

According to an IMF (1998: 45) report, the public sector of Egypt in 1995 accounted for about one-third of economic output and employment, and the share has not really diminished over time (see Table 6-4). The performance of the public enterprises (under Law 203) in the late 1980s and 1990s was very poor. Aggregate profits declined sharply and indebtedness rose, while a number of indicators signalled deteriorating competitiveness.

The public sector in Egypt comprises a wide variety of entities and economic activities. According to the IMF (Ibid.: 45-46) report, the main elements of the public sector in early 1996 were classified as follows:

1) The central government, comprising all line ministries, and local government

2) The service authorities, about 100 in number and consisting of ⓐ various regulatory bodies in agriculture, transportation and communication, trade, finance, housing and reconstruction ⓑ the educational institutions, including the universities; and ⓒ assorted other bodies in culture, tourism, and presidential services

3) The economic authorities, over 60 in number, including those responsible for power generation, telecommunications, the Suez Canal, the petroleum company (EGPC), the railways and national airline, the post office, government supplies, and water and port authorities

4) The nonfinancial public economic enterprises, about 314 in number (called affiliated companies) covered by Law 203. These companies are mostly concentrated in the industrial sector, but also include hotels, electricity distribution companies, and transport and port-related companies. These companies are controlled by 16 holding companies, and in turn own holdings in about 184 joint-venture companies. In addition, a few large industrial enterprises in military production, iron and steel, and so forth fall under Law 97.

5) The banking sector, comprised of the 4 public commercial banks, 26 joint-venture banks, and 21 public specialised banks.

6) The insurance sector, comprised of the three public-insurance companies, a reinsurance company, and five joint venture insurance companies, which are supervised by the Egyptian Insurance Supervisory Authority (EISA)

7) The public pension fund and social security system, and the National Investment Bank

6-3-4. Plans and Targets for Privatisation

On the verge of the signing of the standby agreement with the IMF, in April 1990, the Egyptian government announced the priorities for privatisation. Various public sector entities under the control of local governments were to be privatised first through lease, sale, or liquidation. Then, 150 out of 250 joint-venture companies operating under the then Law 43, would sell their shares, thus leading to the increase of private sector shares in those companies up to 49 percent (Sherif and Soos, 1992: 73).

For this, a special Committee on Privatisation was set up, headed by presidential aide and former Defence Minister Abu Ghazala. The task of this committee was to investigate the priorities and legal considerations in privatisation. In the following months, there was a great deal of intra-governmental debate over the selection of entities to be privatised However, according to Sherif and Soos (1996: 73), there was unanimous agreement that the large public sector companies in textiles, iron and steel, chemicals, and other strategic industries would not be put on the agenda for any type of privatisation.

Despite all the plans and announcements, there was little progress in privatisation during the following two years. President Mubarak repeatedly warned of social unrest and political disorder if reforms were implemented too abruptly (Weiss and Wurzel, 1998: 111).   This situation provoked criticism from the IMF and the World Bank, and as a result, there were serious conflicts over the renewal of the agreement.

An important development in the early years of the SAP was that a significant legal framework was prepared for privatisation. Law 203 of 1991, the so-called Public Sector Business Law, regrouped public enterprises under 22 new Holding Companies. (The number of these holding companies was increased to 27, then reduced to 17 and finally to 16.) The Capital Market Law 95 of 1992 was intended to reactivate the stock exchanges.

Table 6-3 Changes in the Legislation on Public Enterprises

Legislation	Contents
Military Order No.5/1956	Sequester societies, foundations, and associations representing British or French interests
Law 22, 23, 24/1957	Nationalise all commercial banks, insurance companies, and commercial agencies for foreign trade
/1960	Nationalise Belgian interests Nationalise the Bank of Egypt and Bank Misr
Law 117, 118, 119 /1961 (Socialist Laws)	Nationalise all large and medium sized companies Sequester the assets of 150 reactionary capitalists
Law 32/1966	Grant more flexibility to public sector managers Allow the private sector to invest in public enterprises
Law 60/1971	Replace Law 32/1966 Allow public enterprises to retain profitability goals
Law 65/1971	Encourage foreign investment Establish Free Zones
Law 111, 112/1971	Replace the General Organizations, or the supervisory body of public enterprises, with the more flexible Higher Sectoral Councils Allow the sale of government shares in public enterprises
Law 43/1974 (Infitah)	Expand incentives to foreign investment Foreign capital joint venture with public enterprises considered to be private foreign investment
Law 159/1981	Grant the same rights and incentives of the Law 43 companies to Egyptian private investors
Law 230/1989	Replace all previous Infitah laws Abolish all discrimination between Egyptian and foreign capital investment
Law 203/1991	Realign public enterprises under 27 Holding Companies, which were subsequently reduced to 16 Consider previously public enterprises with less than 51% of outstanding government shares (held by the HCs) to be private joint-stock companies

Source: excerpted mainly from Mourad Wahba (1996)

Table 6-4 Size and Composition of the Public Sector by Type of Entity

Public Entity	Output		Employment (1995)			Output per
	Share (%)	Share in Total GDP(%)	Number (000)	Share (%)	Share in the Labor Force (%)	Employee (£E)
Central and local government and service authorities	19.4	7.3	4,089	73.2	24.9	2,592
Economic authorities	46.7	17.5	455	8.1	2.8	56,044
Public enterprise sector	25.8	9.6	964	17.2	5.9	14,627
Banking Sector	7.0	2.6	65	1.2	0.4	58,462
Insurance	0.1	0.0	16	0.3	0.1	3,438
Social Insurance	0.2	0.1	n.a.	n.a.	n.a.	n.a.
Others	0.9	0.3	n.a.	n.a.	n.a.	n.a.
Total	100.0	37.4	5,589	100.0	34.0	9,779

Source: IMF (1998: 47)

By the time the second agreement with the IMF was signed, a new plan for privatisation was announced. According to the agreement of August 1993, 125 enterprises out of total 314 public companies under Law 203 were selected for privatisation without prior large-scale restructuring. While 75 were to be restructured before privatisation, 51 were to be liquidated. No detailed statement was made concerning the remaining public companies (Weiss and Wurzel, 1998: 117).

This plan was also not easily implemented and subsequent conflicts with the donor community followed. The pace of the privatisation was increased only from 1996, facing the third agreement with the IMF and the tied debt reduction. By 1998, a major process in the public reform programme was still underway containing the following elements (IMF, 1998 48):

1)   Civil service reform: reduce the size of the civil service by 2 percent a year.

2) Privatisation of nonfinancial enterprises: reduce the size of Law 203 companies by about one-third in each of the two years of the program.

3) Privatisation of the banking system: privatise the joint-venture banks and one of the public sector banks, thus bringing roughly half the sector into private sector control

4) Privatisation of insurance companies: bring another third of the sector into private hands.

5) Privatisation of infrastructure: although not strictly part of the Standby Agreement, the Egyptian government had vowed greater private sector involvement in the infrastructure sector. Thus, in electricity, airports, and some port facilities, new investments were expected to be open to greater private sector involvement.

Chapter 7

The Process of the Reform

Throughout the ERSAP, the Egyptian government tried to control the pace of the reform, while principally conforming to the pressures of international donor groups to spur it on. Being careful about the potential domestic resistance to the orthodoxy type reform, the Egyptian government tried to proceed with a gradual approach, while the IMF and the World Bank preferred a shock therapy. As a result, frequent conflicts over the range and pace of the reform between the Egyptian government and the donor group had been reported, and such conflicts had frequently threatened the overall progress of the reform.

The Egyptian government in the process took full advantage of Egypt's strategic role in the Middle East and managed to secure enough support to carry on the reform. Even the violent activities of militant Islamists in Egypt during the 1990s had provided the Egyptian government with an excuse for delaying the reforms.

In this chapter, the overall process of the structural adjustment programme will be outlined chronologically in the first section. In the second section, the responses of the internal and external interest groups to this process will be analysed. These groups pressed the Egyptian state, the implementer of the reform, to protect and maximise their own interests. The focus of the second section will be placed on the analysis of the strategies and tactics of each group and the interactions between them and the Egyptian state.

7-1. Chronology of the Reform

As noted in the previous chapter, the ERSAP of the 1990s had been implemented in three phases, based on renewed loan agreements with the IMF. Starting with the May 1991 standby agreement, each agreement in 1993 and 1996 signalled the launch of a new phase of the ERSAP. However, as the May 1991 agreement was negotiated and reached as a replacement for the aborted 1987 agreement, it accompanied many requirements. Because of the 1987 affair, the Fund now insisted that many reforms be implemented prior to the signing of a new agreement, terms with which the Egyptian government eventually complied. Accordingly, the long-protracted negotiation period between 1988 and 1991 can be seen as a preliminary phase of the ERSAP during which some important reform measures were implemented.

7-1-1. The Preliminary Phase (1988-91)

After the breakdown of the 1987 agreement, negotiations with the IMF were resumed in the summer of 1988. This time, the IMF took a harder line and insisted that it would not budge until it had seen results. The Egyptian government tried to ease the terms of the conditionality, while at the same time had to prove its willingness to reform. As a result, some important reform measures had been taken prior to the signing of the 1991 Standby loan agreement.

The first major reform taken by the Egyptian government was the revision of the investment law. In July 1989, a new investment law (Law 230) was passed by the People's Assembly and went into effect in October. This law was intended to replace the Law 43 of 1974 (Infitah law) and all its amendments. It eliminated all discrimination between local and foreign investors, and opened the way for 100 percent foreign ownership. It also expanded tax incentives and reaffirmed basic protections against expropriation. The law also simplified the procedures for investment administration, giving a full legal authority to a single organisation, the General Authority for Foreign Investment and free zones (GAFI).

One major aim of the IMF was the immediate reduction of the budget deficit, which was around 20% of GDP at the end of the 1980s. The Fund demanded a drastic cut of the deficit to 10.1% by 1991/92. Even though the Egyptian government hesitated to cut the subsidies on basic commodities, it eventually complied with the demands of the IMF.

In May 1990, prices for various items including cooking gas, cigarettes, wheat, petrol and kerosene were raised by between 10-130 %. In the following months, a series of price rises followed on other various items. With the subsidy cuts, the capital expenditure had to be also cut down. For this purpose, the disbursement of investment funds for public enterprises from the state treasury was banned from FY 1990/91 (OECF, 1999: 21).

On the revenue side, a number of measures were implemented to increase the tax and other revenues. From the middle of 1990, various public service fees were raised including railway fares, school fees, ports and airports fees, and other public service charges. In April 1991, a new value added tax of 10% was introduced as a general sales tax replacing the previous consumption tax. It was expected to yield more than £E 1 billion of additional receipts (Weiss and Wurzel, 1998: 43).

Reform of monetary policies was also regarded as an important step towards a free market economy and a number of significant changes were introduced in this regard. In January 1991, banks were allowed to freely determine interest rates. Credit ceilings were to be eliminated and subsequently abolished in the following years. The old multiple exchange rate system was ended in February 1991 and was replaced temporarily by a dual exchange rate system. In October 1991, the two rates were unified and non-bank dealers were allowed to deal in foreign exchange (Korayem, 1997: 5).

Finally, the Egyptian government also had to demonstrate its will for privatisation. In this field, the tourism sector spearheaded reforms under the advocacy of the Minister of Tourism, Fouad Sultan. In 1989, two hotels were sold to the private sector and in April 1990, another two hotels were offered for sale and one hotel was leased to a private company. By April 1990, the priorities for privatisation were announced and a special committee to steer privatisation was set up, headed by a presidential aide and former Minister of Defence, Abu Al-Ghazala.

In May 1991, the government submitted to parliament the legislation necessary to proceed with the privatisation of larger industrial establishments. Known as the "Public Enterprise Law", it was needed to override Law 111 of 1975. The IMF eventually signalled its approval of the Egyptian government's reform efforts by signing the standby agreement in that month. The public enterprise legislation was passed as Law 203 in June 1991 (Posusney, 1997: 213).

7-1-2. The First Phase (1991-93)

With the signing of the standby agreement on May 17, 1991, the ERSAP of Egypt was officially launched. This agreement was originally to be effective for 18 months, but after two extensions, expired in May 31, 1993. The reason for these extensions was the conflict between the IMF and Egypt over the performance of the reform. As a positive evaluation by the IMF was required for the continued renewal of successive agreements, and this in turn was a precondition for debt reduction from the Paris Club, the Egyptian side could not let the agreement expire without a positive evaluation by the IMF. The result of diplomatic efforts to resolve this problem was the extension of the expiration and the successful renewal of the agreement in September 1993.

As is typical in most SAPs, the signing of the standby agreement with the IMF opened up the way for another loan agreement with the World Bank. On June 24, 1991, the World Bank approved a Structural Adjustment Loan of $300 million, with repayment over 20 years, including a five-year grace period. Subsequently, the IMF, the World Bank and the Egyptian Government jointly set up the Structural Monitoring Programme to monitor the process of the reform in Egypt. In the process, the World Bank assumed responsibility for monitoring structural matters, such as institutional reform and privatisation, while the Fund concentrated on macro-economic stabilisation.

The focus of the reform in the first phase was on stabilisation of the macro-economy. Major policy targets during this period were 1) improving public finances 2) liberalisation of the exchange rate 3) lowering inflation 4) curbing monetary expansion, and 5) deregulation of prices, markets and investment (Ministry of Economy, 1999).[1]

Concerning the public finances, the IMF pressed for a further reduction of the budget deficit, demanding the abolition of subsidies altogether. According to Mahdi (1997: 28-29), the food subsidy took up 9.2% of total government expenditure in 1989/90, and by 1993/94 was reduced to 5.3%. Achieving this reduction meant the rise of prices for basic commodities "targeted to the poor". In May 1991, prices for petroleum products were raised by 14-100%. The price of butane gas, which is a basic necessity for cooking in low-income households was raised by 66.6%. The IMF kept pushing for an adjustment towards world prices, and petrochemicals were to reach world market prices by June 1995. Electricity prices were to increase annually to reach 100% of their long-run marginal cost, also by June 1995.

This rise in prices meant a deterioration of living standard especially for the

---

[1]   See the chapter titled "The Stabilization Program – Phase 1" in the homepage address
   http://interoz.com/economygoveg/English/quarterly/2_1_1Stabiliz.htm

poor, and social tensions were on the rise. Recognising this tension, President Mubarak once again preferred to avoid social risks rather than to keep the government's commitment. On 18 January 1992, the Petroleum Minister declared in the Industry Committee of the People's Assembly that President Mubarak himself had decided to postpone the increase of the butane gas price by six months (Weiss and Wurzel, 1998: 50).

On the revenue side, further measures to increase taxes were pursued. Besides the introduction of the general sales tax previously mentioned, in May 1991, customs duties were raised by up to 20% in higher brackets, causing conflicts with the goal of foreign trade liberalisation. At the same time, improvements in the taxation system were also pursued. Helped by these measures, revenues from taxes increased from 12.2% of GDP in 1990 to 17.5% in 1992 (OECF, 1999: 24).

The fiscal adjustment programme was accompanied by measures to control monetary expansion and inflation. The overall domestic liquidity growth rate was reined in from a peak of 27.5% in 1990/91 to 14-16% during the following two years. In order to finance the budget deficit through non-inflationary measures, the government issued Treasury Bills (TBs) following IMF recommendations. Three types of short-term maturity TBs were issued from 1991 and they financed about half of the total deficit (CBE, 1995).[2]

Major reforms in the monetary sector were institutionalised with the passing of the new Banking Law (Law 37) and the new Capital Market Law (Law 95) during 1992. With the new Banking Law, credit ceilings on private and public

---

[2] The first and majority type of TBs was 91 day TBs, which was issued as of Jan.3, 1991. This type took up 40.5% of total covered face value during the five years from 1991. The second and third types were 182 day TBs and 364 day TBs, which took up 30.4% and 29.1% of total covered face value during the same period. As from April 1995, long-term "Treasury Bonds" with a maturity ranging from 5-15 years were issued. See Central Bank of Egypt (1995).

companies were abolished on October 1, 1992 and on July 1, 1993. For its part, the new Capital Market Law provided a legal framework for the reactivation of the almost defunct stock exchanges.

The IMF and the World Bank demanded reform in other areas too. In July 1992, a new agrarian law (Law 96) was enacted to replace the old Agrarian Reform Law 178 of 1952. Arguably, it aimed for the modernisation of agricultural sector by abolishing all the Nasserite regulations on land tenure and rents, which were originally intended to protect the socially and economically weak tenants. Under the new law, all the existing tenancy contracts were to be defunct by the end of 1996/97, and the land holdings and rents were to be liberalised.

In the trade sector, the donors demanded the abolition of all import restrictions by the end of 1992. Due to this pressure, in August 1992, the number of import-prohibited items was reduced from 105 to 78. In the following months, a number of trade liberalisation measures were gradually implemented.

However, the IMF and the World Bank were not satisfied with the performance of the reform in general. The main conflicts arose over the issues such as the budget, trade and investment liberalisation, and especially over privatisation. Still sensitive to domestic resistance, the Egyptian government did not accelerate the more institutional aspects of the reform. In September 1992, President Mubarak continued to say that privatisation would be "a long-term process" and that "no worker will be released by the restructuring of the public sector" (Weiss and Wurzel, 1998: 55).

As the 1991 Standby Agreement was originally set to expire in November 1992, this situation implied that the IMF would not produce a positive evaluation of the reform and that the renewal of the agreement would be very difficult. However, after a large earthquake in Cairo in October 1992 that caused 561 deaths and some 10 thousand injured, the IMF initially announced that it would prolong the current agreement to February 1993, in light of Egypt's additional burden following the disaster. And in 1993, the Fund once again prolonged the agreement until the end of May.

In the meantime, President Mubarak visited Washington, DC in April 1993 and met with President Clinton and the IMF Director General Michel Camdessus. What ensued was a great deal of diplomatic and political manoeuvring over the renewal of the IMF agreement, which was finally signed in September 1993 (see Ibid.: 51-63).

7-1-3. The Second Phase (1993-96)

After several months of negotiations and political manoeuvring, the Egyptian government reached a new agreement with the IMF in September 1993. Under the terms of this agreement, Egypt could draw on an Extended Fund Facility of 400 million SDRs ($569 million) in half-yearly tranches until the end of the agreement in September 1996. As this agreement meant that the IMF approved reforms in the first phase, the Paris Club agreed to the second instalment of the 15% debt relief for Egypt, amounting to 4.4 billion dollars (see Table 5-2).

With this agreement, the ERSAP of Egypt entered into its second phase. However, the process of the reform in this phase was much delayed and the conflicts with the donor groups became more serious than in the previous phase. As was described in the previous chapter, the foreign currency reserve position of Egypt in the meantime had significantly improved, and the Egyptian government did not draw upon the agreed facility at all. As such, the policy leverage of the donors became weaker.

The main function of the agreement remained only in the sense that it was the precondition for the third instalment of the 20% debt relief, amounting to 6.4 billion dollars. According to the original schedule, the third instalment was to be made in July 1994, but it actually came more than two years later in October 1996.

The delay was caused by the IMF's refusal to approve the performance of the reform.

The first major conflict arose over the issue of devaluation. The IMF demanded a 25-30% devaluation of the Egyptian pound as it believed the overvalued pound, and the weakness of Egyptian exports, justified it. But the Egyptian government was concerned about the inflationary effect of the devaluation. And, as the majority of the Egyptian business community was more interested in maintaining inexpensive import goods rather than in increasing exports, the Egyptian Businessmen's Association firmly opposed the devaluation (Ibid.: 69).

As a result of these pressures and following rumours in the local press that the government was about to devalue the pound, in July 1994, the pound fell to a record low of LE 3.425 per dollar. Following this, the Central Bank intervened with $150 million to bring the rate back to £E 3.39. In a matter of days the market went back to normal (*The Middle East*, January 1995: 26). In September 1994, shortly after an announcement by the IMF to call for the devaluation, President Mubarak said that it was not under consideration (Weiss and Wurzel, 1998: 69).

Throughout the years 1994-95, other aspects of the reform also did not proceed as well as was expected by the donors. The privatisation plan did not materialise in detail until the end of 1995, and the trade liberalisation process fell far behind the agreed-upon timetable. The Egyptian government committed itself to dropping the standard maximum tariff to 50% and to reducing all other tariffs in the 30-50% range by 10% points by the end of 1995. But it only reduced the maximum tariff from 80% to 70% in February 1994, and did not meet further requirements (EIU, 1st Quarter 1996: 7). As for the subsidy cuts, the electricity prices were to be raised gradually to their production costs by June 1995. However, President Mubarak blocked the increase of electricity rates for industrial use after a request from the Federation of Industries (Weiss and Wurzel, 1998: 70).

The delay in the overall process of the reform in the second phase was closely tied with the domestic political situation. From the early 1990s, the Islamic militants in Egypt launched a new wave of violent campaigns. The two major militant Islamic groups, Gamaat al-Islamiyah and the Jihad began to wage violent attacks on government targets and tourists. During 1993-94, 930 people including 12 western tourists, were killed in the incidents related to their activities. Many high-ranking government officials became the target of their attacks, and even the President Mubarak himself escaped an assassination attempt in June 1995.[3] Due to this situation, tourist receipts dropped sharply from $3 billion in 1992 to $1.3 and $1.5 billion in 1993 and 1994 respectively (Weiss and Wurzel, 1998: 75).

The new wave of militant activities by the Islamists during the 1990s has been explained by many factors. Besides the political and international situation, it was evident that the long-term economic decline and the social tensions arising from the structural adjustment process had provided another impetus for the militants.[4] Even though the militants did not attract public support and were severely

---

[3]   In October 1992, Speaker of the People's Assembly, Rifaat Mahjub was assassinated in an ambush by four gunmen. In November 1993, an assassination attempt was carried out against Prime Minister Atif Sidqi in Northern Cairo. On June 26, 1995, President Mubarak was en route to a meeting of the Organization for African Unity in Addis Ababa, Ethiopia, when his motorcade was attacked by unknown assailants. (see the chronology of *Middle East Journal*)

[4]   At the end of 1990, the Gamaat spokesman Ala Muhi ad-Din was shot dead in Giza. This incident became the most direct cause of the new wave of militant activities. By November 1993, the two militant groups agreed an outline agreement to restore their relationship. And after the end of the Afghanistan war in May 1992, many of the some 1,000 Egyptian Islamists who were involved in the war returned to Egypt to join the militant groups. All these factors reinforced the military capability of the Islamist groups. However, the long-term economic decline from the 1980s and the growth of the socially and economically uprooted poor class worked as a background for the spread of the political Islam. See George Joffé (1996).

repressed and marginalized, the Mubarak regime had to seriously consider the socio-political impact of the reforms. Consequently, the government used this as an argument to delay reform.

The situation had changed somewhat rapidly from the late 1995. In the first place, the IMF was sharply criticised for its inflexible stance by its own executive board in September 1995. After, the IMF dropped the contentious issue of devaluation and stressed instead the need for accelerated structural reform (EIU, 1st Quarter, 1996: 18).[5] This change of position by the IMF led the Egyptian government to concentrate on structural adjustment, especially on privatisation. After reshuffling his cabinet in January 1996, President Mubarak for the first time spoke out clearly in favour of privatisation. Then, the new Prime Minister Kamal al-Ganzouri began to proceed with the privatisation more actively. Also, the Egyptian government had to pass the IMF review to receive the third instalment of debt relief from the Paris Club. The delay of the debt relief had been costing an extra $200 million per year in debt servicing (EIU, 2nd Quarter 1996: 18).

In February 1996, the cabinet approved the sale of 100 public companies, and reactivated the stalled privatisation programme. In March, Public Enterprise Minister Atef Obeid announced a new phase of the privatisation scheme. In May, the government sold a majority stake of one public company through the stock market. This was the first case of its kind, and it worked as a catalyst for privatisation.[6] By the end of 1996, fifteen public companies were privatised in the

---

[5] In October 25, the IMF's first Deputy Managing Director, Stanley Fischer confirmed this change of the IMF's position by saying that "There is nothing in the Egyptian economy now that indicates the need for a change in the exchange rate or the exchange system that we see." (EIU, 1st Quarter, 1996: 18).

[6] According to a report in the *Middle East* (Jul./Aug. 1997: 24), with this successful floatation of the government's 75% stake in the highly profitable Medinet Nasr Housing and Development Company, the privatisation programme "moved from rhetoric to reality".

same way (Ministry of Economy, 1999)[7].

Negotiations between the IMF and Egypt for review of the reform and renewal of the current agreement were resumed in March 1996. As the devaluation was dropped from the agenda and privatisation was being accelerated, a new issue arose over trade liberalisation. The IMF demanded immediate and hefty tariff cuts, but the Egyptian government was worried about negative effects that might arise from these reforms (EIU, 3rd Quarter 1996: 18). The negotiations lasted for more than a half- year and finally on October 11, 1996, both sides concluded a new agreement.

7-1-4. The Third Phase (1996-1998)

Before the signing of the new agreement, in July 1996, President Mubarak made a four-day visit to Washington DC to meet President Clinton. They discussed the renewal issue, and subsequent political manoeuvring followed to soften the conditions for the renewal. As the Egyptian government was keen on having a new agreement in place in time for the third Middle East and North Africa Economic summit to be held in Cairo during November 12-14, such concern had also affected the timing of the deal.

The new agreement was signed as a 24-month standby agreement, by which Egypt could draw SDR 274.1 ($391) million However, in view of Egypt's strong foreign reserve position that had reached $18 billion at the time, it was understood that Egypt would not draw this facility (EIU, 4th Quarter, 1996: 19-20). With this agreement, the third and final instalment of the Paris Club's debt relief was

---

[7] See the "Overview" table in the sub-chapter titled "(B) Privatization" in the homepage address

http://interoz.com/economygoveg/English/quarterly/3_3_b1Overview.htm

implemented.

The third phase of the reform targeted the intensification of the structural reform agenda through privatisation, deregulation, trade liberalisation, and fiscal and financial sector reforms. As the IMF revealed, the central goal of the programme was to "bring about a fundamental change in the ownership structure of the Egyptian economy". To this end, the programme envisaged significant divesture of non-financial public sector enterprises (IMF, 1996).

The IMF demanded that the Egyptian government present a plan of action for the reforms before signing the agreement. To meet this demand, the Egyptian government implemented significant trade liberalisation measures in September 1996. The standard maximum tariff was reduced from 70 to 55 %, and other tariffs were reduced by 10-25 %. At the same time, a new privatisation plan was announced. According to this plan, 91 public enterprises, with a total value of £E 18 billion, were to be privatised before June 1998 (EIU, 4th Quarter 1996: 21-22).

In the following years, the structural side of the reform was more aggressively promoted. In May 1997, a new Investment Guarantee and Incentive Law (Law 81) was enacted. It provided greater incentives for priority investment sectors and longer tax holidays for projects in selected regions. In July 1997, further trade liberalisation measures followed. The standard maximum tariff rate was reduced from 55 to 50 % and other tariffs were also reduced by 5 percentage points.

Both the speed and the scope of the privatisation were enhanced to encompass almost all public sector enterprises, including banks and insurance companies, as well as infrastructure industries. During 1996-97, 74 public sector companies were privatised in various ways: 5 by outright sales to anchor investors, 28 by majority sales through the stock market, and 21 via sales of assets, which primarily meant liquidation (Ministry of Economy, 1999)[8]

---

[8] See the same above internet homepage

The reason for the acceleration of reform during the third phase can be explained by some factors. First, the Mubarak regime regained confidence as economic and political conditions improved. Helped by the economic stabilisation programmes, the macro-economic situation of Egypt had improved quite significantly. The GDP grew in real terms by more than 5% annually during 1995/96-97/98. Annual Inflation declined from 20% level during the early 1990s to 6.2 % in 1996/97 and again to 3.8% in 1997/98. The fiscal deficit also decreased from 18% of GDP in 1990/91 to a mere 1% by the mid-1990s (Ibid.)[9]

Politically, the much feared public resistance against the reform had not been realised. Despite sporadic incidents, the general public and labour unions remained largely calm over the reform process. The militant Islamists had been severely repressed and contained in small rural areas of Upper Egypt. Their militancy and atrocity cost them public support, and after the Luxor massacre of November 1997 that killed 58 foreign tourists, the basis for their support had decisively waned (Gerges, 2000). These factors, together with the constant pressure from the donor and the increasing involvement of foreign capital in the Egyptian market, made the Egyptian government proceed with the reform more actively.[10]

In October 1997, Land Law 96/1992 came into effect after a five-year transitional period. This law put an end to the perpetual lease and strict rent control arranged in the Nasser era, liberalising the rents. As farmers' protests against this law took place, social tensions in the countryside intensified. However, due to the

---

[9] See the <Selected Economic Indicators> in the homepage address
http://interoz.com/economygoveg/English/quarterly/1_1Indicators.htm

[10] During 1995-98, foreign direct investment (FDI) increased annually 21.6% from 598 million dollars to 1,076 million dollars (IMF, 1999). Portfolio investment also increased sharply, representing 31 % of the Egyptian stock exchange in 1996, compared with about 2% in 1995 (EIU, 4th Quarter, 1996: 28).

government's harsh repression, occasional compromises, and farmers' lack of effective political leadership, all incidents were easily resolved (EIU, 4th Quarter, 1997: 13-14).

In 1998, the last year of the whole ERSAP process, still many significant reform measures were implemented. In January, the ban on imported textiles was lifted to comply with the WTO rules, of which Egypt had become a member in June 1995. Also in January, a major amendment to Companies Law 159 was made. It aimed at facilitating new business establishment by simplifying the notoriously bureaucratic business environment. To facilitate foreign investment, the law also removed the requirement that the majority of board members must be Egyptian (EIU, 1st Quarter 1998: 16).

In June, the People's Assembly passed two laws concerning the privatisation of the financial sector. Law 155 allowed the government to sell shares in the country's dominant state banks to private investors. Under the IMF agreement, the government was committed to the sale of one of the four big public sector banks by the end of the year.[11] Law 156 allowed the privatisation of the three public insurance companies (EIU, 3rd Quarter, 1997: 16-17).

Finally, the last of Egypt's major commitments under the IMF accord was implemented the day before the agreement expired on September 30, 1998. Import tariffs, covering 300 import items, were cut by 5-10% points, and import surcharges were dropped from 3% to 2%. After this, as the Egyptian government had already announced that it would not need another loan from the Fund, the eight-year long economic reform programme under the IMF and the World Bank sponsorship officially ended (EIU, 4th Quarter, 1998: 16-17). The performance of

---

[11] Although the privatisation of state banks remained politically difficult, in November 1998, the government came to terms with the UK's Barclays Bank to sell its majority stake of the Banque du Caire (EIU, 1st Quarter, 1999: 19).

the reform, especially during the third phase, was by-and-large highly appraised by the donor groups.

7-2. Interactions between the Stakeholders

As the reform progressed, all the involved stakeholders tried to protect and expand their interests. The IMF and the World Bank, as well as other international donor groups, stepped up their pressure to spur on the reform, while domestic Egyptian groups either welcomed or resisted the reform according to their interests. The Egyptian state, as the implementing authority of the reform, had to respond to pressures coming from every direction. In this respect, it has remained as "the site of struggle" for interest groups, as is properly described by Cox (2000: 25) when he applied this term to explain the role of the state in the globalising world. The direction and characteristics of the interactions among the stakeholders are illustrated in Figure 7-1. These interactions will be further discussed in this section.

Figure 7-1 Interactions between Stakeholders

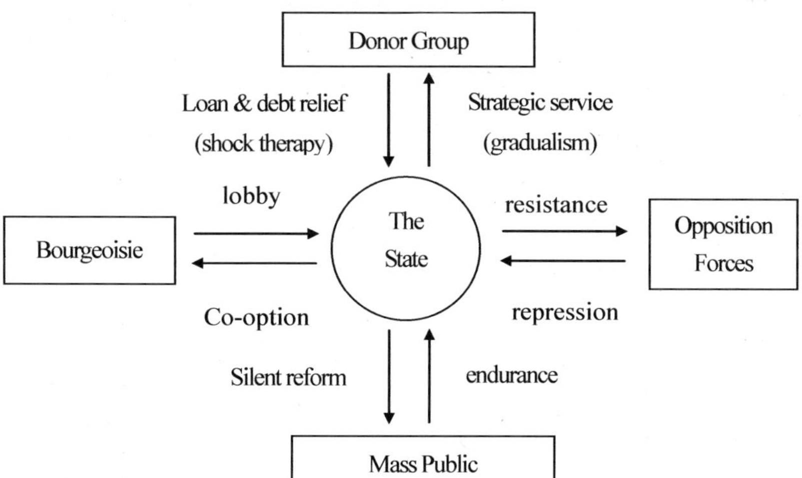

7-2-1. Power Relations between the Stakeholders

Hinnebusch (1993), while analysing the influence of interest groups on the reforms in Egypt, has attempted to apply an analytical model based on state-society power relations. According to him, the reform can be viewed through four different power relation models. In the <Strong State – Strong Society> model, reform originates from a societal consensus. In the <Strong State – Weak Society> model, the state can initiate a reform according to its own will. In the <Weak State – Strong Society> model, the bourgeoisie is able to force its preference for economic reform on the state. And finally, in the <Weak State – Weak Society> model, unresolved domestic problems increase the vulnerability of the nation to external forces allowing them to impose a reform.

As Hinnebusch admitted, none of these four models adequately explains the situation of Egypt with regard to the structural adjustment in the 1990s. However, if these models are applied to the case of Egypt, it seems that the last <Weak State – Weak Society> model is the most plausible. None of the other three models correlates with the situation of Egypt, especially with respect to the reform, where it did not originate from a societal consensus, the state's own will, or the bourgeoisie's preference.

As shown so far, the necessity of reform arose mainly due to domestic economic conditions. However, because neither the state nor the society could solve the problems on their own, Egypt finally brought in external forces to impose the reform. In this sense, the <Weak State – Weak Society> model as presented by Hinnebusch appears to be applicable in explaining the case of Egypt.[12]

---

[12] Hinnebsch himself just briefly presented the four models, and did not apply any of them in explaining the reform of Egypt.

This model captures the basic character of the reform and the status of the Egyptian state and society. There is no doubt that the reform of Egypt in the 1990s was not voluntarily undertaken, but rather an unwilling obligation imposed by donor groups. The Egyptian state and society were weak enough to accept the externally imposed reform. However, as the implementing authority of the reform, the Egyptian state was strong enough domestically against the society. In this respect, the Hinnebusch model reveals the limitation of its applicability. It seems that the power relation model should be expanded to consider the outside force, rather than dealing with only the two actors.

This thesis presented Egypt as a "presidential state", where the Egyptian state has always been the dominant player in the Egyptian politics, with no other societal groups able to effectively challenge its power and authority. Even in times when the regime was suffering from opposition forces, the situation never came to the point of threatening the regime itself, as of yet. This point is well illustrated in the following passages of a report in *The Middle East* (July 1990: 30):

"Is the Mubarak regime threatened in the sense of being embarrassed, bled and bruised? Yes" …. "Is it threatened in the sense of being overthrown? No."

So, with this power and authority, the Egyptian state could bring the imposed reform to the scheduled end. In the process, the state had used tools for co-option of potential dissidents and harshly repressed apparent resistances. In short, examining the power relations among stakeholders, the Egyptian state was vulnerable to external forces due to the heavy debt and economic problems, but at the same time, it was strong enough domestically to carry out its role as the agency of the reform.

7-2-2. Gradualism versus Shock Therapy

In early 1990, when the Egyptian government and the IMF were still arguing in regards to the first standby agreement, a report in *The Middle East* (January, 1990: 18) stated the following: "The IMF calls for acceleration of economic reform, Mubarak wants to slow down and the opposition says turn around. One thing everyone agrees is that the future of the Egyptian economy looks grim." This passage exactly described the positions of the actors in the reform, which remained unchanged over time and lasted throughout the reform. From the beginning, the Egyptian government was not keen on the reform. It worried about the adverse social effects of contractionary economic stabilisation programmes, as well as the negative impacts of privatisation on employment. The possibility of mass resistance, similar to the riot of 1977, had always been a significant concern for the Egyptian government.

As it turned out, the mass public rather endured the bitter policies of stabilisation programmes, not turning to the streets. The resistance from a more organised part of the labour was rather meek and easily controlled. The Islamic militants did not draw popular support, and were harshly repressed and marginalized.

However, the memory of the 1977 experience and the careful style of Mubarak made the government proceed with the reform quite slowly. Throughout the whole process of the reform, "gradualism" was the implicit and explicit position of the Egyptian government. President Mubarak said many times over the years that the economic reform would be a long process, and many of his high-ranking officials publicly repeated this position. The following words of Cabinet Minister Atef Obeid in 1993 about the conflict with the donor group were widely quoted as one example:

"The adviser will not be driving the car, but he might be visiting us in hospital if we crash it." (*Middle East Times*, 15-21 June 1993)

In contrast, the IMF and the World Bank preferred a shock therapy approach, and consistently demanded that the Egyptian government speed up the reform. They remembered the past violation of reform commitments by the Egyptian government, and this time wanted to see a clear progress. The following words of Caio Koch Weser, the World Bank's Vice-President for the Middle East and North Africa in 1993 seems to have expressed the position of the donor group clearly: "I believe that the pace issue is so important because of the momentum that is needed... To make this economy grow again, to make sure private investors don't sit on the fence." (Ibid.)

Due to the differences in their basic positions, the Egyptian government and the donor group frequently had serious conflicts. Even before the very start of the reform, the negotiation process went on for almost three years until the signing of the 1991 standby agreement. Afterwards, the suspension of the IMF's evaluation of the reform and the resultant delays in the renewal of follow-up agreements were caused by such conflicts.

Nonetheless, the Egyptian government managed to secure enough support to carry out the reform to the end, and this led to the reduction by half of its foreign debt owed to the Paris Club. In this context, the deftness of the Egyptian government's diplomatic skills can be rated rather highly.

It bargained over its strategic position in the Middle East and its role as a "peace broker" in the volatile region. During the Gulf War in 1991, it sided with the American-led multinational coalition against Iraq, thus providing a buffer for the US government against the pro-Iraqi sentiments amongst Arab people. After the signing of the peace agreement between Israel and the PLO in September 1993, Egypt led the support activities among Arab states, thus covering anti-Israeli Arab voices. Besides, when the anti-Western Islamists were on the march in the region, the Egyptian government firmly stood as a buttress for the pro-Western secular regimes.

This vital role of Egypt was not lost with the US government under Bill Clinton, which gave crucial 'go-ahead' signs for the reform each time there was a deadlock between the Egyptian government and the donor groups. From the viewpoint of the donor group, it seems that the technocrats of the IMF and the World Bank were much more dissatisfied with the progress of the reform in Egypt. However, in crucial times, their positions were overwhelmed by political considerations from the upper level.

This process was vividly illustrated by the renewal of the 1991 and 1993 agreements. Each time, the IMF and the World Bank refused to produce a positive evaluation for the reform, which caused the delay of the renewal of the follow-up agreements and the resultant delay of the debt reduction. And each time, this situation was changed after US – Egypt summit meetings and after some face-saving reform measures from the Egyptian side (see Weiss and Wurzel, 1998: 59-91).

In short, if the conflict between the gradualist versus shock therapy proponents is examined, it can be said that the gradualists triumphed over the shock therapists. The victory was not one-sided, however, and so the latter largely regulated the overall direction of the reform.

7-2-3. Co-option and Repression: the Bourgeoisie

While the conflict over the pace of the reform was the main external concern of the Egyptian state, internally, it also had to mediate between conflicting interests among domestic groups. The Egyptian bourgeoisie generally welcomed the reform, but their responses varied according to the impacts of specific measures on their interests. The formal opposition parties were principally divided according to their orientations, but were mostly critical on the practical aspects of the reform. The militant Islamists targeted the overthrow of the regime, and so criticised the whole aspects of political economy under the current regime (Awad, 1991; Ibrahim, 1994; Kassem, 2001).

The Egyptian state's position and strategy against these domestic forces can be characterised as "co-option and repression". As noted in Chapter 4, the clientelist and patronage system is one of the most salient features of formal Egyptian politics. In this sphere, as Kassem (1999) indicated, the mechanism of co-option functions widely, incorporating the bourgeoisie, the formal opposition parties, and the labour union leaders. Outside this sphere, where the mechanism of co-option does not work, the Egyptian state harshly represses opponents.

As for the state's relationship with the bourgeoisie, it may be this area where the mechanism of co-option operates most smoothly. Since the Infitah of the Sadat era, the power of the Egyptian bourgeoisie has grown consistently. This fact is symbolically reflected in Table 7-1, which displays the constant increase of the number of "Business parliamentarians" in the People's Assembly. Since the entry to the People's Assembly as a member of the ruling NDP provides unlimited access to central government and the patronage and contacts it commands, prominent businessmen mostly want to get this opportunity (Kassem, 2001: 11).

The bourgeoisie is represented by some national organisations such as the Egyptian Businessmen's Association (EBA) and the Federation of Egyptian Industries (FEI). As a co-opted part of the Establishment, these organisations basically welcomed the economic reforms. One private organisation, representing the interests of professionals and businessmen, the New Civic Forum (NCF), publicly announced their main objective as the promotion of liberal reform (Gomaa, 1996: 169). However, their responses were more of an ad hoc basis and ambivalent than ideologically consistent.

Table 7-1 Parliament Composition since 1981

Parliament Session	Total Elected Seats	Business MPs	Partisan Composition							
			NDP	Amal	Lib.	Tag.	Indep	Wafd	Mos. Br.	Nas
1979-84	382	7	339	30	3	0	10	Bo	Bo	NE
1984-87	448	?	389	0	0	0	0	58	*	NE
1987-90	448	14	349	25	3	0	6	35	**	NE
1990-95	444	31	360	Bo	Bo	5	79	Bo	Bo	NE
1995-00	444	71	417	0	1	5	13	6	1	1

Source: Hashem and El-Mikawy (2001: unpublished)

Notes: Amal = The Socialist Labor Party, established 1978

Lib. = The Liberal Party, established 1976

Tag. = The Progressive Unionist Party (Tagammu), established 1976

Indep = non-partisan independent candidates, were not allowed to run in 1984

Wafd = The New Wafd Party, established 1978

Mos.Br. = Moslem Brother's affiliated members, not legal party; in alliance with Wafd in 1984 and with Amal since 1987

Nas = The Arab Nasserist Party, established 1993

Bo = boycotted

NE = Party was not existent then

* = Its members were on Wafd list ** = Its members were on the Amal list

The bourgeoisie welcomed the liberalisation and the retreat of the state in areas where such measures could provide more opportunity for them. However, many of the bourgeoisies were aware of the advantages of operating in a protected domestic market with limited competition from rather inefficient state enterprises (Weiss and Wurzel, 1998: 119). Thus, they objected to devaluation and were mostly critical of privatisation.

But, as described in Chapter 5, the bourgeoisie was not a coherent group, and conflicting interests sometimes led to intra-bourgeoisie struggles. Against the formal objection of the EBA to devaluation, the more outward-oriented Alexandria Businessmen's Association criticised the emotional approach to the matter, calling for a more analytical approach to be adopted (Ibid.: 69). Likewise, on many reform measures including privatisation, the bourgeoisie did not produce distinct harmonised voices.

In fact, some researchers tend to discount the role of business organisations as well as the power play of the bourgeoisie as a whole. The study by Hashem and El-Mikawy (2001) shows that business MPs did not participate actively in economic law-making processes in the parliament and the business society as a congregation did not play a distinct role as a pressure group. The analysis of Elah (1996) on the debates over economic reform in the parliament partially supports this claim.

The interview by Kassem (2001) with one prominent Egyptian businessman reveals this point very clearly: "I am not a member of any [business] association. These channels are not necessary to get through to government. If there is a problem, it is better to go directly to government, to one of the Ministers or the Prime Minister. He is accessible, so there is no need for organization".

In Egypt, where civil society is weak and the decision-making process is more dependent on personal relations rather than rules or system (Kassem, 2001; Beshara, 1999), this kind of individual contact can be more useful than collective bargaining. These conditions easily lead to the association of politics with business and to corruption from both sides.

It was mentioned in the previous chapters that the profit-seeking "munfatihuns" corrupted and derailed the Infitah from the originally planned "productive reform" to a "speculative and consumptive liberalisation". The role and activities of the bourgeoisie in the 1990s were not much different from their predecessors. Corruption was rampant, and rumours about widespread corruption were prevalent. As a result, the public image of the bourgeoisie is that they are corrupt, involved in speculation, conspicuous consumption, tax evasion, and drug dealing (Hashem and El-Mikawy, 2001).

However, one basic difference between the reform in the 1990s and the Infitah of the past era is that the former was imposed and controlled by strong external forces. As the course of the reform was directed externally and the weak state had to follow, the bourgeoisie in the 1990s could not affect seriously the main course of the reform. Rather, they affected the pace of the reform, as did other domestic interest groups.

7-2-4. Co-option and Repression: Opposition Forces

During the early 1990s when the reform had progressed, the activities of militant Islamists had been on the rise, and this had caused the government's concern that the orthodox reform measures such as the reduction of subsidies and privatisation might increase public support for Islamist activists. Thus, even in 1995, the donors complained that the Egyptian government was sacrificing reform due to political concerns (Brumberg, 1995). However, the Islamists were severely cracked down upon and by the mid-1990s, their bases of activities had been confined to some rural areas of Upper Egypt including Ashyut and Minya. As a result, their influence on the mass public had been limited, and as mentioned in 4, they had waned decisively after the Luxor incident in November 1997.

In the meantime the roles of formal opposition parties and labour unions remained minimal. As regards the official opposition parties, most parties except the leftist Tagammu (The Progressive Unionist Party) boycotted the election in 1990 demanding fairer election rules and the lifting of the Emergency which had been in effect since the assassination of Sadat in 1981. But this boycott movement did not bring any significant response from the public, and the Tagammu won only 5 of the 444 seats in the People's Assembly. As a result, the voices of even the meek, controlled opposition parties almost disappeared in the political arena (Kassem, 1999).

As for the labour unions, the co-opted nature of the leaders, which was mentioned in Chapter 5, restricted their anti-government activities. However, as the union leaders had to maintain some semblance of credibility with the rank and file, they took more oppositional postures when the economic reform began. They concentrated their concern on the social impact of privatisation and the new labour law, and warned that massive layoffs could provoke "social explosion". But their actions, as in the past, were confined to public statements and behind-the-scenes lobbying of other regime elites (Posunsey, 1997:228). Though Gomaa (1996: 167) notes that the workers organised more than 65 strikes, sit-ins, or demonstrations during 1991-95, most of these incidents took place spontaneously by rank-and-file workers, when assaults on their wages, benefits or job security appeared imminent (Posusney, 1997: 230).

These spontaneous workers' struggles won some immediate rollback of the government policy and contributed to the regime's hesitancy to push through new policies. However, as countervailing pressures from the donor groups intensified, the regime offered fewer concessions to rank and file protests, and its responses to them became more repressive and violent (Ibid.)

Overall, after the structural adjustment was launched in 1991, the long-feared reform measures including the subsidy reduction created little visible unrest in the following years. Even the long-time taboo, privatisation caused little resistance when it was accelerated in the later years. Throughout the long period of the economic reform up to 1998, no serious mass riot like that of 1977 had been reported.

In fact, the relative silence of the opposition forces toward the structural adjustment in the 1990s was rather surprising considering the seemingly strong resistance to the reform during the 1980s. Hinnebusch (1993) explained this phenomenon by the retreat of the democratisation and the marginalisation of opposition parties and labour unions and so on. He also indicated the ambivalent attitudes of the Islamists and the general public.

It should be noted that, in some sense, the Egyptian government seems to have deliberately expressed these concerns as an excuse for its delay in the reform and as a leverage to ask for a respite from the demands of the donors. In fact, this tactic was useful for the Egyptian government to secure generous economic assistance and more lenient reform programmes.

However, according to Hinnebusch, the dwindled resistance in the early 1990s could be largely ascribed to the retreat of democratisation process. According to him, the paralysis of reform in the 1980s coincided with a period of widening democratisation, which gave a variety of interests increased access to influence. But, by the 1990s, democratisation had reached an impasse and the government was no longer under pressure to expand it.

Cassandra (1995) showed how the Egyptian government had relied on the repression of opposition forces instead of expanding democratic participation. According to Cassandra, about 86 percent of the casualties resulting from civil disorder in the 41 years up to 1993 occurred during the Mubarak era, 92 percent of which occurred between 1990-93. This seems to back up the claims of Hinnebusch on the retreat of democratisation.

It is true that the Egyptian government had expanded its control on opposition forces in parallel with the progress of the reform. It had harshly cracked down on the militant Islamists and suppressed all other potential opposition forces. During the early to mid 1990s, the state had violently engaged the militant Islamists, and by 1997 had contained the Islamists in small areas of Upper Egypt. During this period, more than 1,100 people were killed and 17,000 political detainees were taken. 83 Islamists were sentenced to death from 1992 to 1996. (EIU, 1st Quarter, 1997: 15)

As the moderate wing of Islamic fundamentalist, the Muslim Brotherhood was taking control of big professional associations, or "syndicates", through elections, the state issued a new law (No.100/1993), which required a 50 percent quorum of all members for syndicate election results to be valid. Otherwise, the government would appoint provisional boards of its own choice (Ibrahim, 1996: 166: also see Fahmy, 1998).

During the economic reform period 1991-98, the government expanded and strengthened its control on most aspects of civil life. To control the opposition inside universities, the government in May 1994 amended the Universities Law (No. 49/1972) so as to replace the election system of deans and departmental chairs with a system of   appointment by the minister of education (Ibrahim:167). In December 1996, the government made it illegal to preach in a mosque without a license from the Ministry of Awqaf (religious endowments), the penalty for violation being a fine of up to £E300 ($76) and a month in jail (EIU, 1st Quarter 1997: 15). Similarly, controls on most private organisations' activities were strengthened.

In this way, while economic liberalisation was in progress, liberalisation in the political arena was apparently on a backward trend. Ibrahim (1996: 166) contends that through such "politics of alienation", the Mubarak regime missed the opportunity to create a national consensus over the reforms and other major public policies. Anyway, it seems that this severe repression on opposition forces could explain many parts of the silence of them.

However, other sources claim that the silence could be explained by the introduction of more democratic measures of the government rather than the repression. Dr. Mokhtar Khattab (1998) from the Ministry of Public Enterprise indicated the way in which the government tried to persuade the opposition forces of the benefits of privatisation. According to his argument, the government tried to induce a consensus through strengthened contacts with the press and the opposition leaders. Apparently, the government gave workers special privileges in the privatisation programme through the preferential rights of the Employee

Shareholders Associations and the lump-sum early retirement fee. These had eased the concern of the union members.

As for the silence of the mass public, some other explanations sound more plausible, and these will be presented in the following section. What is certain is that throughout the reform period of the 1990s, the opposition forces apparently remained weak and marginalised, and that this had helped the smooth progress of the reform.

7-2-5. Reform without Fanfare: The Public

Considering that the 1977 riot was caused by a cut in food subsidies, the public response in the early 1990s to the structural adjustment programme was of special concern to all stakeholders and observers. As mentioned in Chapter 5, the Egyptian government had heeded more on the responses of the unorganised public rather than the controlled formal organisations. However, throughout the whole reform period, the Egyptian mass public remained rather calm. During the first years of the ERSAP, when the reform was more concentrated on stabilisation measures, the public had to bear the brunt of subsidy cuts and the resultant price hikes of most commodities. However, the public had been "commonly calm" as a report in *The Middle East* (July 1990: 29-30) described.

Hans Löfgren (1993: 412-413) ascribed this quiescence of the mass public to the policy management skills of the Mubarak regime. The Mubarak regime carefully chose the timing and the manner in which unpopular policies were introduced. And most of such policies were taken gradually with little public notice, so that the public could not understand the significance of the changes. Ibrahim (1996: 145-146) agrees with this view and he illustrates some cases of the "reform by stealth" as dubbed by Löfgren: subsidies were maintained but the subsidized items themselves gradually disappeared and were replaced by slightly modified and costlier items. Another practice was to choose major holidays as the time to introduce unpopular new polices under the assumption that people are less likely to take to the streets at such a time.

Many evidence support these points. In 1977, when the government suddenly raised prices "they were instigating revolts". According to a report in *The Middle East* (Ibid.), "People read the newspapers at the same time and decided to go into the streets at the same time". By comparison, Mubarak raised prices periodically and inconspicuously – during Ramadan while people were fasting, and over the Eid el Fitr holiday while people were celebrating.

Mubarak's image manipulation was also very skilful. As the conclusion on the IMF agreement was imminent, in December 1990, Mubarak suddenly announced the "Thousand Days Program for the Liberalisation of Egypt's Economy" in the People's Assembly, of which the details have never been revealed. According to Ibrahim (1996: 145), this was to make the economic reform more palatable by giving it a "stamp of Egyptianness". At the same time, Mubarak used the media to portray the government as a defender against invading Western institutions, fending off rapid price increases and other excessive measures. According to an observer, "It looked as if Egypt was in a state of war vis-à-vis the IMF and World Bank" (*The Middle East*, July 1990: 30). Even after the signing of the 1991 standby agreement, Mubarak and the official government documents made no reference to the agreement (Elah, 1996: 245-255).

It is certain that all these tactical approaches by the regime helped to avert social upheaval. However, from a social perspective, other important factors are also indicated. According to the author of a report in *The Middle East* (1990), during the post-war era in 1977, after Egypt's impressive performance in the 1973 conflict with Israel, the public had high expectations for the future. The Egyptians in the 1990s, however, were fully aware of the hardship that lay ahead. They had heard it on television, read it in newspapers, and felt it in their daily life. As such, they had developed some of their own cushions for survival: unreported income through the informal market, second or third jobs, etc. Thus, they were better prepared for future difficulties than the 1977-generation was. In short, even if the population was blindfolded by the tactical manoeuvring of the regime, they felt the slow impact of the ongoing economic reforms in their daily life, but had endured the changes rather than rioted against them

Chapter **8**

The Performance of the Reform

The ERSAP over the last decade has brought significant changes in various sectors of the Egyptian economy. The economic stabilisation packages of the ERSAP led to the stabilisation and recovery of the macroeconomic situation, dissolving much of the concern over the economic crisis that prevailed during the pre-reform years. Towards the mid-1990s, macroeconomic conditions had remarkably improved and this trend continued throughout the decade. However, from the very early 2000s, the Egyptian economy fell into a liquidity problem and subsequent depression, which cast doubts on the long-term macroeconomic effects of the reform.

There have been many significant institutional changes as well. New legislations and changes in various regulations led to the liberalisation of trade and foreign investment environment. In the financial sector, a unified exchange rate system was introduced and interest rates were liberalised. Privatisation was also accelerated during the last phase of the ERSAP and brought in the expansion of private sector involvement in the economy.

In this chapter, an analysis of the overall performance of the reforms will be made. After introducing a general assessment in the first section, the results of the macroeconomic stabilisation packages and the institutional reforms will be examined in separate sections, based on the 'before and after' methodology. Finally, the issue of privatisation will be analysed separately in the last section.

8-1. An Overall Assessment of the Performance

Towards the end of the 1990s, the evaluation on the reform has been highly positive, endorsed by the conspicuous improvement in the economic situation. For example, in a report published in May 1998, four months before the expiration of the ERSAP, the IMF (1998:1) described the effects of the reform in Egypt as follows:

> "By the standards of recent experience with economic stabilisation, Egypt in the 1990s is a remarkable success story. Determined macroeconomic policy, together with some favorable external developments, has brought much reduced inflation, led to improved public finances, a stable currency, and a strengthened banking system, together with a sound balance of payments position."

Similarly, an UNCTAD report published in 1999 (1999:1) said that "macroeconomic adjustment and stabilization efforts, pursued since 1991, have successfully redressed internal and external imbalances" and commented that "Egypt is experiencing a take-off".

This kind of praise was even more manifest in the publications of the Egyptian government. The following statement from the Ministry of Economy (1999) shows clearly how the Egyptian government viewed the results of the reform at the time when the reform just finished:

- Phase three of the economic reform programme has now been successfully implemented. Much of the recent robust economic performance is the result of these reform policies, and the government's agenda continues to support and build on these achievements.

- The outcome of the reform programme has been to fundamentally and irreversibly alter the economic fabric of Egypt, giving rise to a new society where private initiative is respected, where government is the mediator of progress, the architect of an enabling environment, and where prosperity is shared, and steady growth ensured.
- Against the background of the impressive progress in stabilization, Egypt's challenge is to sustain and accelerate growth in order to overcome unemployment and to pursue integration in the global economy.

However, from early 2000, the atmosphere has changed rapidly due to the liquidity crisis and the ensuing recession. This change is succinctly described in the following comments of Ibrahim El-Eissawi (2000) in his article titled "From Reform to Recession":

> "Not so long ago, government officials as well as many liberal economists and politicians were boasting tirelessly about the success of Egypt's economic reform programme, which started in 1990. ... Today, government and business circles are speaking of a 'liquidity problem', and even of 'recession'."

In fact, this change was detected directly during the three fieldwork visits to Egypt. In November 1996, many were talking about the successful transformation of the Egyptian economy, and were generally optimistic about the prospects of economic development. In February 2001, it seemed that the much-praised economic performance of the reform became a story of the past, and that pessimistic views on the future prospects were dominant again. In December 2002, the recession seemed to be entrenched and the more negative aspects of economic development such as unemployment, shortage of foreign currency and the revival of the black market, were major issues of discussion. The following comments of Nader Fergany, in an interview in December 2002, show how the critics of liberalisation felt about the current situation and the above-mentioned changes of atmosphere:

> "Everybody was lying until they could not lie any more, so they keep silent now. The factual situation is that economy has been in a very bad shape for a long time. … Those in charge should recognise and admit the gravity of the situation. We are in a very grave economic situation."

Though his views seemed inclined much to the pessimists, it still reflects the changes of situation. Due to this rather rapid change of the situation, it became very difficult to assess the effects of the reform, and the first draft of this chapter had to be revised considerably to incorporate the changes of situation.

As will be shown in the following section, it is clear that major macroeconomic indicators showed constant improvement of the economic situation during the 1990s. It was not only the official sources but many private analysts also praised the successful transformation of the Egyptian economy. For example, in its issue of 15 March 1997, *The Economist* described the economic ambience of Egypt as a "champagne atmosphere" and noted that "Egypt is beginning to blossom into a vibrant emerging market". Before that, in 1996, international market analysts of Robert Flemming and Merrill Lynch issued reports on the Egyptian economy with such evocative titles as "Egypt: The Sleeping Beauty" and "Egypt: The Investment Jewel on the Nile" (quoted from Moore, 1997: 3).

Indeed, considering the pessimistic atmosphere during the late 1980s and early 1990s, this change of situation from the mid-1990s looked rather impressive. If it was a feeling of crisis that made the hesitant Egyptian government accept the reform in 1991, it was the optimism in the late 1990s that prompted the official termination of the reform.

However, the Egyptian economy rather abruptly fell into a liquidity crisis in early 2000, and the situation has changed a lot since then. Due to the liquidity shortage, interest rates rose and investment fell. As the economy slowed down, the stock market performed poorly, reaching a six-year low in October 2001 and losing 50% of its value since January. Though official statistical data are not available yet, the EIU (2000) estimates the real GDP growth rate of 2000 to be as low as 3.9%, compared to 6.0% in the previous year. The recession continued until the time of this writing in December 2002.

Debates are going on the causes of the liquidity crisis and the recession, and on whether it has to do with the structural adjustment programme. Most government officials interviewed commented that the recession has more to do with the worldwide recession and the regional instability in the Middle East, while critics view that it has more to do with specific domestic policies.

According to Abdel-Razek (2000), the liquidity problem did not happen all of a sudden, but its causes have been accumulating over the years. In the view of El-Eissawi (2000), the roots of the current predicament lie deep in the structures of investment and production, in current industrial and trade policies, the pattern of income distribution and poverty-generating forces, and the lack of a proper mix between market forces and planning. He indicated that the concentration of investment in the construction sector and the rapid growth of imports were the major causes of the current situation. According to El-Eissawi, imports of goods have grown to around four times the value of exports in 1998/99, from around three times the value five years ago. The swelling public debt and the excess supply of consumer goods and nontradables are also seen by El-Eissawi as causes of the current problem.

Alia El-Mahdi, professor of economics in Cairo University, said that while the recession is partly a cyclical phenomenon, it has also to do with the unstable interest rate policy and exchange rate policy that made the expectations of business and consumers difficult (Interview on December 16, 2002).

Indicators that have been associated especially with the negative impacts of the structural adjustment programme are the trade deficit and the unemployment rate. By many critics, the expansion of the trade deficit has been ascribed to the liberalisation of trade and the rapid increase of imports of nontradables and luxury consumer goods. Although the impacts of privatisation on unemployment seem uncertain, many had the perception that it had caused the increase in unemployment. It is claimed that the reduction of subsidies has affected the growth of poverty, and the resultant decrease of purchasing power. The social impacts of the ERSAP including poverty will be more closely examined in Chapter 9.

However, there are also views that disassociate the current recession with the structural adjustment programme. Heba El-Laithy, a professor of economics in Cairo University, takes the view that the Egyptian economy would have been unsustainable with the swelling budget deficit and the foreign debts, had it not been for structural adjustment reforms. Mohammad Selim indicated that the official termination of the reform and the withdrawal of the IMF surveillance have caused the moral hazards of banking sector, which brought in the expansion of inappropriate credits and massive corruption (Both were interviewed twice in 2001 and 2002).

These conflicting views indicated how difficult it is to assess the relationship between the structural adjustment programme and the current economic situation in Egypt. They certainly affected the explicit recovery of the economy during the 1990s, and also seem to explain parts of the recession in the early 2000s. With regard to this, the following comments of Mahmoud Abdel-Fadil, professor of economics at the American University in Cairo, seem to compactly summarise the basic characteristics of the structural adjustment programme and the utility of it in the Egyptian economy:

"Structural Adjustment Programme is a programme about the stabilisation of the economy, not about growth. … On the stabilisation side, it succeeded. Budget deficit is lower, inflation rate is lower, and balance of payment deficit is lower. But what remains to reform and that cannot be solved by the structural adjustment is unemployment, which is serious problem, export problem, and technological advance. And this is not a whole part of the structural adjustment programme, neither in Egypt nor anywhere." (Interview on December 20, 2002).

8-2. Macroeconomic Stabilisation

In this part, the effects of the stabilisation packages of the ERSAP will be examined. As mentioned earlier, during the 1990s, the macroeconomic situation of Egypt had largely improved with the implementation of the ERSAP. However, after the official termination of the reform, the economy fell into a recession from the early 2000s and many indictors began to worsen again. This situation can be seen through Table 8-1 and 8-2, which will be explained in the following sections along the lines of major macroeconomic sectors. Due to the availability of more recent data, and to focus more on the direct effects of specific reform measures, the analysis here will be more concentrated on the period up to the late 1990s.

8-2-1. Growth, Inflation and Employment

During the 1990s, the trend of indicators in growth, inflation, and employment was quite positive. The records of these indicators before and after the reform improved greatly, which was quoted as evidence of the "success story" of the Egyptian reforms. After some initial shock effects in the first years of the reform, the real GDP growth rate rebounded from a low 1.9% in 1991/92 and had consistently increased to annually over 5% in the last three years of the reforms, reaching a high 5.7% in 1997/98.

Figure 8-1 Trends of Investment Rates

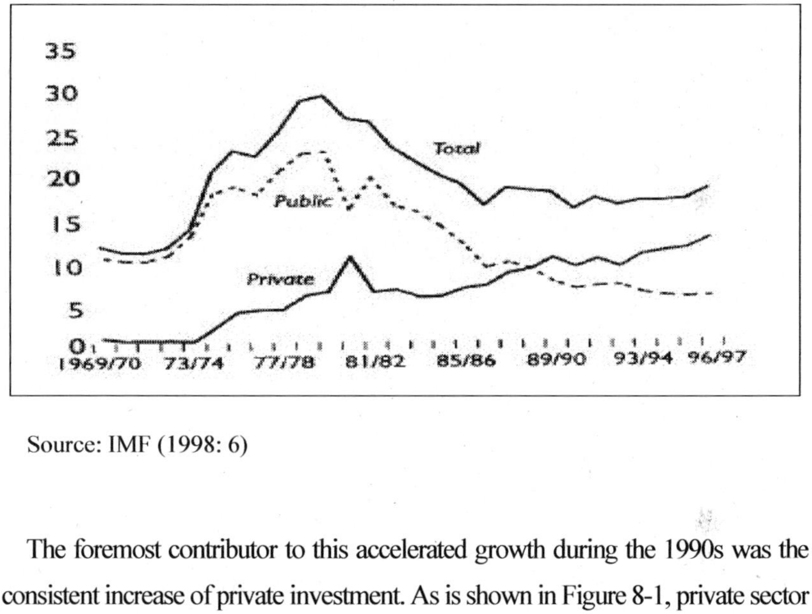

Source: IMF (1998: 6)

The foremost contributor to this accelerated growth during the 1990s was the consistent increase of private investment. As is shown in Figure 8-1, private sector investment exceeded the previously dominant public sector investment from the late 1980s, and contributed to the continued increase of total investment despite the decline of public sector investment. According to the IMF (1998:7), private investment accounted for more than 65% of the total investment during 1993-97. This expansion of the private sector investment was attributed to the stabilisation of the investment environment, which by itself signified the successful effects of the stabilisation programme.

The reduction of inflation was even more remarkable. The annual average inflation rate recorded 21.1% in 1991/92 and then declined continuously to reach a record low 3.8% in 1997/98. The main source of this successful containment of inflation was the improved fiscal stance, which had over the years alleviated the pressure on domestic liquidity growth coming from the financing of the government deficit: liquidity growth was halved in the first three years of stabilisation (Ibid. : 3)

Table 8-1 Selected Economic Indicators 1986/87-97/98

	1986/87	1987/88	1988/89	1989/90	1990/91	1991/92	1992/93	1993/94	1994/95	1995/96	1996/97	1997/98
	Pre-reform		Preliminary Reform			Phase 1		Phase 2			Phase 3	
Real GDP Growth Rate(%)	4.6	5.1	4.7	4.8	3.7	1.9	2.5	3.9	4.7	5.0	5.3	5.7
Average Annual Inflation (%)*	25.2	18.6	16.7	21.2	14.7	21.1	11.1	9.1	9.3	7.3	6.2	3.8
Unemployment Rate (%)	7.4	5.6	7.0	8.6	9.3	9.2	10.0	9.8	9.6	9.2	8.8	8.3
Fiscal Deficit (% GDP)	21.0	20.8	15.4	15.1	17.7	5.4	3.5	2.1	1.2	1.3	0.9	1.0
Current Account (% GDP)	n.a	n.a	n.a	n.a	10.2	6.4	4.9	0.8	0.6	(0.3)	0.2	(3.4)
Foreign Debt (% GDP)	205.9	209.3	185.2	157.0	106.9	77.9	64.6	59.8	54.8	45.9	38.0	34.0
Total Debt (% Exports)	1,631.0	1,205.0	1,031.0	390.0	311.1	270.1	251.2	257.1	227.1	203.6	173.5	180.3
Debt Service Ratio (%)	91.7	35.1	49.2	25.8	23.2	24.6	11.7	13.8	12.7	12	7.2	7.2
Reserves (Months of Imports)	2.0	1.6	2.1	2.8	6.3	12.1	16.1	18.8	16.4	15.7	15.7	14.3

* Starting July 1998, the relevant authority CAPMAS started applying a new basket of commodities with new weights and base period (1995/96).   This was reflected in a statistical increase in inflation.

Source: Ministry of Economy, *Quarterly Economic Digest*, April-June 1999, from the Internet Homepage

(http://interoz.com/economygoveg/English/quarterly/1_1Indicators.htm)

Table 8-2 Trends of Selected Indicators after the Reform

		1999	2000	2001	2002 (forecast)
Real GDP growth	%	6.0	3.2	2.5	0.8
Consumer Prices	%	3.1	2.7	2.2	5.4
Exchange Rates	£E/US$	3.40	3.69	4.49	5.18
Current Account	Million Dollars	-1,606	-926	-736	-1,683
	% of GDP	-1.8	-1.0	-0.9	-2.3
Exports	Million Dollars	5,237	7,061	7,093	7,533
Imports	Million Dollars	15,165	17,569	16,427	16,378
Trade Balance	Million Dollars	-9,900	-10,468	-9,329	-8,841
Total Debt	Million Dollars	30,404	29,484	29,219	30,614
Total Debt Service	Million Dollars	1,733	2,335	2,189	2,138
Debt Service Ratio	%	8.5	10.6	10.3	10.8

Source: EIU (2002)

The employment situation did not improve as rapidly as the two indicators above. It is generally believed that the impact of typical reform programmes on employment is negative, at least in the short term, and an early survey proved that the employment situation in Egypt worsened after the reforms (Korayem, 1997). However, according to the official statistics, the unemployment rate fell down from a peak of 10.0% in 1992/93 and slowly moved down afterwards.

Though there are some doubts about the credibility of the official statistics,[1] it appeared that the accelerated economic growth and the increased investment rates had provided more opportunities for employment.

---

[1] Many sources claim that the real unemployment level in Egypt is estimated to be much higher than the government statistics. International organisations including the World Bank and the IMF generally put the unemployment rate in Egypt higher than the government statistics. See OECF (1999: 52-53)

From 2000, the economy began to worsen again. As is shown in Table 8-2, the growth slowed down, and the inflation rate rose again. Due to the recession and dwindling economic activities, it looks that the employment situation has also deteriorated. As mentioned in the previous section, it is not clear whether this recession is just a cyclical phenomenon or a result of the failures of domestic policies. The worldwide recession especially after the September 11, 2001 terror incident in America, and the successive regional instability in the Middle East also helped to deepen the recession in Egypt.

On the depth of the current recession, there are also different views. According to Abdel-Fadil, current situation is a "mild' recession, not a serious one, and general macroeconomic situation is still much better compared to that of the pre-reform era (Interview in December 2002). But, as quoted earlier, Fergany asserts that the situation is much grave. It is yet to be seen whether the economy will rebound in the near future, or will slowly fall back into the crisis that caused the implementation of the reform.

8-2-2. Fiscal Adjustment

As the IMF (1997:8) has indicated, at the very heart of the stabilisation effort was the rectification of fiscal imbalances, and it was a cornerstone of the whole stabilisation programme. Over the reform period, consistent efforts were made to reduce the chronic fiscal deficit. As shown in Table 8-3, the effects of these efforts were remarkable. In just one year alone, between 1990/91 and 1991/92, during which the bulk of fiscal adjustment efforts were concentrated, the fiscal deficit was reduced to less than half, from a huge 20.0% to 6.4% of GDP. Then, over the years, it had been consistently reduced to reach as low as 1.0% in 1997/98.

This successful reduction of fiscal deficit was obtained through both an increase in revenue and expenditure reduction. On the revenue side, the largest single element of the policy effort was the exchange rate change in early 1991. This raised revenues from oil receipts, Suez Canal receipts, and from taxes on international trade. In addition, the introduction of the sales tax in 1991 and its subsequent expansion contributed to the revenue increase as well (Ibid. :12).

On the expenditure side, the focus was the reduction of subsidies and investment. During the first three years from 1990/91 to 1993/94, government investment expenditure had been continuously reduced not only as a percentage of GDP, but in absolute amounts as well. As a result, the weight of investment expenditure decreased from 15.3% of GDP in 1990/91 to 6.2% in 1993/94.

During the same period, subsidies had also been reduced from 6.0% to 2.0%.[2]

Table 8-3 National Budget Operations

(as percent of GDP)

	1990/91	1991/92	1992/93	1993/94	1994/95	1995/96	1996/97	1997/98
Total Revenues	31.1	36.7	35.1	30.4	27.8	27.0	25.7	24.4
Tax	15.7	20.5	20.6	18.1	17.1	17.0	16.1	25.4
Total Expenditure	51.1	41.1	39.3	32.5	29.1	28.4	26.6	15.8
Current	27.8	28.3	30.8	26.5	23.4	22.7	21.1	19.9
(Wages)	6.4	6.8	7.4	6.4	6.2	6.2	6.1	6.1
(Subsidies)	6.0	4.1	3.2	2.0	1.8	1.8	1.7	1.6
Investment	15.3	13.3	8.3	6.2	5.6	5.6	5.6	5.6
Overall Balance	-18.3	-6.4	-4.2	-2.1	-1.3	-1.3	-0.9	-1.0

Source: Ministry of Economy (1999)

As a whole, the weight of the government budget in the national economy had been consistently reduced over the years. The weight of total government

---

[2] Concrete numbers in the relevant statistics differ from source to source. I crosschecked closely the statistics from the Ministry of Economy (1999), Ministry of Economy and Foreign Trade (2000a), IMF (1998), OECF (1999). Then, mainly for consistency, I relied on the statistics from the Ministry of Economy (1999).

expenditure as a percentage of GDP decreased from 51.1% in 1990/91 to almost a half level, 25.4% in 1997/98. The weight of total revenue also decreased from 31.1% to 24.4% over the same period. This seems to imply that a significant retreat in the role of the state in the economy has taken place during the reform.

More recently, the fiscal deficit seems to have risen slowly after the termination of the ERSAP in 1998. According to a government source (Ministry of Economy and Foreign Trade, 2000c), the fiscal deficit as percent of GDP in 1998/99 has slightly increased to 1.3% from 1.0% in the previous year. Another source (Korean Embassy in Cairo, 2002) revealed that it reached 5.4% in the year 2000/01.

8-2-3. External Balances

The impact of ERSAP on the external balances were double-faced. Through the debt relief from the Paris Club, which was connected to the ERSAP and finally reduced the debt owed to them by half, the total foreign debt of Egypt fell from $45.6 billion in 1989/90 to $28.1 billion in 1997/98. This massive debt reduction had brought in many positive effects in the external balances. As is shown in Table 8-1, the ratio of the total debt to GDP had continuously fallen from 209.3% in 1987/88 to a mere 34.0% in 1997/98. It had also helped to reduce the Debt Service Ratio from a high 91.7% in 1986/87 to a low 7.2% in 1997/98. According to Subramanian (IMF, 1997; 47), the debt relief had improved the balance of payments by an estimated $15.5 billion (cumulative) between 1990/91 and 1996/97, accounting for all the increase in gross reserves between the two dates. He estimated that this figure represented an annual improvement in the BOP of about $2.2 billion.

Table 8-4 Balance of Payments

(Billion US Dollars)

	1990/91	1991/92	1992/93	1993/94	1994/95	1995/96	1996/97	1997/98
Trade Balance	-7.2	-6.2	-7.0	-7.3	-7.9	-9.5	-10.2	-11.8
Exports	4.3	3.9	3.7	3.3	5.0	4.6	5.3	5.1
Imports	11.4	10.1	10.7	10.6	12.8	14.1	15.6	16.9
Current Account	2.8	2.7	2.3	0.4	3.9	-0.2	0.1	-2.8
Capital Account	0.5	-0.0	1.8	2.5	4.3	1.0	2.0	3.8
Direct Investment	1.1	1.2	1.1	1.3	0.8	0.6	0.8	1.0
Portfolio Investment	0.0	0.0	0.0	0.0	0.0	0.3	1.5	0.2
Overall Balance	3.8	4.0	4.3	2.1	0.7	0.6	1.9	-0.1
Foreign Reserve	5.3	10.1	14.4	16.7	17.5	18.5	20.3	20.1
Total Debt	.32.9	32.6	30.2	30.9	33.0	31.0	28.8	28.1
Exchange Rate (£E/$)	3.33	3.34	3.37	3.39	3.39	3.39	3.39	3.39

Source: Ministry of Economy (1999)

However, since this improvement in the BOP had been made by debt relief, or a kind of windfall, rather than through an improvement in the structure of the economy, it seems doubtful whether this effect will be persistent. In fact, during the reform period, the chronic trade deficit had worsened despite tight monetary and fiscal policies. This is because commodity imports had increased rapidly, helped by the trade liberalisation measures and the improved foreign reserves, without compensating increases in exports.

As is seen in Table 8-3, the deficit in the trade account increased from $6.2 billion to $11.8 billion between 1991/92 and 1997/98. Traditionally, this deficit in the trade sector has been offset by receipts from service sector, especially through the Suez Canal receipt, tourism, and remittances by Egyptian workers overseas. However, with the simple export structure, of which petroleum takes up annually around half of the total, and with fluctuating service sector receipts, the whole economy is quite vulnerable to external shocks. As El-Mahdi (1997: 37-38) has indicated, this situation did not change over the reform period, and the apparent positive changes in the BOP could not be envisaged as being permanent. The more recent external balances data in Table 8-2 show that Egypt is still suffering from massive trade deficit and fluctuating current account receipts.

8-3. Institutional Reform

With the launch of the ERSAP, significant changes have been made to economic laws and institutions. According to Moore (1997: 4), in 1996 alone, 36 new laws were passed aimed at promoting investment and economic liberalisation. He contends that it is doubtful whether any country not undergoing revolutionary political change, such as those in the former communist bloc at the start of the 1990s, has ever engineered such extreme and far-reaching changes to its legal system within so short a space of time.

Most of the official sources from the Egyptian government and international organisations evaluate reforms on the institutional side very highly. The IMF's 1998 report said that "Against the background of impressive progress on stabilisation, there has been also a reinvigoration of a program of structural reform". The report further stated that "considerable progress has been made in privatization, deregulating protected sectors, reducing distortions from pricing and subsidy policies, and removing other obstacles to trade and investment" (IMF, 1998: 1).

However, it should be noted that there are many critical views on this aspect as well. Heba Handoussa, formerly a professor of economics at the American University in Cairo and now a managing director of an NGO, the Economic Research Forum, commented in an interview in February 2001 that despite the successful economic policy change in the 1990s toward a market-oriented economy, reform consolidation has been hampered by resilient institutional features that have survived the past thirty years. Handoussa (2001: unpublished) presented this view in her forthcoming article, stating that Egypt's story in the 1990s is one of policy change with a lag in institutional reform on the legislative and bureaucratic fronts.[3] El-Mikawy (2001: unpublished) concurs with Handoussa's view, stating that: "The 1990s in Egypt tell a story of tremendous governmental efforts to reorient statist economic policies toward an open free market. But this positive record has been tarnished by a lack of political will to effect institutional reform, either on the economic or on the political levels".

In the following parts, the aspects of institutional reforms in major economic spheres including financial sector, trade and investment liberalisation will be looked at more closely.

8-3-1. Financial Sector

Since the beginning of the ERSAP, many significant changes have taken place in the financial sector, including banking and insurance, stock exchanges and foreign exchange market. As a catalyst for market-oriented reforms, the IMF regarded an early rectification of market distortions in this sector as very important. As a result, a number of reform measures were introduced from a very early stage of the ERSAP. In January 1991, the government liberalised bank lending and deposit rates. Subsequently, ceilings on bank lending to the private sector and public sector companies were removed in October 1992 and July 1993,

---

[3]   She was interviewed by me during my fieldwork study in Egypt in February 2001, and gave me a complete set of copies of unpublished articles, which were to subsequently appear in her edited book (2001). All my referrals to the articles in her book (2001) are made from the unpublished edition.

respectively. In the following years, many liberalisation measures also followed. To redress the dominance of the public sector banks, public sector companies were authorised to deal with all banks without prior permission from a public sector bank. Law No. 101 of 1993 allowed for a branch of a foreign bank to operate in Egypt in local currency, without the need to take the form of an Egyptian joint stock company.

Privatisation of the state-owned banks was also promoted. In 1996, the government requested each of the Big Four state banks, with ownership of 49% or less in joint venture banks, to dilute their ownership to no more than 20% by the end of the year, which was duly carried out by two banks. Law No. 97 of 1996, amending the Banking Law 163 of 1957, allowed foreigners to own more than 49% equity shares in a bank. Then, Law No. 155 of 1998 allowed the private sector, including foreigners, to own shares in public sector banks up to 100% (Ministry of Economy and Foreign Trade, 2000b: 106).

As for the capital market, the government adopted a new Capital Market Law (Law 95) in 1992, streamlining all pre-existing regulations. This law provided a comprehensive framework for the revitalisation of the security industry, charging the Capital Market Authority (CMA) with new functions and responsibilities. In 1994, the stock exchanges in Cairo and Alexandria were unified and linked for real-time trading. In 1995, the annually levied stamp duty was abolished by a new law (Law 11). Similarly, in 1996, a new law (Law 89) abolished the 2% capital gains tax.

Helped by these legislations and the acceleration of the privatisation of public enterprises, the stock market activities increased conspicuously from the mid-1990s, with turnover rising from an annual average of £E 531 million during 1991-93 to over £E 10 billion in 1996. During this period, the stock market began to rival the banking system as a means of financial intermediation: new issues as a percentage of new bank credit rose from 18% to about 80% in 1997 (IMF,

1998: 59).

In the foreign exchange market, the IMF pressed for an immediate reform as an important part of the stabilisation programme. In 1991, by Ministerial Decree No. 117, the multiple exchange rate system was abolished and was replaced temporarily by a dual exchange rate system, and finally by a single unified exchange rate system. The nominal exchange rate was devalued by 23%, and buying and selling foreign currencies were allowed outside the banking system, upon obtaining proper licenses. Since the unification of the exchange market, the exchange rate of the Egyptian Pound has been virtually unchanged (see Table 8-3). The nominal rate is determined by market forces in the free exchange market. However, the Central Bank of Egypt intervenes if the value of the pound fluctuates above or below the bands specified by the government. In late 1998, the band was 3%, around a central rate of about £E 3.39 per U.S. dollar (WTO, 1999: 6).

As was discussed in the previous chapter, during 1994-95, the IMF demanded a 20-30% depreciation of the nominal exchange rate, as the inflation differentials with major partners had resulted in an appreciation of the pound's real effective exchange rate. The Egyptian government refused this demand and has kept the existing policy. Accordingly, it is widely indicated that the appreciation of the real exchange rate has negatively affected the competitiveness of Egyptian exports (Ibid.: 7, Al-Shawarby, 2000).

Finally, another important indicator showing the performance of financial sector reforms is the "dollarisation" rate. Since the Sadat regime allowed free holdings of foreign currency accounts, people have preferred to save in foreign currencies rather than the Egyptian currency (see Chapter 6). As a result, the dollarisation rate, or the foreign currency deposits as percentage of liquidity, reached as high as 50% prior to the 1991 reform. According to Subramanian (IMF, 1997: 27), this rate fell to 37% in 1991/92, and steadily to around 20% in

1996/97. This successful de-dollarisation is said to be ascribed to the stabilisation of the financial sector: diminishing fears of inflation and exchange rate instability, together with large interest differentials between Egyptian and dollar-denominated assets.

However, more recently, the stability of the foreign exchange market has been considerably shaken. It could be directly felt in the field from the revival of the black market and the bouncing back of the dollarisation. In December 2002, the US dollar could be exchanged in restaurants and shops in Cairo with exchange rates ranging from £E 5.00 to £E 5.20 per dollar, while the official exchange rate in the banking sector was £E 4.64. Apparently, people seemed to prefer to hold the US dollars, expecting rapid depreciation of the Egyptian Pound in the near future. This phenomenon could be ascribed to the accumulated current account deficits and the resultant shortage of the foreign currency.

8-3-2. Trade Liberalisation

The early focus in trade liberalisation was to remove various non-tariff barriers such as import bans and export controls, thus making the tariff the only trade policy instrument. Then, the focus naturally moved towards reducing the tariff rates and rationalising the tariff structure. During the reform period, considerable progress has been made in this sector. Thus, the Trade Policy Review for Egypt by the WTO in 1999 commented:

> "Members congratulated Egypt on its wide-ranging trade reform. They noted that most non-tariff barriers had been removed, tariff rates had been reduced and rationalized, although a degree of escalation remained."

As for the non-tariff barriers, the significance of these barriers has remarkably decreased as is shown in Table 8-4. The imports bans, which covered 52.9% of domestic production before the reform, covered less than 4% of domestic production in 1997. The import ban list now covers only poultry parts, certain textiles and apparel items, down from 210 items in 1990 (Refaat, 1999: 9).

All other non-tariff barriers (NTBs) except quality control, such as prior approvals, special conditions, suspension of letter of credits, servicing requirements, were abolished after 1991 and no longer exist. However, quality control has been increasingly gaining importance as a NTB to trade, and now covers 131 items including foodstuffs, spare parts, construction parts, electronic devices, and many consumer goods. Products removed from the import ban list are sometimes subject to high duty rates: the tariff on whole poultry, removed from the ban in July 1997, was set at 80%, which is outside the boundary of the maximum tariff as an exception.

As regards the tariff rates, a series of tariff reduction measures had effectively lowered the nominal and effective rates of protection. The maximum tariff rates declined from 110% in 1986 to 100% in 1992, 80% in 1993, 70% in 1994, 50% in 1997 and 40% in 1998. The standard deviation of tariffs also declined (Ibid.: 6). As part of the tariff structure rationalisation, in 1994, the Harmonised System (HS) was introduced, replacing the Customs Commodity Classification Nomenclature (CCCN).

Table 8-5 Production Coverage of NTBs on Egyptian Imports

(percentage of domestic production)

	Before 1991			After 1991 Trade Reform		1997	
	Public Sector	Private Sector	Total	Public Sector	Private Sector	Total	Total
Import bans	47.5	64.0	52.9	43.7	32.9	40.7	<4
Quality control	3.6	21.4	15.8	19.9	21.9	20.5	NA
Prior Approvals	12.4	9.5	11.5	0	0	0	0
Special Conditions	8.4	2.6	6.8	0.56	0.51	0.55	0
Suspension L/C	9.2	7.9	8.8	0	0	0	0
Servicing requirement	6.8	1.5	5.4	0	0	0	0

Source: Amal Refaat (1999)

Despite this progress, however, the IMF's appraisal of the trade liberalisation was rather mixed. Not withstanding the progress, the IMF (1998: 65) indicated that Egypt's trade system still remained relatively restrictive. According to the IMF, Egypt's weighted average tariff rate as of March 1996 was 28.0%, higher than the developing countries' average of 21.4%, and much higher than the world average of 8.2%. As a result, the report presents the view that, over the period between the mid-1980 and 1996, Egypt had not maximized the potential benefits from the liberalisation of the trade regime and consequently, was becoming less integrated in the world economy. Refaat (1999: 12) presented a similar view stating that Egypt's trade profile was comparatively low over the reform period, and that its economy had become less open and less integrated in the world economy over time.

El-Mikawy (2001: unpublished) presents the Egyptian/European relations as an illustrative case of the lag in institutional reform. According to El-Mikawy, Egyptian and European negotiators finalised a partnership agreement in June 1999. However, the Egyptian leaders hesitated to approve and ratify the agreement for fear that such an agreement would increase European imports into Egypt without achieving the desired increase in Egyptian exports to Europe. As such, it can be said that Egypt's trade regime still has comparatively high barriers despite the considerable liberalisation measures taken during the 1990s.

8-3-3. Investment Liberalisation

The legal and policy framework for foreign investment in Egypt has changed considerably during the reform period. As was noted in the previous chapter, even before the official launch of the ERSAP, in July 1989, the Egyptian government enacted a new Investment Law (Law 230), as a signal to present its will to reform to the donors. And in May 1997, another new law, the Investment Guarantees Incentive Law (Law 81), was enacted to attract foreign investors. Through these measures, the regulatory framework for foreign investment changed very favourably for investors.

These changes have drawn a favourable response by donors and foreign investors. According to the Investment Policy Review for Egypt by UNCTAD (1999: 2), when international business executives were asked whether changes to government policies in a country had improved competitiveness in the past year, Egypt was ranked as the first of the 58 countries surveyed.

The changes in the policy framework have certainly contributed to the increase in foreign direct investment into Egypt. According to UNCTAD (1999: 4), FDI into Egypt had steadily increased in the 1990s. Annual inflows, which were below $200 million in 1990, reached nearly $2 billion in 1997. Although higher peaks had been reached in the past, the recent inflows had been more stable than in earlier years.

Egypt has strong advantages to attract foreign investment: its strategic location as a bridge to Asia, Africa and Europe; the large size of domestic market; the low cost labour and natural resources. However, there are still many weaknesses. As is shown in Table 8-6, the UNCTAD survey indicated that bureaucracy, financial risk and business information constituted significant weaknesses.

Table 8-6 Evaluation of the FDI environment in Egypt

(○ Strengths x Weakness)

Economic Determinants	Factors	Evaluation
Market	● Market size/Growth Potential	○
	● Proximity to other nearby markets	○
	● Strategic business location	○
	● Potential return on investment	○
	● Financial Risk	x
Cost	● Low cost labour	○
Policy framework	● Generally friendly regulatory environment	○
	● Preferential access to third markets	○
	● Political Instability	x
	● Bureaucracy	x
	● Investment and business establishment procedures	x
	● Dispute settlements/judicial system	x
Business support	● Linkage/partnerships	x
	● Business Information	x

Source: UNCTAD (1999: 29)

In practice, these weaknesses considerably offset the strength of the FDI environment in Egypt, thus hindering potential capital inflows. According to UNCTAD (Ibid.: 2), while FDI flows to Egypt had been increasing, flows to other countries had been increasing more rapidly. As a result, between 1990 and 1997, Egypt no longer ranked among the 20 largest recipients of FDI among developing countries; "it should", the UNCTAD report says.

Many surveys have pointed out that these weaknesses have seriously undermined business activities and potential investment. In a survey of this researcher (Joo, 1997), Korean companies operating in Egypt expressed their difficulties arising from local financing, high taxes, ineffective administrational procedures, and strict labour law restrictions as major factors hampering their business in Egypt. According to the survey of Abu Shnief (2001: unpublished), most of the surveyed business community members replied that investment incentives and related legislation were relatively favourable. However, they pointed out that restrictiveness of the bureaucracy, the tax administration and land tenure-related procedures were also important constraints.

Criticisms over the performance of the Egyptian bureaucracy have been abundant from the past, and recently complaints of bureaucratic opposition to economic liberalisation have abounded in the Egyptian press (Palmer, et.al., 1986; El-Sayyid, 1996: 115).[4] Putting the political economy of bureaucracy aside, complaints of inefficient bureaucracy and tax administration are very prominent.

According to Giugale and Mobarak (1996: 5), the Egyptian tax administration system lacks predictability and transparency. As a result, incentives granted by the government to foster private investment, such as tax holidays, are rendered meaningless as their benefits are outweighed by the tax uncertainty. The arbitrariness and virtually unlimited discretionary powers of the tax collectors seriously distort tax collection and make tax payers seek or accept informal settlements. Tohamy (1998) has presented similar views through research into tax

---

[4]   Monte Palmer, et.al. (1986) claimed that assessment of bureaucratic performance in the Middle East offer little hope that Middle Eastern bureaucracies would serve as positive force of economic and social development in the region. They pointed to Egypt's pervasive influence in the bureaucratic system of the whole region. According to El-Sayyid (1996), the Egyptian bureaucracy was largely at odds with the new scheme of structural adjustment promoted by the international financial institutions, as it required reductions both in government expenditure and in the size of the bureaucracy, as well as insisting that other economic agents be allowed to assume a larger share of national resources.

administration and transaction costs. According to Tohamy, tax evasion in Egypt is consistent, to a great extent, with the country's economic and institutional conditions. Correspondingly, Tohamy claims, tax issue is ranked as the primary obstacle to doing business in Egypt.

These findings lead to the conclusion that, despite the considerable improvements in the legal and policy framework, the business environment in Egypt remains weak and fragile. These findings also support the claims of Handoussa and El-Mikawy: Egypt's story in the 1990s is one of policy change with a lag in institutional reform on the legislative and bureaucratic fronts.

8-4. Privatisation

Privatisation has been the most sensitive issue in the reform process, and has been a major source of conflicts between all the stakeholders. In view of the unpopularity of the issue, concerns on political instability, fears of worsening unemployment, privatisation of public companies has lagged behind its schedule. It has only been during the last stage of the ERSAP that privatisation has been promoted ardently. However, during the last three years of the ERSAP, the record of privatisation has been remarkable, and has been evaluated by donors very positively. The IMF (1998: 45) stated:

> "The magnitude of the recent privatization effort since January 1996 has been remarkable: the divestiture so far represents about 35 percent of the initial portfolio, and the market value of companies privatized accounts for about 7 percent of GDP. The pace of privatization that has been established also compares very favorably with recent international experience."

In this section, the process and the results of privatisation as well as its economic effects will be discussed in detail.

8-4-1. The Process and Proceeds of Privatisation

As privatisation was one of the most pressing conditionalities of the IMF agreement, the Egyptian government embarked on preparing for privatisation from an early stage of the ERSAP. During the first and second years of reform, the government prepared the legislative and administrational environment for privatisation. In 1991, the Ministry of Public Enterprise (MPE) and its assistant body, the Public Enterprise Office (PEO) were newly set up. And in that year, the Public Enterprise Law 203 was newly enacted. This law regrouped all the 314 public enterprises under 16 Holding Companies (HCs) as affiliated companies and granted the HCs all the powers and responsibilities to control their affiliated companies.

Under the provisions of the old Public Sector Law (Law 97 of 1983), it was prohibited to sell public sector companies except to other public entities. Under the new law, however, the HCs could sell the shares of their affiliated companies to private companies and individuals. Thus, the Law 203 of 1991 paved the way for the privatisation of public enterprises (Ministry of Economy and Foreign Trade, 2000b: 109). In 1992, the Capital Market Law 95 was issued to regulate the stock market and introduce a new framework for share trading. In 1993, a new guideline for privatisation was issued, which was updated in 1996. All these measures were undertaken to help the process of privatisation.

However, during the period 1991-95, the real process of implementing privatisation was slow. The chief problem with this first stage was that it appeared to do little more than pay lip service to the principles of privatisation. Divestitures of state-owned enterprises typically involved the sale, either to strategic investors or through the stock market, of minority stakes, meaning that the government and the existing management retained effective control of strategic decision-making. In addition, sales of these stakes were generally accompanied by legal clauses stipulating that management would undertake not to lay off existing members of the workforce (Moore, 1997: 59).

The breakthrough for the privatisation programme came in April 1996, when the government announced that for the first time, it would sell a majority holding in a state-owned company. This was the Medinet Nasr Housing and Development Company, founded in 1959, which has developed a number of sites in the Nasr City region to the northeast of Cairo, including the national sports stadium. The government floated its equity stake of 75% on the stock market, which was successfully sold at the total sales value of £E 189.63. It was a landmark issue because the government for the first time offered a majority stake to private sector investors. In addition, it was also important because it attracted very heavy foreign buying. It was reported that 36 foreign institutional investors participated in the issue, many of which were investing in Egypt for the first time (Ibid.: 60)

As this successful sale set an important precedent, a wave of similar transactions followed. As is shown in Table 8-7, 20 public companies sold their majority stake through the stock market in 1996 alone, and in 1997 another 13 companies were privatised that way.

It is difficult to analyse the performance of privatisation since government statistics are often conflicting. The data in Table 8-7 are possibly the most reliable. According to this data, a total of 90 public companies were privatised during the reform period of 1994-98. This accounts for 28.7% of the total 314 original Law 203 companies. Among them, 37 companies were privatised through the majority floatation on the stock market, while 16 companies were privatised through minority flotation. 10 companies were sold directly to anchor investors and finally, 27 companies were sold through Employee Shareholder Associations (ESAs).

The business sectors of the privatised companies widely ranged from agriculture, real estate and construction, food and beverages, milling, pharmaceuticals, cement, chemicals and fertilisers, engineering, retail, textiles, tourism and hotels.

In Egypt, if government relinquishes its majority stake (51%) in a particular company, the company will no longer be subject to the provisions of Law 203, but will be subject to the Companies Law 159 of 1981. Accordingly, during 1994-98, 37 companies that were privatised through majority selling were placed under Law 159 (Ministry of Economy and Foreign Trade, 2000b: 109; Khattab, 1999: 2).

Table 8-7 Record of Privatisation

	1994	1995	1996	1997	1998	Total
Total number of companies	6	12	30	20	22	90
Sale to anchor investors	2	1	3	2	2	10
Sale of majority stakes through the stock market	0	0	20	13	4	37
Sale of minority stakes through the stock market	0	5	7	0	4	16
Sale to ESAs	4	6	0	5	12	27
Sale of assets	0	0	0	0	0	0
Proceeds (£E million)	661	1,148	3,697	2,272	1,457	9,235
Percentage of all Law 203 Companies privatised	1.9	3.8	9.6	6.4	7.0	28.7

Source: Ministry of Economy and Foreign Trade (2000c: 20)

The process of privatisation continued even after the ERSAP officially ended in 1998. According to government statistics, by June 1999, the total privatisation effort involved the sale of interests in 127 companies, bringing in proceeds worth £E 10.7 billion, which represents some 3.5% of GDP, and about 71.4% of the current market value of the initial privatisation portfolio of Law 203 companies (Ministry of Economy: 1999).

8-4-2. The Effects of Privatisation

The impact of privatisation can be assessed in various ways based on different standards. Not withstanding the methodological constraints and difficulties, Cook and Kirkpatrick (1995: 18-21) have presented several ways of assessing the effects of privatisation: in terms of the objectives set for the privatisation, macro level indicators, enterprise level indicators, social impacts, and finally economic welfare using a cost-benefit analysis.

It is difficult to measure the impact of privatisation in Egypt in this way owing to the lack of relevant data. Most of the available data are from government sources and they are apt to praise the successful implementation of the privatisation. Even though privatisation lagged behind the original schedule and had caused serious conflicts with the donors, the IMF also evaluated the performance, especially during the final stage of the reform, very positively.

Comparing Egypt's privatisation performance with recent international experience, the IMF (1998: 52) concluded that Egypt's experience ranked among the top four countries. It especially praised the high privatisation receipts of Egypt considering that Egypt's privatisation effort so far did not encompass infrastructure sector, while major share of privatisation receipts for many of the selected countries emanated from this sector.

There are some indicators that help to assess the performance of privatisation in terms of macroeconomic level. According to government data (Ministry of Economy, 1999), the share of private sector output in GDP slightly increased during the years 1991/92 – 95/96, from 61.2% to 63.3%. The consistent increase of private sector investment during the 1990s along with the declining trend of public sector investment, which is shown in Figure 8-1, could be interpreted as another indicator. Even though these indicators by themselves do not represent the effects of privatisation, it would not be far-fetching to say that the privatisation helped to bring in these changes.

There are also very limited data that can help to assess the effects of privatisation in terms of enterprise level indicators. According to data by the IMF (1998: 55), the performance of the companies sold to ESAs generally improved after privatisation. Seven out of ten companies increased their profits after privatisation, and the average increase in profits for those companies that improved their performance was a remarkable 61.1%. Even though this limited data does not say much about the performance of all the privatised companies, they still show that privatisation has partially improved the performance of those companies.

It is just as difficult to assess the social impact of privatisation as the economic impact. On the employment side, the World Bank in 1991 estimated that about one quarter of workers in public enterprises, i.e. 380,000 workers might be laid off with the implementation of public enterprise reform (Korayem, 1997: 20). Due to the lack of any available data, it is still difficult to know how many public sector workers have been laid off during the process of privatisation. However, contrary to the general expectation of worsening unemployment, official government statistics show that the unemployment rate had consistently declined since 1992/93 (See Table 8-1).

Accounting for public fears over unemployment, the government had introduced a number of complementary programmes in parallel with the privatisation. The ESAs, through which the employees could be the new owners of privatised companies, and the Early Retirement Programme that granted three years' wages in a lump sum, were introduced to ease the concerns of workers. The Social Fund for Development, which was established in 1991 with financing from the World Bank, had also helped to absorb the negative social impacts through providing short-term jobs and retraining.

In general, it is still difficult to assess the overall impacts of the privatisation, and the limited data from the Egyptian government and international organisations tend to present affirmative comments. However, it might be useful to refer to a critical view also to comprehend the situation. The following comments of a specialist in Cairo (2002) help to look at the effects of privatisation in a different perspective:

> "What happened is that they were selling successful companies that could invest and provide job opportunities. And the new owner is not very much interested in developing these companies. ... Let's see what we are witnessing in the cement industry. Some of the companies that have been sold were successful companies, but after the privatisation, they went bankrupt. There was a company called Kaha for food processing. They make tomato paste, jams, things like that. One of the most successful companies. It used to produce a total of 18 thousand tons a year. Now they produce only three thousand tons. Lots of people lost their jobs. … In order to prepare the companies for privatisation, the government persuaded workers to take money and leave. Lump-sum and leave. Most people took the money, spent the money, and they are now jobless. And they have become a burden on the economy."

Privatisation has continued even after the official ending of the ERSAP even though the pace has slowed down. Considering that it has been a long term issue raised as a remedy to the ailing economy since the Infitah era, the performance of privatisation during the 1990s has been certainly remarkable and has proven the government's will to reform toward a market economy.

To sum up the chapter, the structural adjustment of Egypt in the 1990s has been implemented fairly in success in achieving its original targets. Macroeconomic situation has considerably improved and significant changes have taken place in institutional side as well. However, it is not yet certain whether these effects will be persistent.

Chapter 9

The Social Impact and Political Implications

Since the mid-1980s, the 'social cost of adjustment' has been raised as a major issue of wide-ranging debates. It has been pointed out by many that the structural adjustment programme has exacerbated the standard of life for the mass of the people in many of the concerned developing countries (See Chapter 3). In the case of Egypt, the results are under dispute. The Egyptian government paid considerable attention to the politically sensitive nature of the social issue, and tried to secure a social safety net against the strict austerity measures demanded by the donors. Government sources claim that this effort has helped to avert the negative social impacts of the structural adjustment. However, critics contend that the reform has aggravated the living conditions of especially the weak social strata. They argue that poverty has grown and equity has been more distorted due to the impacts of the reform. These points are discussed in the first part of this chapter.

The second part of the chapter will discuss some of the political implications of the reform, focusing on who gained through the economic and social impacts that this thesis has analysed so far. In this way, this thesis is approaching its research goal to understand the overall aspects and implications of the structural adjustment in Egypt.

9-1. Public Spending and the Social Protection

The SAP has affected the life conditions of the mass of the people, especially the socially weak strata, in many developing countries. The typical paths of such impacts are identified as follows (Stewart, 1991: Nassar, 2002).:

1) The increase in the prices of basic commodities, which is caused by the removal of subsidies as a result of government expenditure reducing policies

2) The availability of free social services provided by the state, such as health and education, which now face cost recovery schemes

3) The changes of income, which are affected by changes in employment, wages, privatisation policies as well as agricultural policies

What these paths connote is that the more immediate and direct social impacts of the SAP are made through adjustment in public spending, even though other parts of the policy packages can bring more long-term effects. In this section, the trends of public social spending and the ensuing changes in public services, as well as the social protection system of Egypt, will be analysed.

9-1-1. Trends for Public Social Spending during the ERSAP

While Egypt was embarking on the structural adjustment programme, it was generally feared that fiscal austerity would lead to a sharp decline in public expenditure in general, and in social spending in particular. However, according to government sources, these fears proved to be ungrounded. Even though public spending fell as a percentage of GDP, with most cuts related to public investment, social spending rather increased (Institute of National Planning, 1998).

According to the *Human Development Report of Egypt 1997/98*, published by a government agency, the INP, with the help of the UNDP, social spending as a percentage of total government expenditure increased from an average of 19 percent during 1987-93 to 25 percent over 1994-97 (Ibid.: 24). Even though it declined by an average of 15 percent in real terms during the first two years of the ERSAP, real social spending picked up again by an annual average of 6 percent in the following four years, which along with the drop in the overall public spending has assured the reallocation of public resources toward social sector and related activities.

As seen in Table 9-1, public social spending, which includes all government expenditure items related to health, education, social security, and subsidies, increased from an average of 9.9 percent during 1987/88-89/90 to an average of 10.3 percent during the second reform period, or 1994/95-96/97. The table shows that most items, except the subsidies, have either increased or remained constant during the reform period. Only the share of subsidies has declined from 3.3 percent to 1.9 percent during the same period

Based on these statistics, the government source (Ibid.; 25) claimed as follows: "The composition of the social sectors' expenditure shows that the Government of Egypt has not only taken action to protect essential social services during fiscal austerity, but has also given high priority to these sectors."

Since the Government of Egypt is the ultimate producer of all statistical data on the public spending, it is difficult to repudiate these claims or to present different data. Even some government officials interviewed presented similar data, commenting almost the same above. However, it is worth noting that the perception from the field was felt quite different and many were dubious about the claims of the government. Some conflicting views will be presented in the following section.

Table 9-1 Public Social Spending during the Reform Periods.

(percent of GDP)

	1990/91	1996/97	Pre-Reform	1st Phase	2nd Phase
Total	10.3	10.3	9.9	9.8	10.3
Current	7.5	7.6	7.8	7.26	7.25
-Subsidies	2.96	1.75	3.3	2.54	1.9
-Education	3.13	3.95	3.2	3.3	3.92
-Health	1.15	1.06	1.1	1.25	1.24
-Community	0.22	0.29	0.12	0.17	0.20
Investment	2.84	3.26	2.12	2.56	3.04
-Education	0.97	1.5	0.66	1.04	1.45
-Health	0.5	0.48	0.44	0.44	0.40
-Housing	1.36	1.25	1.01	1.06	1.14
-Community	0.014	0.027	0.014	0.014	0.027

Source: INP (1998: 25)

9-1-2. Changes in Public Social Services and Social Safety

Contrary to the claims of the Egyptian government that it had protected essential social services and social safety schemes during the austerity periods, many of the interviewees commented that the quality of essential social services, especially, health and education, has seriously worsened, and that they were sceptical of the reliability of official data. The following comments of a journalist in Cairo refer to this situation.

"I would have my doubts about the reports published by international agencies. They have great interests with the Egyptian government, and want to keep good relationship with the government. So they would come up with such reports that paint rosy pictures with the Egyptian economy. .. The advisor to the Prime Minister told me that poverty percentage has gone down. Maybe, but I do not believe this is true. I can see, from talking to people, that poverty is really acute. They have what we call 'acts of survival'. They survive through acts of survival. They make ends meet with whatever they have. You know, how you would measure this person as poor, below poverty line, is a very tricky issue."

According to Nader Fergany (1999: 17), there is a tendency to exaggerate the success of social safety schemes for political purposes. He claims that assistance schemes such as the Social Development Fund, which will be analysed in the following section, have not proven sufficient to tackle extensive unemployment and widening poverty, and indicates that close monitoring and in-depth research of the social safety net seems to be hampered by political expedience.

Analysts indicate that the worsening of public social services is an important factor accounting for the increase in poverty and a disturbing factor for the whole Egyptian economy. Dr. Mohamed Said (2000) of the Al-Ahram Center for Political and Strategic Studies contends that the vast erosion of the state's capacity to maintain social services led to 'the private appropriation of public assets'. According to him, costly private tutoring thrives due to the deterioration of the public education system, and in the health sector, too, a similar phenomenon is taking place. According to Mohammad Selim, the massive cost of private tutoring (he estimated it as seven billion US dollars referring to a government source) is pressing the households and even disturbing the flow of capital in the Egyptian economy. Heba El-Laithy indicated the increase of the cost in education and health as the negative social effects of the structural adjustment (Interview in December 2002).

Regarding the status of public social protection system in Egypt, Heba Nassar (2002) presented a comprehensive statement. In the following, a synopsis of the status will be introduced based on Nassar's paper and other available sources.

Food Subsidy

As shown previously, the subsidy was the one public social expenditure item that had been most seriously cut during the ERSAP. According to Nassar, the food subsidy system in Egypt was the most extensive in the world. In 1989, approximately 89 per cent of the population received some form of ration card, with most people receiving the full ration (green card) and some portion receiving the partial subsidy (red card). However, the food subsidy was reduced to approximately half during 1990/91-95/96, and according to Nassar (Ibid.: 159), the food price index increased over the period 1986/87-95 by 223.6 percent in urban areas and 206.9 percent in rural areas.

Health

According to Nassar (Ibid.: 164), the ERSAP affected the health sector in Egypt by extending cost recovery programmes in governmental facilities and increasing the cost of health services and pharmaceutical drugs. Even though the data in Table 9-1 shows that the share of public health expenditure to GDP remained almost constant during the ERSAP period, Nassar refers to other statistics, stating that the same ratio had declined from 1.2 percent in 1970 to 0.6 percent in 1995. As a consequence, according to Nassar, a substantial increase occurred in the prices of health services by 170 percent in urban areas and by 166 percent in rural areas over the period 1986/87-95.

Education

According to Nassar (Ibid.: 173), the ERSAP has also brought a direct impact on the educational sector. The ratio of public expenditure in the education sector as a percentage of total public expenditure fell from 15.3 percent in 1966/67 to 10 percent in 1994/95. Nassar also introduced some important measures that accompanied the retreat in the role of the state in the education sector. Some of them are:

- The introduction of moderate fees in schools and free universities, which range 5 percent of the basic annual salary of government employees in the lower grades
- The increase in the density of classes, of which the number of children reached 60-65 per class. This led to the increase in the demand for private teachers and the cost of education
- The introduction of official private teaching groups in different subjects in schools with a high class density

In the view of Nassar, the main consequences of these factors are the high drop out ratio of children and the permanent existence of poverty-related illiteracy. Usually those who drop out from primary education are still illiterate or can hardly read and write. They come from the poorest socio-economic groups.

Even the previously mentioned INP report (1998: 34) refers to this situation by stating as follows: "In practice, there is evidence that the school system is being insidiously privatised, as expenditures on private tutoring as well as on donations for extra-curricula books acquire increasing shares in household budgets."

Insurance and Pensions

In Egypt, it is stipulated in the constitution that each citizen has the right to insurance benefits in old age and sickness. The Egyptian government has been running some social insurance and pension system based on laws. According to Nassar (2002: 143), in 1994/95, the total beneficiary of this system was 27.5 percent of the population, whereas 10.3 percent of the population received a pension. The ERSAP has brought some negative impacts in this system, too. Even though the total numbers of the beneficiaries of the social insurance and pension had increased by 21.7 and 17.7 percent respectively over the period of 1987/88 – 94/95, the most vulnerable social group had been seriously hit by the reduction of the pension specifically targeted for this group.

While the four main schemes of the social insurance and pension (Law 79/1975, Law 108/1976, Law 50/1978, Law 112/1980) have been contributed by beneficiaries, one specific pension, the Sadat Pension, has been financed by direct transfer payments from government expenditure. This pension has been targeting the vulnerable groups with no source of income, mainly widows, divorced women, the disabled, the elderly, children of divorced women and others. With the ERSAP, the number of Sadat Pension beneficiaries sharply declined by 34.8 percent over the period 1987/88-1994/95, which implies that the reform once again had undermined the life conditions of the most vulnerable social groups who were already in absolute poverty (Nassar, 2002: 147).

The Social Fund for Development [1]

The Social Fund for Development (SFD) is a special programme that was

---

[1] About the SFD, some papers related quite in detail. Those are: Heba El-Laithy (2001), "Evaluating the Social Fund for Development Programs to alleviate Poverty", in Heba Nassar and Heba El-Laithy (eds.)(2001), *Socioeconomic Policies and Poverty Alleviation Programs in Egypt*, Cairo: Center for Economic & Financial Research & Studies; Dr. Azita Berar Awad (2002), "Social Funds: A New Approach to Poverty Reduction?", and Dr. Hanna Kheir El-Din (2002), "Assessment of Performance and Impacts", both in Mustapha K. Al-Sayyid (ed.)(2002), *Facing Social Consequences of Structural Adjustment in Latin America and the Arab World*, Cairo: Center of Developing Countries Studies, Cairo University; The homepage of the SFD (http://www.sfdegypt.org/) also provides basic information.

introduced especially for the alleviation of the adverse social impacts of structural adjustment. It was established by Presidential Decree No. 40 in 1991, with an initial US 613.0 million dollars from 17 donors and a five-year mandate. Major donors were the European Union, the World Bank/IDA, Arab organisations (Arab Fund, Abu Dhabi Fund, Kuwait fund), and the Egyptian government.

In the meantime, the SFD has pursued programmes aimed at protecting and improving the status of vulnerable groups, comprising new graduates, unemployed youth, displaced public enterprise workers, and female-headed households. The programmes have been implemented on a project basis, rather than disbursing direct subsidies in cash or in kind to the target groups. Various projects such as public works, community development, enterprise development, employment and retraining, and institutional development have been implemented to create jobs and provide social services for the target groups.

The performance of such activities can be ascertained in a variety of ways. Hanna Kheir El-Din (2002: 267) has commented as follows: "The SFD has succeeded – during the span of five years – in generating over 360 thousand jobs, around 70% of which are permanent. This is a modest figure compared to the number of unemployed. But gauged against the limited resources available, this number is quite substantial." As a consequence of such activities, the SFD has developed into a permanent development agency after its originally scheduled 5-year mandate ended in 1996. However, El-Din has referred to several weaknesses in relation to SFD activities. According to her, too much emphasis has been put on the visibility of those activities, which were meant to portray the accomplishments of the SFD. To reflect this, she indicated, many of the statistics showing the performance were exaggerated or inconsistent. Also, the projects have been male-biased, and the project-based approach used has excluded those who cannot work and those who are too poor to wait for the implementation of the projects.

A Special Projects manager of the SFD, has related this criticism to the lack of public relationship of the SFD with the media and the resultant misunderstanding of its activities by outsiders, despite the presentation of various statistics showing the achievements of the SFD. His following comments during an interview in December 2002 show how officials there feel about their performance:

> "You will have to understand that the Social Fund is a tool in participation for the unemployment. We cannot fight the whole problem of the unemployment. We reached, we solved almost 25 percent of the unemployment till now. This year it will decrease because of the recession, but this is what our role (cannot cope with). When we talk about almost 25 percent as one organisation, which is semi-governmental, I guess it can-be felt."

9-2. Aspects of Social Development

In this part, aspects of social development during the reform period will be examined. Logically, it is assumed that the changes in public social spending and social services that have been analysed so far have affected the social development. After a general overview of the trends of major social indicators, a more detailed analysis of the status of poverty and equality is presented.

9-2-1. Trends in Social Indicators

One way to assess the social impact of the reforms would be to check the development of major social indicators before and after the reforms. Table 9-2 shows the trends of such indicators, which are related to basic human necessities such as education, health, food and gender-related development. Due to problems of data consistency, the time span in the table has been limited to 1993-97. Most indicators relate to education and health status and show that conditions in these fields have been consistently improved during the reform period. The gender-related development index, combining various indicators showing the status of women, also shows that it has consistently improved. A comprehensive index combining income, life expectancy, and educational attainment, the Human Development Index (HDI) introduced by the UNDP, shows that Egypt has made continued progress in social development.

However, a problem with these social indicators is that they show only national average data, concealing important differences at the regional and local levels, and between class and gender distributions. According to the *Human Development Report* published by the UNDP (1998:19), the HDI of Egypt disaggregated by income group shows big discrepancies. Whereas the overall HDI of Egypt in 1997 is 0.616, belonging to the medium group in the world table, the HDI of the 'poor' is only 0.464, belonging to the low human development category. On the contrary, the HDI of the rich is 0.815, belonging to the high category. This implies that the national average data do not reveal much about the social conditions of the general population.

The previously mentioned INP (1998) report presents more detailed statistics about the regional disparities. According to the report, while national average HDI of 1996 was 0.631, that of the Urban Governorates including Cairo, Alexandria, Port Said and Suez was the highest at 0.782, and that of Upper Egypt was the lowest at 0.570. In the middle were the Frontier Governorates (0.700) and the Lower Egypt (0.613). No explanation is given for the differences between the statistics of the UNDP and the INP.

Table 9-2 Trends in Social Indicators of Egypt 1990-97

	1993	1994	1995	1997
Human Development Index	0.611	0.614	0.612	0.616
HDI Ranking	106	109	112	120
Adult literacy rate	49.8	50.5	51.4	52.7
Male	62.4	62.6	63.6	64.7
Female	37.0	36.7	38.8	40.5
School enrolment*	69	69	69	72
Life expectancy index	0.65	0.66	0.66	0.69
Education index	0.56	0.57	0.57	0.59
Gender-related Development Index	0.545	0.555	0.555	0.603
Population with access to				
Health services	99	99	99	99
Safe water	80	79	87	87
Sanitation	50	32	88	88
Daily Calorie supply per capita	3,336	3,336	3,315	3,289
Infant Mortality (per 1,000 live births)	66	63	57	54

Source: UNDP, *Human Development Report*, 1996, 1997, 1998, 1999, 2000

* Combined first, second, and third gross enrolment ratio

** Each data does not necessarily signify that it is the data of the indicated year, but the most recent data available at the time.

Figure 9-1 Human Development and Income Change of Egypt

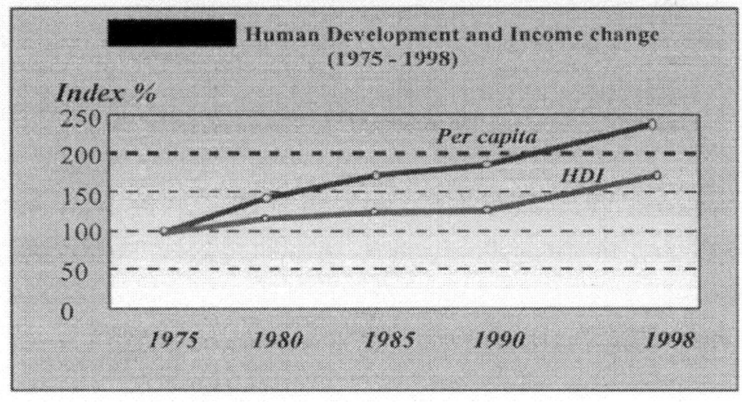

Source: INP (1999)

The speed of human development of Egypt has also been much slower than the speed of per capita income growth. As shown in Figure 9-1, the speed of human development in Egypt has always lagged behind income growth since the mid-1970s, and the gap has been widening during the 1990s. This implies that Egypt has invested much less resources in human development than its potential. Indeed, the HDI rank of Egypt in the world table in 1997 comes at 20 places behind its per capita GDP (PPP) rank, which confirms this point. Also, as shown in Table 9-2, its HDI rank has consistently declined from 106 in 1993 to 120 in 1997, which indicates that, despite the progress in absolute terms, social development has been lagging in relative terms.

9-2-2. Poverty and Equality

In the literature, poverty and equality are most frequently used as the standards to measure the social impacts of structural adjustment (Thiele, 2001). There are conflicting views concerning the development of poverty and equality in Egypt. The Egyptian government and international agencies claim that the poverty situation in Egypt has improved recently, while many others are sceptical about the truth of these claims. The following evaluation from the IMF (1998:42) represents the view of the former group: "The incidence of poverty has remained remarkably stable between 1990/91 and 1995/96. Inequality appears to have fallen in four of the eight regions over the past five years, and overall, the poorest quintiles' share of total income has risen, narrowing the gap between rich and poor." However, the IMF did not present any evidence to support this claim. It simply referred to the author - Cardiff - of a forthcoming publication.

When interviewed, officials in the public sector generally sided with this view. A policy advisor of the UNDP Egypt commented that as far as he knew, poverty had been reduced in Egypt (Interview in December 2002). An economist at the

American Embassy in Cairo also said that the economic as well as the social conditions of Egypt had certainly improved as a result of the reforms. They failed to expound on the factors that accounted for their perception of the reduction.

An alternative view has been expressed by a number of critics. According to Nader Fergany (1999: 17), poverty has been on the rise during the reform in the midst of affluence for a few. Referring to the same forthcoming publication mentioned by the IMF, Fergany asserted that the proportion of the poor has more than doubled between 1990/91 and 1995/96 from about 21%. Based on the results of the 1995/96 Household Income and Expenditure Survey (HIES), Fergany showed that average household income and expenditure in real terms have declined in urban and rural areas alike (see Table 9-3). Considering the changes in household size over time, Fergany indicated that on a per capita basis, real expenditure declined by 3% in urban areas and close to 10% in rural areas. While income per capita rose in the cities by 3%, it fell in the countryside by about a quarter. Applying a crude poverty line of one US dollar per person per day, Fergany states that about 88% of the population could be considered poor (94% in the countryside and 80% in urban areas). Applying a poverty line based on the minimum food requirements, he estimated that at least 44% of Egyptians ought to be considered poor.

Table 9-3 Average household income and expenditure (in £E)

Category	1990/91	1995/96	
		Current prices	Fixed prices
Urban			
Income	6120	8940	5290
Expenditure	5685	7829	4633
Rural			
Income	5125	6461	4089
Expenditure	4741	5712	3615

Source: Nader Fergany (1998)

To sum up, Fergany asserts that a rapid deterioration of the standard of living has taken place since the official SAP started. He reasserts that the reforms have considerably impoverished the people and those in the countryside have paid a heavier price.

Figure 9-2 Changes of the Poor in Rural Areas

The Percentage of the Poor for Rural Areas

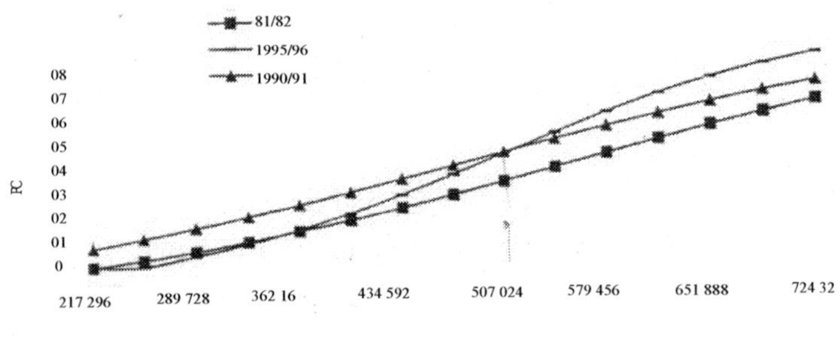

Poverty Line Z

Source: El-laithy and Osman (1996)

Another research by Heba El-Laithy and Osman (1996) shows similar results to that of Fergany. Using the same HIES data and applying more complicated measures, they conclude that poverty has grown during the 1990s, especially in urban areas. However, in rural areas, they indicate that the trend has varied, judged from different levels of poverty lines. Analysing the extent of poverty between three different periods, they conclude that in urban areas, irrespective of poverty measures and at any levels of poverty line, poverty was the least in 1981/82, and was the highest in 1995/96. However, in rural areas, it varied according to which poverty line was applied. As shown in Figure 9-2, at the lowest level poverty line (some £E 217), the percentage of the poor was the highest in 1990/91 and the lowest in 1995/96. As the poverty line is raised (to £E

724), the percentage of the poor was the highest in 1995/96.

More recent research on poverty by a joint Egypt/World Bank team led by Heba El-Laithy (World Bank, 2002) presents a compromising view on the development of poverty situation in Egypt. According to their report (Ibid.: 8-20), poverty decreased in Egypt during the second half of the 1990s, although earlier studies showed that poverty levels increased from the early 1980s to the mid 1990s. In 1999/2000, the poor in Egypt - those who could not meet their basic food and non-foods needs - was 16.7 percent of the population or approximately 10.7 million individuals. This ratio is lower than the results of many earlier studies, and it proves, according to the report, that the poverty situation in Egypt has improved. According to the report, when using the internationally comparable $2/day measure, the poverty incidence was 19.4 percent, which was relatively low by international standards.

However, according to the report, while poverty decreased during 1995/96-1999/2000 in Egypt as a whole, regional patterns were significantly different. While poverty declined rapidly in the Metropolitan areas, the decline was moderate in Lower Egypt, and poverty actually rose in Upper Egypt. At the same time, during the 1995-2000 period, inequality in Egypt as a whole rose slightly, with the Gini index rising from 35 to 38. But the effects of this worsening distribution were outweighed by large increases in per capita expenditure. The average per capita expenditure in 1999/2000 at a national level (evaluated at 1995/96 Metropolitan prices) was £E 1,599 per year, compared to £E 1,408 in 1995/96 – an annual increase in real average per capita expenditure of 3.2 percent.

As mentioned earlier, critics are quite dubious about the authenticity of official reports, including government publications and this World Bank report. The comments of the journalist cited earlier refer to this situation. The following comments of a professor at the Cairo University summarise the critics' view:

"I agree with Nader Fergany. Poverty has increased, although Heba El-Laithy says otherwise. She says it hasn't increased. But from what we see, either it has increased or remains the same. The problem is that unemployment rate is increasing. So, if you relate unemployment to poverty, then we can talk about increasing poverty. Heba El-Laithy is talking about more increase in income. But, to our knowledge, whether this increase in income has been equitable is not clear. The income could be increasing by small fraction, by small percentage (of population), but it could be in an inequitable way. So, the situation could be improving, but if you look at the distribution of income, it may be inequitable, more towards a higher Gini coefficient, more towards inequality."

Heba El-Laithy (World Bank, 2002: 73) mentioned the differences of methodology used to assess poverty and the resultant variations of perspectives, stating:

"The assessment of poverty changes and evolution is essentially arbitrary. On the one hand, the assessment of poverty changes over time depends on, and varies with, the poverty line chosen. We are not certain whether we would obtain the same conclusions if we used a different poverty line. The previous comparisons of poverty changes over time are therefore partial than complete. To assess robustness of the poverty measurements to the poverty lines used, dominance analysis is carried out to examine whether or not the same conclusions are obtained if the poverty line is changed."

And on this stance, the conclusion of the work of her team on poverty is as follows:

"To conclude, testing dominance within regions showed that the conclusion that poverty changes is robust to the choice of poverty line and poverty measure

for Upper Egypt regions, in the period 1995/96-1999/2000. However, poverty in
the Metropolitan and Lower Egypt regions dominated the increases in poverty in
Upper Egypt regions, resulting in a decline in overall poverty during 1999/2000-
1995/96 period." (Ibid.; 74)

For this researcher, it is not easy to judge whose opinion is closer to the truth, or
the reality of the Egyptian society. However, it can be said that the perceptions of
many Egyptians and foreigners, whom this researcher could see more frequently
during the fieldwork period, seemed to sympathise with the claims that the social
conditions of ordinary Egyptian people in recent times have deteriorated. The
comment of the earlier mentioned journalist seems to succinctly express the
prevalent perceptions of the general public.

> "For the people on the streets, the reform means just the rise of prices and the
> worsening of their life conditions."

9-2-3. Perceptions from the Field

Although it cannot be presented in calculable ways, the impacts of the reform
could be seen in many aspects of social development, too. More conspicuously,
the impacts could be seen in the consumption spree of the upper class. The effects
of improved macroeconomic performance and the liberalisation measures have
been reflected in the flooding of luxury imports goods into the Egyptian market
and the consumption boom of the elite class. According to Emad Mekay's (1996)
description, the 'new genies' of the society, or the newest elite businessmen, roam
Cairo's streets in fancy cars, wear the best suits, and live in imposing mansions.
But as they carry a corruption-tainted history and scandals of corruption and
business excesses are widespread, such excesses fuel the perception of the mass

public that the economic reform is redistributing wealth even more inequitably, in favour of the already affluent elites.

According to McKee (1999), while TV channels and newspapers pour out lavish advertisements for luxury goods and expensive new suburban residences, some 12 million Egyptians are believed to be living in unhygienic conditions or slums. The government's plan to ease the housing problems of the overcrowded capital through building new satellite towns caused a real estate boom and provided profiteering chances for the new business elites. However, it hardly offered a solution for the need for housing. As the urban drift, mainly into Cairo, continues at an estimated rate of 150,000 people a year, the metropolis of some 16 million people is now almost bursting at the seams.

As Cassandra (1995) indicated, while economists are persuaded by data on balance of payments, levels of indebtedness, budget deficits, and other macroeconomic indicators, such data mean little to ordinary people who are concerned about the scarcity of jobs, low wages, high prices, and inadequate profits. Since this microeconomic performance has deteriorated quickly, the public in general feel that their lives have become harder than before.

Dr. Mohamed El-Sayed Said (2000) presented the "private appropriation of public assets and the rising inequality" as the most serious illness in the recent social development in Egypt. According to him, the vast erosion of the state's capacity to maintain social services led to the private appropriation of public assets. As mentioned earlier, costly private tutoring and also costly private health services are an indicator of such phenomenon. The cancerous proliferation of urban settlements, which makes the evolution of cities and city life a true absurdity, is another sign of the erosion of state functions. It results from, Said says, systematic payment of bribes in return for unfreezing construction regulations and rules, or the usurpation of public land. In his opinion, this situation has led to a sense of social chaos with a mix of public responses such as political apathy, despair and moral decay, which in turn urges people to look out for their own individual interests only, frequently at the expense of public interests.

According to Mervat Hatem (1992), the reform has also negatively affected the status of women. With the retreat of the state as an agent of social and economic change, many official commitments to gender equality were either ignored or abandoned within and outside the state sector. The ideological and economic vacuum caused by the retreat of the state has not been effectively filled by local and international private enterprises, who have declined to hire women on the grounds that the provision of maternity leave and child care, stipulated by laws, has made their labour expensive. In a stark contrast, Hatem says, economic liberalisation has enhanced the prospects of upper-class and upper-middle-class women. College graduates with knowledge of foreign languages have found lucrative jobs in international enterprises, many of which had an unwritten policy of not hiring veiled women because they did not fit the image these companies wanted to project. However, even these well-paid positions tended to be concentrated in clerical ranks with very limited prospects for professional advancement.

Though Hatem's paper describes the situation that had developed until the early 1990s, it seems that the situation has not changed much even after then. All the phenomenon could be seen and heard in the same manner as Hatem has described even in the Korean Embassy and Korean companies operating in Egypt, ie, Samsung, LG, Hyundai and others, with whom this researcher was closely associated.

To conclude, the perception that the reform has widened the inequality between the affluent and the poor, and that it has worsened the life conditions of mass public was very strong and widespread. And it seemed to this researcher that this perception was a strong reflection of a real phenomenon in the society.

9-3. Political Implications of the Reform

Due to the different distributional consequences, economic reform inevitably brings about political effects: it fosters more favorable socio-economic environments for certain socio-economic groups, while certain groups come to face less favorable conditions. As mentioned in Chapter 1 in the comments of Stephen Haggard et. al. (1995: 12), this very effect is what renders an economic reform a political process.

In the previous chapters, the roles and interests of major actors as well as their responses to the reform process were examined. Now, in this section of the chapter, the results of their interactions will be analysed by focusing on who are the final winners and who are the losers. And some implications of the results will be examined with regard to the socio-political development of Egypt.

9-3-1. The Winner: the Bourgeoisies

As indicated in Haggard's statement, economically successful programmes require political success in building the bases of support and managing resistance. In this regard, the Egyptian state manipulated the political process of the reform deftly and so successfully implemented the reform to the scheduled end. It has secured enough support from the IFIs and international donor groups, and has managed domestic groups' responses through cooption and repression.

As the reform is not a simple game, it is not easy to say simply who won and who lost. Since the ERSAP finished quite recently, academic studies on this aspect are still rare. However, compiling from available reports in various journals and interviews from the field, it seems rather clear that who gained the most benefits from the reform and who lost: the former is the elite bourgeoisies and the latter is the mass public. The state and international interests also took their shares, but they eventually helped to boost the power of the bourgeoisies by creating a more private sector-based, business-friendly environment.

As described in the previous chapters, the power of the bourgeoisies has been rising since the days of the Infitah. However, in the last decade, it has more dramatically increased. As a crude indicator of this phenomenon, the number of businessmen-parliamentarians has more than doubled from 31 in the 1990-95 session to 71 in the 1995-2000 session, or from 7.0% to 16.0% of the total elected seats (see Table 6-1).

According to Abdel-Latif (2001), this led many observers to predict that the 1995 parliament heralded the beginning of the age of liberalisation in Egypt. And the parliament lived up to this expectation, passing 19 market economy-related laws, thereby liberalising the banking and insurance sectors. However, this officially expressed role and power of the bourgeoisies in the rather powerless parliament presents only part of their influence. As was mentioned in Chapter 7, it is more privately exerted through private networking and lobbying, even bypassing official business societies such as the EBA. Indeed, several prominent businessmen came to be known for their privileged relations with "powers", and it is said that businessmen enjoy "extra immunities and privileges" (*Ibid.*).

In Abdel-Latif's opinion again, there is, in fact, a near consensus that never in the history of Egyptian politics has the entrepreneurial influence on politics been so obvious as it has been in the last decade or so. The following comments from Mahmoud Abdel-Fadil, explain this point succinctly: *(Ibid.)*

> "That they become part of the entourage of the economy minister or the prime minister on foreign trips or that they get invited to attend ministerial meetings where important decisions are discussed is unprecedented in the history of Egyptian politics".

David Hirst (1999), a correspondent from the British paper, *The Guardian*, straightforwardly pointed out the winners and losers of the Egyptian reform in the following description:

> "Who Egypt's winners are is clear. Just go to the Katameya Heights. To get there, you pass through Old Cairo and its cemeteries, where a half million people live. This is losers' territory … At the Katameya Heights Golf and Tennis Club, the 18-hole course meanders through landscaped fairways of Bermuda turf flown out in refrigerated crates from Atlanta, Georgia …"

According to Hirst, these "walled and gated" communities in Cairo not merely typify the new rich's social behaviour and conspicuous consumption; they are an intrinsic, structural feature of the new economics.

Traditionally, the army has played a very important role in Egyptian politics. But since the Sadat era and more decisively during the Mubarak reign, the power of the army has been contained in the military sector, and has been overwhelmed by the growth of the private business sector (Library of Congress, 1991; Springborg, 1989). An economic researcher quoted by Hirst stressed this point clearly:

> "At first sight, it might seem that power has moved from the barracks to the boardroom. More to the point, the army has moved into business."

Ever since the days of Nasser, the Egyptian constitution has stipulated that 50% of the total elected seats in the People's Assembly should go to workers and peasants. With the growth of the bourgeoisies, this clause has been put under serious pressure for amendment. Recently, many sought to eliminate this quota entirely, arguing that it prevents the state from offering incentives to investors, restructuring the economy and privatising the public sector. Though this movement was repulsed by Mubarak, it still reflects the changes in the power structure between classes in Egypt (Shafiq, 2000).

However, regarding the power relationship between the bourgeoisies and the state, many have observed that the bourgeoisies is still under the state's control. Abdel-Latif, citing the comments of others, said that this "class" of businessmen is not considered to be part of the ruling system, but to be seeking to join it. Regarding this, she added as follows: "I wouldn't say one part is putting pressure on the other. Both are putting pressure on another. But I would still say that the government, or the state, still has the upper hand." (Interview in December 2002). David Hirst also pointed out the collaborative but still subordinate status of the bourgeoisies by saying that the businessmen would be nowhere without the army and bureaucracy.

To sum up, all the evidence so far supports the conclusion that private sector businessmen, or the bourgeoisies as a class, are the biggest beneficiaries of the reform. As mentioned in Chapter 5, the power of the bourgeoisie emanates from its ability to disrupt the economy, its payoffs to the press, and its connections to the ruling elite as well as opposition parties. The reform has boosted the power of the bourgeoisie through liberalisation and the retreat of the state in economic spheres.

9-3-2. The Share of the Other Actors

If the bourgeoisies is deemed to be the biggest beneficiary of the reform, what did the other actors get out of it? Even though the reform might not necessarily result in a zero-sum game, it seems rather apparent that there is a loser. And it is the poor as directly indicated by David Hirst. For the mass public, the growth of the whole economy and per capita income does not have serious meaning as it does not show distributional effects. For them, as indicated by Abdel-Latif, the reform implanted its meaning more as the rise of prices and the worsening of their life conditions.

Many observers have noted that the economic and political growth of the bourgeoisies has been achieved at the expense of the other segments of Egyptian society. According to El-Eisawi, "social groups such as consumers and workers and other civil society groupings which should take part in the process of governance are rarely there on the political scene." (Abdel-Latif, 2001)

As was presented in Chapter 7, the mass public has been almost completely alienated in the process of the so-called "reform by stealth". The activities of civil organisations have been strictly controlled. The co-opted part of the formal opposition parties and the labour unions have not represented the mass public faithfully. This situation is properly captured in the phrase cited by Abdel-Latif (2000): "parties without followers for people without parties." The only true oppositional force, the militant Islamists, has been severely cracked down upon and marginalized.

As such, the mass public has not had any socio-political apparatus through which to represent their will, which, in turn, led to the unequal distributional effects of the reform. And the situation has not been restricted to urban poor people. The socio-economic status of some six million rural tenants has also been threatened by the Law 96 of 1992 and following reform measures, which have abolished all legal constraints on land leases and liberalised the rents. As was shown in Chapter 7, protests from tenants have been harshly dealt with.[2]

Then, what did the Egyptian state and the international donor group, represented by the IFIs, achieve through the reform? As mentioned in the previous chapter, the Egyptian state and the IFIs alike evaluated the results of the

---

[2]   The socio-political effects of the ERSAP, especially on the agricultural sector and rural development, are analysed in-depth in Ray Bush (1999)

reform quite positively. This implies that, as the original designer and implementer of the reform, they are satisfied with what they achieved through the reforms.

First and foremost, the Egyptian state secured enough financial support to escape from the economic crisis, which had enfeebled the resource base of its power and ultimately threatened the stability of the regime. Throughout the late 1980s and early 1990s, the Egyptian state had been suffering from a declining economy, and this situation led to an "impending crisis", which, according to Cassandra (1995), implied the "potential collapse" of the political and economic system. Thereafter, with the improvement of the macroeconomic situation and with some $18 billion in foreign reserves by 1998, the regime gained a respite from the crisis. This was achieved through, most of all, the massive debt reduction and the infusion of financial assistance by the international donor group, given as a reward for the reform. The political and financial support from the international group also helped the Egyptian state to suppress the militant Islamists and to maintain political stability, seemingly at least.

Regarding the political implication of the structural adjustment especially on the states in Africa, Jeffrey Herbst (1990) raised a significant issue: the retreat of the state through private sector and market-oriented reform will lead to the weakening of the central apparatus of the state on which the rulers have long relied on to stay in power, thus making the political climate much more volatile and riskier. According to Herbst, the rulers in African states have long used public enterprises and state intervention in economic affairs as a political conduit through which they can distribute valuable resources for their clients. However, as the structural adjustment has severely reduced the state's ability to provide patronage, it will also make the state much less flexible in dealing with a political crisis.

In the case of Egypt, the same situation might have different implications.

Instead of depending on the malfunctioning, resource-consuming public enterprises, the state now can use the bourgeoning private sector enterprises as a new instrument of patronage and political manoeuvring. The following comments by Robert Bianchi (quoted in Abdel-Latif, 2000) seem to indicate this point clearly:

> "The emergence of more autonomous private capitalists may provide the ruling elite with an important new coalition partner whose support can be particularly welcome since the traditional populist slogans of the 1952 Revolution lose what little remains of their credibility."

As the private entrepreneurs are granted foreign rents through collaboration with the state, and as they are eager to join the ruling system themselves, the state can still control the private sector and use them as an alternative source of patronage. In fact, even the state itself is demanding the private sector to replace the state as the major source of employment and provider of social safety net.

Finally, what has the international donor group gained as a consequence of the reform in Egypt? As was mentioned previously, the official evaluation of the reform by the IFIs was very positive and as late as May 14, 2001, the Managing Director of the IMF, Horst Kohler still commented that, "Egypt's political and social stability under President Hosni Mubarak led to successful economic program". (http://www.arabicnews.com)

This implies that the IFIs and the international forces behind them are content with the results of the reform in Egypt. In Chapter 5, this thesis assumed that the international donor group, of which the US is the most important actor, had a stake in keeping the Egyptian state as a partner against anti-Western regional powers such as Iraq and Iran, and as a bulwark against the militant Islamic fundamentalists. It also assumed that the incorporation of the Egyptian economy into the capitalist economic order to be a major motive in the reform.

Then, by providing much needed financial assistance and pressing the implementation of the reform, the donor group has achieved these targets. Most of the goals in economic stabilisation and institutional reform have been successfully met, rendering the Egyptian economy more market-based and susceptive to the international order. By helping the Egyptian state escape from the economic crisis, the donor group also helped it to restore the seeming political stability. And this kept the Egyptian state to play its expected role in the region.

To date, all these findings lead to the conclusion that despite the relatively successful macroeconomic performance, the social effects and political implications of the reform are not so positive. Rather, it seems that many negative factors are looming in the socio-political development of Egypt in the future. Some prospects on this aspect will be presented in the next chapter.

Chapter 10

Conclusion

This chapter is composed of three parts. In the first section, the overall findings of the research will be presented. In the second section, views on the prospects of the economic and socio-political development of Egypt, together with some policy implications of such prospects, will be delivered. In the final section, some personal remarks closing the research will be given.

10-1. Findings of the Research

The goal in this research was to understand the overall development process and the impacts of the structural adjustment programme in Egypt that had been implemented during the period 1991-98. For this purpose, this thesis has analysed the background and causes of the economic reform, the main contents of its policy measures, the process of its implementation, and the resultant economic performance as well as the social impacts and political implications. These topics were presented in the relevant chapters.

Since this thesis adopted an approach of political economy, which assumes that economic reform is motivated and developed by political factors, especially through the influence of major interest groups, it has attempted to show the influence of such interest groups. The influences of major actors including the Egyptian state, the international donor group, the bourgeoisies, the opposition forces and the mass public were analysed and presented in proper chapters.

As the reform did not originate by domestic social consensus in Egypt but was imposed by the IFIs as a condition for providing needed financial assistance, it had all the characteristic features of typical SAPs implemented elsewhere in developing countries. In this respect, this thesis also tried to present the characteristics of the SAP so as to illuminate the features of the ERSAP in a global context.

The main findings concern the cases of reform in Egypt and its economic and social impacts. They are summarised below:

Background and Causes of the Reform

As analysed in Chapters 4 and 5, the most direct cause of the economic reform of the 1990s was the prolonged economic depression and the foreign debt service crisis of the earlier decade. The Egyptian economy had not performed well for a long time since the late 1960s, and the accumulated foreign debt that reached 209% of GDP by 1987/88 (see Table 7-1) hampered normal operations of the economy. With the low productivity of the largely public sector-dominated industries that had been a legacy of the statist policies of the Nasser era (1952-70), it seemed that the economy could not sustain itself in the long-term, especially with the rapidly increasing population.

Under this situation, the former presidents Nasser and Sadat (1970-81) had each tried to introduce reforms in their economic policies. Especially, the Infitah, or the Open-Door Policy, introduced by Sadat in 1974, signified a full-scale turnaround of the economic policies from the statist to a liberalist system, which envisaged a leading role of the private sector and foreign capital in economic development. However, except for the short boom in the following years, which was largely helped by the oil price increase in the mid-1970s, the Infitah had failed to bring a positive transformation of the economy. Rather, with the rapid increase of consumption and imports and the corresponding expansion of trade deficits, the foreign debt problem had surfaced.

Against this negative performance of the Infitah, Sadat planned an adjustment, which was materialised with the Standby Agreement with the IMF in 1977. However, this adjustment policy, which started with the reduction of subsidies and the price increase of some basic commodities, had immediately caused a severe mass resistance and was soon rescinded. Mubarak, who succeeded Sadat in 1981, tried to introduce another IMF programme in 1987. However, Mubarak was conscious of the 1977 riot and lacked the full commitment to carry out the reform. Accordingly, the 1987 IMF programme was aborted soon after.

With the collapse of oil prices in 1986 and the continued deterioration of the economic conditions, the Egyptian government had no other alternative than to rely on the international donors. The government resumed talks with the IMF in 1988, which lasted almost three years to reach another Standby Agreement in May 1991. This agreement signified the launch of the full-scale economic reforms, which is the main object of this research.

To sum up, the economic reform of Egypt in the 1990s was precipitated by the continued deterioration of the economic situation and the balance of payment crisis. In this respect, it presents another case of the 'Crisis Hypothesis" introduced in Chapter 1.

Main Contents of the Policy Measures

The agreement with the IMF was followed soon by another agreement with the World Bank in June 1991. These two agreements regulated the overall framework of the reform in Egypt, or the ERSAP. As is typical in the Structural Adjustment Programmes elsewhere, there was the division of the roles between the two IFIs in monitoring the Egyptian reforms. While the IMF took care of the macroeconomic stabilisation part, the World Bank took charge in the institutional reform side.

In the macroeconomic stabilisation part, the main target was reducing the budget deficit mainly by cuts in subsidies and investment. Also, reducing the balance of payments deficit and lowering inflation were important targets. To achieve these goals, reforms in taxation and the issuance of Treasury Bills followed. In the institutional reform side, the unification of foreign exchange rates, deregulation of the banking sector, liberalisation of trade and foreign direct investment, and privatisation of public companies were pursued as the primary concerns. To achieve these goals, various reform measures such as lowering the tariff rates, abolishing major non-tariff barriers, abolition of the negative foreign investment list, and the expansion of incentives for foreign investment were introduced.

Overall, the ERSAP was just another case of the typical SAPs that contained all the major elements of the Washington Consensus.

Process of the Implementation

The ERSAP had been implemented officially in three phases during 1991-98. As the 1991 Standby Agreement expired in 1993, the Egyptian government signed a new loan agreement with the IMF in September 1993, which was successively renewed again in July 1996. Each of these three agreements signalled the launch of a new phase of the ERSAP. In addition, the period from 1988 to the 1991 agreement can be seen as another preliminary phase, because, during this period, the Egyptian government complied with many of the demands for reform by the IMF. During this preliminary phase, a new investment law (Law 230) was enacted to liberalise foreign direct investment. Also, some measures to redress the budget deficit, including the cuts in subsidies and capital expenditure, were implemented.

In the first phase (1991-93), the focus was put on the macroeconomic stabilisation. Some fiscal adjustment programmes were implemented such as the continued reduction of subsidies and the introduction of a new taxation system. Also, a new Banking Law (Law 37) and Capital Market Law (Law 95) were enacted to adjust the financial sector. A new Agrarian Law (Law 96) liberalised land tenure and rents. Various trade liberalisation measures also followed.

In the second phase (1993-96), the reform did not proceed easily, as the focus was moving from macroeconomic stabilisation to institutional reforms. Over some issues including devaluation and privatisation, the Egyptian government did not comply with the donors demands. Only from 1996, some measures in privatisation were more actively pursued. Since the IMF and the World Bank were discontent with the performance of the Egyptian reforms during this phase, it took intensive diplomatic and political manoeuvring for the Egyptian government to get a positive evaluation from them.

In the third phase (1996-98), the structural reforms agenda including privatisation, deregulation, and trade liberalisation was more aggressively promoted. A new Investment Guarantees Law (Law 81) was enacted and further trade liberalisation measures were introduced. Privatisation of public companies was also more actively pursued, resulting in the privatisation of 74 public companies during 1996-97.

Throughout the whole process of the reform, the basic position and attitude of the Egyptian government was gradualism, while the donors preferred a shock therapy. Accordingly, conflicts arose frequently between the Egyptian government and the donors over the issue of the pace and range of the reforms. One important factor that made the hesitant Egyptian government carry out the reforms to the last phase was the massive debt reduction scheme by the Paris Club. In 1991, the Paris Club promised to cut the Egyptian debt owed to them by half.

However, this debt reduction was to be made in three stages according to the evaluation of the IMF on the performance of the Egyptian reforms. As the Egyptian government carried out the reforms to the last phase and finally got a positive evaluation of its performance from the IMF, a total of 14.2 billion dollars was written off and the same amount of remaining debts were rescheduled. This massive debt reduction contributed positively to the balance of payment situations in Egypt, and it was in fact the most important economic factor that kept the reform going for nearly a decade.

Economic Performance of the Reform

The economic reforms over most of the 1990s have brought many significant changes to the Egyptian economy. Towards the mid-1990s, macroeconomic conditions had remarkably improved, and this trend continued throughout the decade. Many significant institutional changes have also taken place including a more liberalised trade and foreign investment environment. Privatisation of many public companies has also been completed. When the ERSAP officially ended in 1998, many analysts, internal or external, praised the high performance of the reforms. However, from the early 2000s, the Egyptian economy fell into a liquidity problem and subsequent depression, which cast doubt over the long-term macroeconomic effects of the reforms.

As for macroeconomic stabilisation, the ERSAP led to the stabilisation and recovery of the economy, dissolving much of the concern over the economic crisis that prevailed in the pre-reform years. The trends of major macroeconomic indicators developed quite positively during the 1990s. After some initial shock effects in the first years, the real GDP growth rate rebounded from a low 1.9% in 1991/92 and had consistently increased to annually over 5% in the last three years of the reforms. The reduction of the fiscal deficit was also remarkable. In the very first year of the reform alone, between 1990/91 and 1991/92, the fiscal deficit was reduced from a huge 20.0% to 6.4% of GDP. Then, over the years, it had been consistently reduced to reach as low as 1.0% in 1997/98. This improved fiscal stance helped to contain inflation, which was lowered remarkably from a high 21.1% in 1991/92 to a low 3.8% in 1997/98.

However, the impacts of the ERSAP on the external balances were double-faced. The massive debt reduction by the Paris Club helped to reduce the foreign debt from 209% of GDP in 1987/88 to a mere 34% in 1997/98. The Debt Service Ratio also fell from a high 91.7% in 1986/87 to a low 7.2% in 1997/98. But the trade liberalisation measures led to the rapid expansion of imports without compensating increases in exports. Accordingly, the chronic trade deficit had increased from 6.2 billion dollars in 1991/92 to 11.8 billion dollars in 1997/98.

The economic situation after the ending of the ERSAP began to worsen again, mainly due to the liquidity crisis of early 2000 and the ensuing recession. In the 2000s up to the time of this writing in late 2002, the growth slowed down and inflation, as well as unemployment, rose again. It is not clear whether this recession is just a cyclical phenomenon or a result of the failures of economic policies. It is yet to be seen whether the economy will rebound or fall back to the crisis situation of the pre-reform years.

On the institutional side, the ERSAP has also brought in many significant changes. During the very early stage of the reform, the multiple foreign exchange rate system was abolished and replaced with a single unified exchange rate system. Bank activities and deposit rates were liberalised. By streamlining all regulations, capital market activities were revitalised. Most import bans and export controls were removed and tariff rates were lowered year by year. The imports bans, which covered 52.9% of domestic production before the reform, covered less than 4% in 1997. The maximum tariff rates were lowered in several stages from a high 110% in 1986 to 40% in 1998. The environment for foreign direct investment was also significantly liberalised. Through the 1989 Investment Law, 100% foreign ownership was allowed and all discrimination between local and foreign investors was eliminated. A new law in 1997 further expanded incentives for foreign investors. Helped by these measures, FDI into Egypt slowly increased in the 1990s, from below $200 million in 1990 to around $2 billion in 1997.

The record with privatisation was also remarkable by many standards. During 1994-98, a total of 90 among the total 314 public companies (Law 203 companies) were privatised by various means. Among them, 37 companies were privatised through a majority flotation on the stock market. Regarding the proceeds of privatisation, the IMF (1998: 52) commented that Egypt's experience ranked among the top four. However, the macro and micro economic impacts of the privatisation were not clear at the time of this writing.

Despite the relative success of the institutional reforms, reform consolidation had been hampered by resilient institutional features. Not withstanding the recent liberalisation measures, the IMF (1998: 65) indicated that Egypt's trade system still remained relatively restrictive. In spite of Egypt's strong advantages to attract foreign investment, many surveys indicated that bureaucracy and other weaknesses still were restricting business activities in Egypt (See Chapter 8).

Social Impacts

The ERSAP has also brought many social impacts. The main paths of the social impacts were the changes to public social spending and social services. According to Egyptian government sources, the relative weight of social spending in the government expenditures during the reform period did not decrease at all, despite the reduction of overall public expenditure. Government sources claimed that this fact proved the government's will to protect essential social services during fiscal austerity.

However, scepticism on the reliability of such official data was very strong and critics contended that many of the social safety schemes had been seriously damaged by the fiscal adjustment measures. According to private sources (See Chapter 9), food subsidies were seriously cut, resulting in the high rise of food prices. Health and education sectors were also negatively affected by the reduction of public expenditure. Despite the increase in the overall numbers of the beneficiaries of insurance and pensions, the most vulnerable social group had been seriously hit by the reduction of the pension especially targeted to this group. Though the Social Fund for Development was set up especially to absorb the negative social impacts of the reform, some weaknesses of its activities were also indicated.

Despite the general improvement in major social indicators, significant gaps existed in the regional and class distributions. Some data showed that the social development of Egypt has been lagging compared to its potential and international standards. The trends for poverty and equality were also ambiguous. The Egyptian government sources and the World Bank claimed that poverty had declined recently, while critics reputed these claims. For this researcher, it seemed that the perception of the deterioration of the living conditions of the socially weak strata was very strong in the field. And it seemed that this perception is a strong reflection of the real phenomenon in the society.

The Stakeholders and the Political Aspects of the Reform

Based on the assumptions of the political economy introduced in Chapter 1, this thesis analysed the interests and roles of major political forces in the formulation and implementation of the reform. Five broad categories of the political forces were the targets of the analysis: The Egyptian state, the international donor group, the bourgeoisie, the opposition forces, and the mass public. The analyses so far revealed that the Egyptian state, as the implementer of the reforms, had to confront and deal with all the pressures from the other groups. Among them, the study concluded that, the Egyptian bourgeoisie was the ultimate beneficiary. The mass public was the loser who had been completely alienated in the process and suffered most from the negative impacts of the reform. Other groups benefited but to varying degrees.

For the Egyptian state, or the regime, the primary concern was the stability of the regime itself. The economic crisis had enfeebled the resource base of its power and so jeopardised the stability of the regime. In the 1980s, the regime had feared the reaction on the streets to the reforms. However, when Egypt accepted the reform package in 1991, its calculation of the payoffs had changed. It seemed that without certain economic reforms, the economy could not sustain itself in the long run. Falling real incomes and rising unemployment threatened to produce exactly what the ruling elites feared would be the result of orthodox economic reforms: riots and political instability.

As the failure of the socialist policies was clearly manifested by the successive breakdown of the communist regimes in the Eastern Block from the late 1980s, and as it became clear that the international order had changed into a unipolar world under the American hegemony, the orthodox reforms came to be perceived as the only feasible alternative for the Egyptian elite. The massive debt reduction and financial assistances provided by the Western donors had also induced the Egyptian state into undertaking neo-liberal type reforms.

However, since the Egyptian ruling elite had watched the politically volatile impacts of the shock reforms in the Eastern Europe, and since they were still conscious of the 1977 riot against the IMF programme, they preferred a gradual approach to reform, and had bargained hard with the donor group over this issue.

When the reform ended in 1998, the Egyptian state had acquired the share it wanted. Through the massive debt reduction and the infusion of financial assistance by the international donor group, the regime gained a respite from the economic crisis that had threatened its power base. The political and financial support by the international donor group helped the state to suppress the militant Islamists and maintain political stability, seemingly at least. In this respect, the ERSAP in the 1990s was apparently an economic reform adopted by political imperative.

The international donor group represented by the IMF and the World Bank, of which the United States and its Western allies are the major stakeholders, also had distinct political interests in the reforms of Egypt. This study has revealed that the donors had a stake in keeping the Egyptian state as a partner against anti-Western regional powers such as Iraq and Iran, and as a bulwark against the militant Islamic fundamentalists. It also revealed that the incorporation of the Egyptian economy into the capitalist economic order was a major motive in the reform. By providing much needed financial assistance and pressing the implementation of the reform, the donor group achieved these targets. They helped to make the Egyptian economy more susceptive to the capitalist international order through a more open and market-based economic system, and helped to restore political stability in Egypt so that Egypt may carry on its expected role in the region.

To secure the implementation of the reforms, the donor group demanded a shock therapy approach, and linked the massive debt reduction to reform performance. Considering the fact that the reform had been carried out to its expected end, and the donor group finally evaluated the performance of the reform positively, it can be inferred that the donor group were satisfied with the results of the Egyptian reforms.

The power of the Egyptian bourgeoisie, or the elite business groups, has been on the rise since the Infitah years of the Sadat regime. This study has revealed that the basic interests of the bourgeoisie in the reforms lay in securing the legal framework that could guarantee a stable business environment and profit-making.

Also it is the conclusion of this study that the ERSAP had ultimately benefited this bourgeoisie group most by creating a more private sector-based and business-friendly environment. This fact is symbolically manifested by the rise of the power of business circles in the parliament and their association with the ruling elite. The business circles affected the course of the reform more through private access to power than by official manifestation of their power through organisations.

The influences of the opposition forces and the mass public on the process of the reform had remained minimal. The official opposition parties and labour unions that had been working as the co-opted part of the establishment had done little, except issuing public statements and behind-the-scenes-lobbying. The militant Islamists, the true opposition force, had launched harsh military activities during the early 1990s, but they had been severely cracked down upon and marginalized.

Though the Egyptian government had been conscious of the public responses to the reforms, the public had remained rather calm throughout the whole process of the reforms. This was partly because the state had implemented reforms gradually in the hopes that the public would not notice the impacts. Also, it was because the public in the 1990s had been more accustomed to economic hardships than the previous generation. In any case, the public had been completely alienated in processes of the reform, and had to face the bitter impacts of the reforms.

10-2. Prospects and Policy Implications

In this part, views on the prospects of economic and socio-political development of Egypt are presented, and some policy implications are explored.

10-2-1. Prospects of Economic Development

As stated in Chapter 8, recent views on the prospects of the Egyptian economy have largely turned to be pessimistic, mainly influenced by the ongoing recession. There still are views that see the current recession as a cyclical phenomenon. The recent edition of the Country Risk Service issued by the Economist Intelligence Unit (2002) forecasts that the real GDP growth rate of Egypt will rebound to 2.7% in 2003 from the low of 0.8% in 2002. Aside from these short-term views, views on the long-term prospects for economic development are more or less in tune with the perspectives that evaluate the effects of the economic reforms in the past decade.

One point of view, which was more prevalent in the late 1990s, but seems to have waned recently, is that the reform has effectively changed the rules and institutions of the Egyptian economy toward liberalisation and the incorporation of the economy into the world economic system. This view naturally assumes there will be increased inflows of capital into the Egyptian market and an increased role for private sector industries for sustained economic growth and development. The following comments of the Egyptian Prime Minister Atef Obeid in the foreword of a government publication (Ministry of Economy & Foreign Trade, 2000) undoubtedly show this perspective:

> "Today, the economic fabric of Egypt has been fundamentally reconstructed; the role of government in the life of Egyptians has been redefined to intervene only where needed. The Egyptian economy has entered a new phase instigated by its deliberate journey of reforms; where its infrastructure is up to the needs of a modern economy, where financial balances have been restored in a lasting sustainable fashion, and where foreign investment is welcomed, profitable and secure."

Another point of view sees the effects of the reforms negatively, and contends that the ERSAP of the 1990s was a replication of the failed Infitah of the 1970s. The following statement of Bromley and Bush (1994: 212) shows that the ERSAP had already displayed many aspects of the negative development of the Infitah at the time of their writing as early as 1994:

> "It is tempting to conclude that history is repeating itself in Egypt. There are many parallels between the themes of Sadat's *infitah* and the current push of the IFI to liberalise the Egyptian political economy. ….. the *infitah* began with optimism but led to a fourfold increase in imports, especially in food, without a corresponding level of domestic production and exports. Its principal effect, aside from an oil-financed boom in infrastructure and construction, was to provide the opportunity for speculative investment and consolidation of Cairo as a place for Gulf Arabs to spend the summer. Equally the promises of the IFIs in the 1990s regarding the much more dramatic liberalisation of investment and trade are similar to those made by Sadat."

At the time of this writing, these comments by Bromley and Bush seem to be quite resounding. By and large, the current development of the Egyptian economy shows many similarities with that of the Infitah era. During the late 1970s and early 1980s, the Egyptian economy enjoyed a boom, with the real GDP growth rate reaching 7-8% annually. However, during this period, investment was mostly concentrated in speculative construction and the service sectors rather than in productive sectors. Imports of goods had rapidly grown while export growth had remained stagnant. The boom ended with the collapse of oil prices and economic crisis followed.

The current development of the Egyptian economy has displayed many similarities with this picture. One difference is that the boom in the late 1970s and early 1980s had been financed by the abrupt increase in oil prices, while the short boom in the mid-1990s had been financed by huge foreign rents. The common point is that the economic upturn during the two periods did not result from improvement in the productivity of the Egyptian economy, but rather from windfall-type financial inflows. This is the point that the sceptics of the reforms in the 1990s have been indicating. It is succinctly described in the following passage by Said (2000):

> "The flood of foreign capital during the last 25 years has coincided with generally modest economic performance. The enormous volume of foreign financial flows failed to empower the country to take-off or to achieve levels of economic growth adequate for passing major bottlenecks. … It is a mockery of history that a truly poor country could use so much foreign capital in order not to improve its productivity and foreign competitiveness but, on the contrary, to finance very high levels of consumption, basically through importation."

Even some critics contended that the reforms of the 1990s were not genuine reforms but were superficial changes unwillingly performed, and when the imposed reforms had officially ended, many of the economic policies were rolled back to the practices of the pre-reform years. The following statement by the EIU (2002: 2) supports the case by showing that recent government policies revived the use of subsidies in response to the recession:

> "The government will respond to domestic grievances with its tried and tested 'carrot and stick' approach. It will continue to spend heavily on subsidies, providing basic goods and commodities such as bread, sugar, fuel and electricity at below-market rates"

In late 2002, the Egyptian government was negotiating with the IMF for another loan agreement. It is rather surprising to see how the issues and situation are very similar to those of the ERSAP years of the last decade:

> "The government laid out an economic policy framework in a document presented to donors at the February 2002 Consultative Group meeting, promising to address a number of long-standing structural issues, most notably by 'maintaining' an appropriate exchange rate, keeping the fiscal deficit within acceptable international levels and pushing ahead with privatisation, including of the state-owned banks. However, many of the key policies outlined were broad, vaguely worded and without a timetable, representing a general reiteration of the government's commitment to continue along the path of economic liberalisation rather than its willingness to be tied down to specific dates and measures." (EIU, 2002: 3)

To conclude, despite the praises of the optimists about the effects of the reforms in the 1990s, the problems that have hampered economic development and caused to bring in the reforms still remain persistent. The economic structure, which is heavily dependent on the fluctuating foreign exchange incomes, has not changed significantly. The development of export industries remains stagnant. All these conditions lead to the conclusion that the economic prospects for the medium-term do not look so bright, and it will need more full-fledged reforms to make the economy take-off into a consistent development path.

10-2-2. Socio-Political Perspective

Prospects for the socio-political development of Egypt do not look so bright either. Not withstanding the conflicting views of specialists on the social impacts of the ERSAP, there is almost no doubt that the poverty situation of Egypt is still serious. As mentioned in the previous chapter, there is the widespread perception among the general public that the reforms have expanded and entrenched poverty, while reinforcing the status of the already affluent elite business class. According to the United Nations, roughly half the population of Egypt is classified as "poor". These range from the "moderately poor", living on two to three Egyptian pounds a day (less than 1 US dollar), to the "ultra poor", scraping by on less than one pound (quoted from Hirst, 1999).

This situation has been related to the rise of the militant Islamists. As Ibrahim (1988: 632) has said, the resurgence of political Islam since the 1980s has been related to multiple causes, such as questions of identity, modernisation, cultural authenticity, socio-economic grievances, political participation, and foreign domination, and so it is neither wise nor accurate to oversimplify the phenomenon. However, the current economic plight of the mass public is especially related to the recent militant Islamic upsurge. The following passage by Phebe Marr (1994) reveals this point:

> "The Islamic movements are being created by multiple crises. These include rising unemployment, growing class differences resulting from market reforms and an inadequate social safety net, sluggish democratization, and the growth of a 'lumpen proletariat' – the fastest growing pool of recruits for violent movements."

In addition, the authoritarian political system that blocks the participation of the mass public and opposition forces in the political process reinforces the political apathy in one side of society and the extremism on the other side. In contrast to economic liberalisation, the Egyptian government has relied on severe crackdown and repression in the political arena. The Emergency has never been lifted since

1981. In 1998, the Egyptian government imprisoned some journalists and passed a new law (Law 3) that would further restrict the freedom of the press. In May 1999, it enacted another new law (Law 153) that would severely control the activities of NGOs.

After harsh military engagements, the state crushed the militant Islamists and restored seeming political stability. Yet, as Hirst has put it, the 'terror' may have been defeated but the conditions that bred it remain. Unless the government introduces political reform to give its opponents fair representation, as one lawyer has stated, "a new generation will come and call for the taking up of arms again" (Financial Times, 2000).

Views on the prospects for socio-political development are largely grim. According to Weiss and Wurzel (1998: 194, 208), the ruling establishment in Egypt is identified with extensive corruption and the new class of private businessmen are strikingly in their lack of awareness and sensitivity regarding the political risks of rising mass poverty. Since the ruling elite is depending on the "politics of alienation" (Ibrahim, 1994), the opposition forces and mass public seem to have no proper means of expanding their roles peacefully in the political process. As Abdel-Fadil and El-Eisawi have pointed out, the newly emerging class of private businessmen have no interest in defending the democratisation process. According to them, "It will work against their own interests because democracy means more transparency and growing opposition to the kind of capitalism they represent" (quoted from Abdel-Latif, 2001). As this situation leads to the 'delegitimation' of the ruling system (Cassandra, 1995), the discontent of people might erupt abruptly. In this respect, despite the appearance of political stability, the situation is still volatile, and the warnings of Cassandra on the "impending crisis" seem to be still resounding.

Overall, despite the market-oriented reforms of nearly one decade, the prospects for economic and socio-political development of Egypt look dim. The effects of macroeconomic stabilisation are impermanent, and the institutional reforms are incomplete. Dependence of the economy on fluctuating sources of foreign exchange and foreign assistance remains persistent. The ruling elite lacks the full commitment to achieve economic self-reliance, as well as democracy, and improve the welfare of the public. This situation implies that the socio-political and economic situation of Egypt in the future may not develop in ways that will provide improved living conditions for the Egyptian people, and points to the need for a more effective remedy for the ailing economic and political system.

10-2-3. Some Policy Implications

Certainly, it is not easy to find and propose appropriate remedies to these complex problems. Since many of the economic problems facing Egypt are related to the authoritarian nature of the political system, a broader perspective for the approach to be taken is needed. This ought to encompass political, as well as economic reforms. This point is attested to by the comments of Abdel-Nour, an opposition leader from the Wafdist group (quoted from El-Din, 2001):

> "Many of the problems in the Egyptian economy are largely due to the lack of democratisation and transparency and the lack of effective supervision for economic institutions. Economic liberalisation can never be viable without achieving political liberalisation at the same time."

To Abdel-Nour, the most urgent priority issue is the revision of the constitution, which was drawn up in 1970. According to Abdel-Nour, Egypt now requires a constitution that is in harmony with the developments that have taken place, particularly in the areas of democratisation and human rights. This would entail the repealing of the emergency law, the lifting of restrictions on political parties, and freeing the press from government control.

The reason why these political aspects are related to the issue of economic development can be found in the recent international debates on a "Good Governance". For example, in September 1996, the IMF's Interim Committee adopted the *Declaration of Partnership for Sustainable Global Growth,* which identified "promoting good governance in all its aspects, including the rule of law, improving the efficiency and accountability of the public sector, and tackling corruption" as an essential element of a framework within which economies can prosper (IMF, 1997).

Good governance emphasises the creation of systems that limit the scope for ad hoc decision making, rent seeking, and undesirable preferential treatment of individuals or organisations. As long as economic policies are decided by a small group of ruling elite without the proper participation of relevant interest groups and the public, such decision-making may lead to corruption and undesirable results that disproportionately favour certain groups and harm the public welfare.

The case of Egypt seems not much different. Many of the earlier named interviewees commented that without transparency and accountability in the formulation as well as implementation process of the policies, any economic reform may not produce the results originally expected. Rumours about the corruption of the power elite and their families were rampant, and stories about how such corruption affected government policies and business deals could be easily heard. The socio-political problems, such as the militant Islamists, are also related to the authoritarian nature of the political system. In this regard, good governance, or political reforms towards a more liberalised and democratic political process appear to be requisite for successful economic policies.

In economic areas, the most serious problem throughout the last few decades is related to the simple trade structure. Dependence on a few sources of earnings, notably petroleum exports, tourism, the Suez Canal receipts, and workers remittance, continues to make Egypt susceptible to exogenous shocks. Chronic trade deficits lead to perpetual balance of payment problems, which in turn brings about the debt crisis. To redress this problem, it seems that priority should be placed on improving the competitiveness of export industries.

Finally, on social issues, more active poverty reduction programmes are urgently needed. The growth in poverty undermines the potential of human resources needed for economic growth and disrupts the socio-political stability of the society. To cope with this problem, a greater commitment on the part of the Egyptian government will be needed, recognising the significance of the issue and putting policies in place. Also, international assistance ought to focus more on this issue.

Recently, the World Bank presented a general framework for action with regard to the global poverty reduction schemes. As presented in the *World Development Report 2000/01,* the three important areas for poverty reduction are as follows:

● Promoting opportunity: expanding economic opportunities for poor people by stimulating overall growth and by building up their assets and increasing the returns on these assets. Human capabilities such as health and education are important to build up their assets.

● Facilitating the empowerment: making state institutions more accountable and responsive to poor people, strengthening the participation of poor people in political processes, and removing the social barriers that results from distinctions of gender, ethnicity, race, and social status.

● Enhancing security: reducing poor people's vulnerability to ill health, economic shocks, policy-induced dislocations, natural disasters, and violence.

In the context of Egypt, the World Bank (2002) report mentioned in Chapter 9 has also presented detailed action programmes. Even though it is not certain whether these action programmes could actually be implemented, the increased concern of the international organisation on poverty alleviation looks desirable by itself.

So far, this thesis has revealed that the structural adjustment of Egypt has been implemented at the expense of the poorer classes. This implies that, despite the decade-long debates on the social cost of the adjustment and the modification of SAPs to take such debates into consideration, the agenda of the so-called "Structural Adjustment with a Human Face" has still many parts of it to be applied even in the case of Egypt.

10-3. Closing Remarks

As the ERSAP was implemented only recently, and was still progressing when this research started in 1998, assessing the overall progress and results was difficult and challenging. Research materials were scarce and evaluations were either premature or self-praising. Most existing materials focused on specific aspects of the progress, and fell short of providing a comprehensive view. Indeed, as far as I can ascertain, this research is a rare case of a study that has attempted to analyse the ERSAP from start to finish in a comprehensive socio-political and economic perspective. A detailed compilation of the progress of the ERSAP, in its economic and socio-political aspects, will contribute to our understanding of the ways in which economic reforms have been approached in specific country context.

A limitation of the study is that fieldwork has relied on interviews only. As a self-financing foreign student studying in a third country, it was difficult to arrange alternative methods of fieldwork other than interviews. In the future, it may be possible to incorporate more sophisticated research methods, including the use of quantitative analysis based on structured questionnaires. It seems that there are many rooms for such studies especially related to the social impacts, and further studies will be pursued in those ways.

Bibliography

Abdallah, Ali and Brown, Michael (1988), "The Economy", Chapter 3 in Lillian Craig Harris (ed.), *Egypt: International Challenge and Regional Stability*, London: Routledge & Kegan Paul

Abdel-Latif, Omayma (2000), "Dreaming of better times", *Al-Ahram Weekly*, 23-29 November 2000, Cairo

___________________ (2001), "Political Business", *Al-Ahram Weekly*, 7-13 June 2001, Cairo

Abdel-Razek, Sherine (2000), "Money, money, money", *Al-Ahram Weekly*, 6-12 July 2000, Cairo

Abu Shnief (2001), "Institutional Reform to Encourage Investment", Chapter 11 in Handoussa, Heba and El-Mikawy, Noha (eds.) (2001), *Institutional Reform and Economic Development in Egypt*, Unpublished Edition

Aly, Abdel Monem Said (1992), "Privatization in Egypt: The Regional Dimensions", Chapter 3 in Iliya Harik and Denis J. Sullivan (eds.), *Privatization and Liberalization in the Middle East*, Bloomington: Indiana University Press

Awad, Azita Berar (2002), "Social Funds: A New Approach to Poverty Reduction?" in Mustapha K. Al-Sayyid (ed.), *Facing Social Consequences of Structural Adjustment in Latin America and the Arab World*, Cairo: Center of Developing Countries Studies, Cairo University

Awad, Ibrahim (1991), "Socio-Political Aspects of Economic Reform: A Study of Domestic Actor's Attitudes towards Adjustment Policies in Egypt", Chapter 10 in Heba Handoussa and Gillan Potter (eds.), *Employment and Structural Adjustment: Egypt in the 1990s*, Cairo: The American University in Cairo Press

Ayittey, George B. N. (1995), "Why Structural Adjustment Failed in Africa", Chapter 7 in Daniel M. Schydlowsky (ed.), *Structural Adjustment: Retrospect and Prospect*, London: Praeger

Ayubi, Nazih N. (1988), "Domestic Politics", Chapter 4 in Lillian Craig Harris (ed.), *Egypt: Internal Challenges and Regional Stability*, London: Routledge & Kegan Paul

__________ (1989), "Government and the State in Egypt Today", Chapter 1 in Tripp, Charles and Owen, Roger (eds.), *Egypt under Mubarak*, London: Routledge

__________ (1991), The State and Public Policies in Egypt Since Sadat, Reading: Ithaca Press

__________ (1991), Political Islam: Religion and Politics in the Arab World, London and New York: Routledge

Balassa, Bela (1981), *Structural Adjustment Policies in Developing Economies*, World Bank Staff Working Papers, No. 464

Bates, Robert H., and Krueger, Anne O. (eds.) (1993), Political and Economic Interactions in Economic Policy Reform: Evidence from Eight Countries, Oxford: Blackwell Publishers

Berg, Elliot (1995), "African Adjustment Programs: False Attacks and True Dilemmas", Chapter 6 in Daniel M. Schydlowsky (ed.), *Structural Adjustment: Retrospect and Prospect*, London: Praeger

Beshara, Miranda (1999), "The Egyptian NGO Sector: Prospect and Challenge", in *Civil Society: Democratization in the Arab World*, August 1999, Cairo: Ibn Khaldun Center for Development Studies

Biersteker, Thomas J. (1995), "The triumph of liberal economic ideas in the developing world", Chapter 6 in Barbara Stallings (ed.), *Global Change, Regional Response: The New International Context of Development*, Cambridge: Cambridge University Press

Borthwick, Bruce Maynard (1980), *Comparative Politics of the Middle East: An Introduction*, Englewood Cliffs, NJ: Prentice Hall, Inc.

Bromley, Simon and Bush, Ray (1994), "Adjustment of Egypt? The Political Economy of Reform", *Review of African Political Economy*, No.60

Brumberg, Laurie MacDonald (ed.) (1995), *Stability and Reform in Egypt*, Internet Homepage (http://www.ned.org/pubs/reports/egypt.html).

Buchanan, James M. (1972), "Toward Analysis of Closed Behavioural Systems", in James M. Buchanan and Robert D. Tollison (eds.), *Theory of Public Choice: Political Applications of Economics*, Ann Arbor: The University of Michigan Press

Bush, Ray (1999), *Economic Crisis and The Politics of Reform in Egypt*, Boulder, Colorado: Westview Press

Butter, David (1989) "Debt and Egypt's Financial Policies", in Chapter 5 of Charles Tripp and Roger Owen (eds.), *Egypt Under Mubarak*, Centre for Near and Middle Eastern Studies, School of Oriental and African studies, London: Routledge

Cassandra (1995), "The Impending Crisis in Egypt", *The Middle East Journal*, Vol.49, No.1, Winter 1995, Washington, DC: Middle East Institute

Cassen, Robert (1994), "Structural Adjustment in Sub-Saharan Africa", Chapter 1 in

Willem Van Der Geest (ed.), *Negotiating Structural Adjustment in Africa*, New York: United Nations Development Programme

Central Bank of Egypt (1989), "Economic Development in Africa and Structural Adjustment Programs", *Economic Review*, Vol.XXX, No.4

________________________ (1993a), "Free Foreign Exchange Market (March 1991-December 1992)", *Economic Review*, Vol.XXXIII, No.2, 1992/93

________________________ (1993b), "The Role of the Private Sector in the Economic Development in Egypt (1986/87-1992/93), *Economic Review*, XXXIII, No.4, 1992/93

________________________ (1993c), "The Egyptian Economy and the Economic Liberalization", *Economic Review*, Vol.XXXIII, No.4, 1992/93

Central Bank of Egypt (1995), "The Economics of Egyptian Treasury Bills (Jan.1991-March 1995)", *Economic Review*, Vol.35, No.3, 1994/95

Chege, Michael (1995), "Sub-Saharan Africa: underdevelopment's last stand", Chapter 10 in Barbara Stallings (ed.) (1995), *Global Change, Regional Response: The New International Context of Development*, Cambridge: Cambridge University Press

Clark, Barry (1991), *Political Economy: A Comparative Approach*, New York: Praeger

Colclough, Christopher and Manor, James (eds.), *States or Markets? Neo-liberalism and the Development Policy Debate*, Oxford: Clarendon Press, 1991

Congressional Quarterly Inc. (1991), *The Middle East*, Seventh Edition, Washington, DC

Cook, Paul and Kirkpatrick, Colin (1988), "Privatisation in Less Developed Countries:

An Overview", Chapter 1 in Paul Cook and Colin Kirkpatrick (eds.), *Privatisation in Less Developed Countries*, Sussex: Wheatsheaf Books

Cook, P. and Kirkpatrick, C. (1995) (eds.), *Privatisation Policy and Performance: International Perspectives*, Hertfordshire: Prentice Hall/Harvester Wheatsheaf

Cooper, Mark N. (1983), "State Capitalism, Class Structure, and Social Transformation in the Third World: The Case of Egypt", in Tim Niblock and Rodney Wilson (eds.) (1999), *The Political Economy of the Middle East, Vol. IV: Economic and Political Liberalisation*, Cheltenham, UK: Edward Elgar Publishing Ltd.

Cornea, Giovanni A., Jolly, Richard, and Stewart, Frances (eds.) (1987), *Adjustment with a Human Face, Vol.1: Protecting the Vulnerable and Promoting Growth*, New York: Oxford University Press

Cox, Robert (2000), "Political Economy and World Order: Problems of Power and Knowledge at the Turn of the Millennium", Chapter 1 in Richard Stubbs and Geoffrey R.D. Underhill, *Political Economy and the Changing Global Order*, Ontario: Oxford University Press

Dollar, David and Kraay, Aart (2000), *Growth Is Good for the Poor*, Washington, DC: The World Bank

Ebeid, Mona Makram (1989), "The Role of the Official Opposition", Chapter 2 in Tripp, Charles and Owen, Roger (eds.), *Egypt under Mubarak*, London: Routledge

Eissawi, Ibrahim El- (2000), "From Reform to recession", *Al-Ahram Weekly*, 27 April – 3 May 2000, Cairo

EIU (1996-2000), *Country Report: Egypt* (Quarterly), London: The Economist Intelligence Unit

_______ (2002), *Country Risk Service: Egypt*, April 2002, London: The

Economist Intelligence Unit

Elah, Wafaa Abd El (1996), "An Overall Analysis of Economic Liberalization and Privatization in the People's Assembly", Chapter 5 in Wadouda Badran and Azza Wahby (eds.), *Privatization in Egypt: The Debate in the People's Assembly*, Center for Political Research and Studies, Cairo University

El-Din, Gamal Essam (2001), "The Hidden Issue", *Al-Ahram Weekly*, Issue No. 525, 15-21 March 2001

El-Din, Hanna Kheir (2002), "Social Fund for Development: Assessment of Performance and Impacts", in Mustapha K. Al-Sayyid (ed.), *Facing Social Consequences of Structural Adjustment in Latin America and the Arab World*, Cairo: Center of Developing Countries Studies, Cairo University

Fahmy, Ninette S. (1998), "The Performance of the Muslim Brotherhood in the Egyptian Syndicates: An Alternative Formula for Reform?", *The Middle East Journal*, Vol.52, No.4, Autumn 1998, Washington, DC: Middle East Institute

Fergany, Nader (1998), *The Growth of Poverty in Egypt*, Research Notes No.12, Cairo: Al-Mishkat Center

______________ (1999), *An Assessment of the Unemployment Situation in Egypt*, Research Notes No.13, Cairo: Al-Mishkat Center

Financial Times (2000), "Egypt 2000 – Politics: Islamists - Frustration buried but not removed", *Financial Times Survey*, London (http://specials.ft.com/ln/ftsurveys/country/scdcfe.htm)

Geest, Willem Van Der (ed.) (1994), *Negotiating Structural Adjustment in Africa*, New York: United Nations Development Programme

Gerges, Fawaz, A. (2000), "The End of the Islamist Insurgency in Egypt? Costs and Prospect", *The Middle East Journal*, Vol.4, Fall 2000,

Washington, DC: Middle East Institute

Giddens, Anthony (2001), *Sociology*, 4th Edition, Cambridge: Polity Press

Giugale, Marcelo M. and Mobarak, Hamed (eds.) (1996), *Private Sector Development in Egypt*, Cairo: The American University in Cairo Press

Glavanis, Pandeli M. (2002), "Social Consequences of Structural Adjustment Policies: A Contribution to the Debate", in Mustapha K. Al-Sayyid (ed.), *Facing Social Consequences of Structural Adjustment in Latin America and the Arab World*, Development Issues No. 24, Cairo: Center of Developing Countries Studies, Cairo University

Goddard, C. Roe, Passé-Smith, John T., and Conklin, John G. (eds.) (1996), *International Political Economy: State-Market Relations in the Changing Global Order*, Boulder and London: Lynne Rienner Publishers

Gomaa, Salwa Shaarawi (1996), "The Civil Society Debate over Privatization in Egypt: Conflicting Interpretations and Goals", Chapter 3 in Wadouda and Azza Wahby (eds.), *Privatization in Egypt: The Debate in the People's Assembly*, Center for Political Research and Studies, Cairo: Cairo University

Gray, Matthew (1998), "Economic Reform, Privatization and Tourism in Egypt", *Middle Eastern Studies,* Vol.34, No.2, April 1998

Grindle, Merilee S. and Thomas, John W. (1991), *Public Choices and Policy Change: The Political Economy of Reform in Developing Countries*, Baltimore and London: The Johns Hopkins University Press

Haggard, Stephen, Lafay, Jean-Dominique, and Morrisson, Christian (1995), *Political Economy of Adjustment: The Political Feasibility of Adjustment in Developing Countries*, Development Center Studies, Paris: OECD

Handoussa, Heba and El-Mikawy, Noha (eds.) (2001), *Institutional Reform and Economic Development in Egypt*, Unpublished Edition

Handoussa, Heba and Potter, Gilan (eds.) (1991), *Employment and Structural Adjustment: Egypt in the 1990s*, Cairo: The American University in Cairo Press

Harik, Iliya (1992), "Privatization: The Issue, the Prospects, and the Fears", Chapter 1 in Iliya Harik and Denis J. Sullivan (eds.), *Privatization and Liberalization in the Middle East*, Bloomington: Indiana University Press

Harik, Iliya (1998), *Economic Policy Reform in Egypt*, Cairo: The American University in Cairo Press

Harik, Iliya and Sullivan, Denis J. (eds.) (1992), *Privatization and Liberalization in the Middle East*, Bloomington: Indiana University Press

Harris, Lillian Craig (ed.) (1988), *Egypt: International Challenges and Regional Stability*, London: Routledge & Kegan Paul

Harvey, Charles (ed.) (1996), *Constraints on the Success of Structural Adjustment Programmes in Africa*, Saint Martin's Press, LLC

Hashem, Amir and El-Mikawy, Noha (2001), "Information and Production of Knowledge through Interest Representation: Business MPs", Chapter 5 in Heba Handoussa and Noha El-Mikawy (eds.), *Institutional Reform and Economic Development in Egypt*, Cairo: The Economic Research Forum for the Arab Countries, Iran and Turkey

Hatem, Mervat F. (1992), "Economic and Political Liberation in Egypt and the Demise of State Feminism", *International Journal of Middle East Studies*, Vol.24, 1992, Cambridge University Press

Herbst, Jeffrey (1990), "The Structural Adjustment of Politics in Africa", *World Development*, Vol.18, No.7

Hinnebusch, Raymond A. (1993), "The Politics of Economic Reform in Egypt", *Third World Quarterly*, Vol.14, No.1

Hirst, David (1999), "Egypt stands on feet of clay: A Middle East Indonesia in the Making", *Le Monde diplomatique*, October 1999, Paris

Holt, Robert and Roe, Terry (1993), "The Political Economy of Reform: Egypt in 1980s", Chapter 5 in Robert H. Bates and Anne Krueger (eds.), *Political and Economic Interactions in Economic Policy Reform: Evidence from Eight Countries*, Oxford: Basil Blackwell

Hoogvelt, Ankie (1997), *Globalisation and the Postcolonial World: The New Political Economy of Development*, London: Macmillan Press Ltd.

Hopwood, Derek (1993), *Egypt: Politics and Society 1945-1990*, London and New York: Routledge

Hudson, Michael C. (1996), "To Play the Hegemon: Fifty Years of US Policy toward the Middle East", *The Middle East Journal*, Vol.50, No.3, Summer 1996

Huntington, Samuel P. (1997), *The Clash of Civilizations and the Remaking of World Order*, London and New York: Touchstone Books

Husain, Ishrat and Rashid Faruqee (eds.) (1994), *Adjustment in Africa: Lessons from Country Case Studies*, Washington, D.C.: The World Bank

Ibrahim, Saad Eddin (1988), "Egypt's Islamic Activism in the 1980s", *Third World Quarterly*, April 1988

_________________ (1994), "Governance and Structural Adjustment: The Egyptian Case", Chapter 8 in the same author (1996), *Egypt, Islam and Democracy: Twelve Critical Essays*, Cairo: The American University in Cairo Press

_________________ (1996), *Egypt, Islam and Democracy: Twelve Critical Essays*,

Cairo: The American University in Cairo Press

IMF (1985), *Adjustment Programs in Africa: The Recent Experience*, Occasional Paper 34, Washington, DC: International Monetary Fund

IMF (1992-99), *International Financial Statistics Yearbook*, Washington, DC: International Monetary Fund

_______ (1995), *IMF Conditionality: Experience Under Stand-By and Extended Arrangements, Part 1: Key Issues and Findings*, Occasional Paper 128, Washington, DC: International Monetary Fund

_______ (1996), "IMF Approves 24-month Stand-by Credit for Egypt", Press Release No. 96/50, Washington, DC: International Monetary Fund

_______ (1997), *Good Governance: The IMF's Role*, Address of the Managing Director, Michel Camdessus, to the United Nations Economic and Social Council on July 2, 1997, Washington: International Monetary Fund

_______ (1997), *Conditionality as an Instrument of Borrower Credibility*, PPAA/97/2, Washington, DC: International Monetary Fund

_______ (1997), *The Egyptian Stabilization Experience: An Analytical Retrospective*, Prepared by Arvind Subramanian, Working Paper WP97/105, Washington, DC: International Monetary Fund

_______ (1998), *Egypt: Beyond Stabilization, Toward a Dynamic Market Economy*, Occasional Paper 163, Washington, DC: International Monetary Fund

_______ (1999), *The Egyptian Stock Market: Efficiency Tests and Volatility Effects*, IMF Working Paper WP/99/48, Washington, DC: International Monetary Fund

_______ (2000), *IMF Conditionality and Country Ownership of Programs*, Working Paper WP/01/142, Washington, DC: International Monetary Fund

________ (2001), *Economic Growth and Poverty Reduction in sub-Saharan Africa,* WP/01/112, Washington, DC: International Monetary Fund

INP (1998, 1999), *Egypt: Human Development Report,* Cairo: The Institute of National Planning

Ismael, Tareq Y. and Ismael, Jacqueline S. (1991), *Politics and Government in the Middle East and North Africa,* Miami: Florida International University Press

Joffé, George (1996), "The Islamist Threat to Egypt", *The Middle East and North Africa 1996,* London: Europa Publications Limited

Joo, Dong-Joo (1997), "An Assessment of the Foreign Direct Investment Environment of Egypt from a Korean Perspective", Chapter 7 in Mohammad Selim and Ibrahim Arafat (eds.), *The Egyptian-Korean Dialogue,* Center for Asian Studies, Cairo University

Kassem, Maye (1999), *In the Guise of Democracy: Governance in Contemporary Egypt,* Reading, UK: Garnet Publishing Limited

Kassem, Maye (2001), "Information and Production of Knowledge or Lobbying? Businessmen's Association, Federation of Labor Unions, and the Ministry of Manpower", Chapter 6 in Heba Handoussa and Noha El-Mikawy (eds.), *Institutional Reform and Economic Development in Egypt,* Cairo: The Economic Research Forum for the Arab Countries, Iran and Turkey

Khattab, Dr. Mokhtar (1998), *Constraints of Privatization in the Egyptian Experience,* a paper for the Mediterranean Development Forum held on September 3-6, 1998 in Marrakech, Morocco

Khattab, Mokhtar (1999), *Constraints to Privatization: The Egyptian Experience,* Working Paper No.38, Cairo: The Egyptian Center for Economic Studies

Kienle, Eberhard (1998), "More than a response to Islamism: The Political Deliberalization of Egypt in the 1990s", *Middle East Journal*, Vol.52, No.2, Spring 1998

Killick, Tony (1995), *IMF Programmes in Developing Countries: Design and Impact*, London: Routledge

Korayem, Karima (1997), *Egypt's Economic Reform and Structural Adjustment Program (ERSAP)*, Working Paper No.19, Cairo: The Egyptian Center for Economic Studies

Korean Embassy in Cairo (2002), *Recent Economic Trends of Egypt* (in Korean), unpublished

Krueger, Anne O. (1995), *Political Economy of Policy Reform in Developing Countries*, Cambridge, MA: The MIT Press

Laithy, Heba El- and Osman, Osman M. (1996), *Profile and Trend of Poverty and Economic Growth in Egypt*, A Background Paper prepared for Egypt Human Development Report 1996, UNDP

Lane, Jan-Erik and Ersson, Svante (1990), *Comparative Political Economy*, London and New York: Pinter Publishers

Library of Congress, USA (1991), *Egypt: A Country Study*, (http://lcweb2.loc.gov/frd/cs/egtoc.html)

Little, I.M.D, and three Co-Authors (1993), *Boom, Crisis, and Adjustment: The Macroeconomic Experience of Developing Countries*, Oxford University Press

Löfgren, Hans (1993), "Economic Policy in Egypt: A Breakdown in Reform Resistance?", *International Journal of Middle East Studies*, Vol.25, Cambridge University Press

Mabro, Robert (1974), *The Egyptian Economy 1952-1972*, Oxford University Press

Mahdi, Alia El (1996), "The Economic Reform Program in Egypt: After Four Years of Implementation", Chapter 1 in Alia El Mahdi (ed.) (1997), *Aspects of Structural Adjustment in Africa and Egypt*, Center for the Study of Developing Countries, Cairo University

Marr, Phebe (1994), "U.S.- Egyptian Relations After the Cold War: Egypt's Growing Challenges", *National Defense University Strategic Forum*, No.4, August 1994, (http://www.ndu.edu/inss/strforum/z405.html)

Marx, Karl and Engels, Frederick (1991), *Selected Works in One Volume*, London: Lawrence and Wishart

McDermott, Anthony (1988), *Egypt: From Nasser to Mubarak – A Flawed Revolution*, London: Croom Helm

McKee, E.S. (1999), "Egypt's Promised Lands", *The Jerusalem Report*, July 19, 1999 (http://www.jrep.com/Mideast/Article-10.html)

Mehmet, Ozay (1995), *Westernizing the Third World: The Euro-Centricity of Economic Development Theories*, London and New York: Routledge

Mekay, Emad S. (1996), "Egypt's Economic Reform Releases a New Genie", *Washington Report on Middle East Affairs*, May/June 1996

Metz, Helen Chapin (ed.) (1991), *Country Study: Egypt*, Washington, DC: Library of Congress (The full text can be downloaded from the Internet Homepage http://lcweb2.loc.gov/frd/cs/egtoc.html)

Mikawy, Noha El- (2001), "Institutional Reform to Improve Economic Performance: Challenges and Sequences in the Case of Egypt", Chapter 1 in Handoussa, Heba and El-Mikawy, Noha (eds.) (2001), *Institutional Reform and Economic Development in Egypt*, Unpublished Edition

Ministry of Economy (1999), *Quarterly Economic Digest: April-June 1999*, Internet

Homepage (http://interoz.com/economygoveg/English/quarterly/TocQ.htm)

Ministry of Economy and Foreign Trade (2000a), *Monthly Economic Digest*, January, March and June 2000, Cairo

_______________________________ (2000b), *Investing in Egypt*, Cairo

_______________________________ (2000c), *Egypt 2000*, Cairo

Moore, John (1986), "Why Privatise?", Chapter 3 in J. Kay, C. Mayer, and D. Thompson, (eds.), *Privatisation and Regulation: The UK Experience*, Oxford: Clarendon Press

Moore, Philip (1997), *Egypt: Privatisation and Beyond, Meeting the Challenges of the 21st Century*, Euromoney Publications

Mosley, Paul, Harrigan, Jane, and Toye, John (1995), *Aid and Power: The World Bank & Policy-based Lending*, Second Edition, Vol.1, London, Routledge

Mosley, Paul (2000), *The IMF after the Asian Crisis: Merits and limitations of the 'Long-term Development Partner Role'*, First draft, unpublished material

Nassar, Heba (2002), "Social Protection for the Poor in Egypt", in Mustapha K. Al-Sayyid (ed.) (2002), *Facing Social Consequences of Structural Adjustment in Latin America and the Arab World*, Development Issues 24, Cairo: Center of Developing Countries Studies, Cairo University

Nassar, Heba and El-Laithy, Heba (eds.) (2001), *Socioeconomic Policies and Poverty Alleviation Programs in Egypt*, Cairo: Center for Economic & Financial Research & Studies

Nassar, Heba and Aziz, Alfonse (eds.) (2000), *Egyptian Exports and Challenges of the 21st Century*, Center for Economic & Financial Research and Studies, Cairo University

Nelson, Joan M. (ed.) (1990), *Economic Crisis and Policy Choice: The Politics of Adjustment in the Third World*, Princeton, NJ: Princeton University Press

Nelson, Paul J. (1995), *The World Bank and Non-Governmental Organizations: The Limits of Apolitical Development*, London: Macmillan Press Ltd

Niblock, Tim and Wilson, Rodney (eds.) (1999), *The Political Economy of the Middle East, Vol. IV: Economic and Political Liberalisation*, Cheltenham, UK: Edward Elgar Publishing Ltd.

OECF (1999), *The Egyptian Economy: Its Current Status and Future Challenges*, OECF Research Papers No. 31, Tokyo: The Overseas Economic Cooperation Fund

Owen, Roger and Pamuk, Sevket (1998), *A History of Middle East Economies in the Twentieth Century*, London: I.B. Tauris & Company

Palmer, Monte and 4 Co-Authors (1986), "Bureaucratic and economic development in the Middle East: a study of Egypt, the Sudan and Saudi Arabia", *International Review of Administrative Sciences*, Vol.53, London

Pastor, Jr., Manuel (1996), "The Effects of IMF Programs in the Third World: Debate and Evidence from Latin America", Chapter 16 in C. Roe Goddard, John T Passé-Smith, and John G. Conklin (eds.), *International Political Economy: State-Market Relations in the Changing Global Order*, Boulder and London: Lynne Rienner Publishers

Please, Stanley (1994), "From Structural Adjustment to Structural Transformation", Chapter 2 in Willem Van Der Geest (ed.), *Negotiating Structural Adjustment in Africa*, New York: United Nations Development Programme

Posusney, Marsha Pripstein (1992), "Labor as an Obstacle to Privatization: The Case of Egypt", Chapter 5 in Iliya Harik and Denis J. Sullivan (eds.), *Privatization and Liberalization in the Middle East*, Bloomington: Indiana University Press

______________________ (1997), *Labor and the State in Egypt: Workers, Unions, and Economic Restructuring*, New York: Columbia University Press

Preston, P.W. (1996), *Development Theory: An Introduction*, Oxford: Blackwell Publishers

Reed, David (ed.) (1996*), Structural Adjustment, the Environment, and Sustainable Development*, London: Earthscan Publications Ltd.

Refaat, Amal (1999), *New Trends in Egypt's Trade Policy and Future Challenges*, Working Paper No. 36, Cairo: The Egyptian Center for Economic Studies

Richards, Alan and Waterbury, John (1990), *A Political Economy of The Middle East: State, Class, and Economic Development*, Boulder: Westview Press

Riddel, J. Barry (1992), "Things Fall Apart Again: Structural Adjustment Programmes in Sub-Saharan Africa", *The Journal of Modern African Studies*, Sep. 1992, Vo.30, No. 3, Cambridge University Press

Sagiv, David (1995), *Fundamentalism and Intellectuals in Egypt 1973-1993*, London: Frank Cass

Said, Mohamed El sayed (2000), "Egypt: The Dialectics of State Security and Social Decay", *Politik und Gesellschaft Online: International Politics and Society*, 1/2000, Internet Homepage (http://www.fes.de/ipg/ipg1_2000/arelsayed.html)

Sayyid, El- (1996), "Bureaucracy and Political Change in Egypt", Chapter 7 in Dan Tschirgi (ed.), *Development in the Age of Liberalization: Egypt and Mexico*, Cairo: The American University in Cairo Press

Sayyid, Mustapha Al- (ed.) (2002), *Facing Social Consequences of Structural Adjustment in Latin America and the Arab World*, Development Issues 24, Cairo: Center of Developing Countries Studies, Cairo University

Schydlowsky, Daniel M. (ed.) (1995), *Structural Adjustment: Retrospect and Prospect*, London: Praeger

Selim, Mohammad El-Sayed (2002), *Models of Development in the Arab World*, Unpublished

Shafiq, Amina (2000), "The crucial 50 percent", *Al-Ahram Weekly*, 4-10 May 2000, Cairo

Shaw, Jane (2002), "Public Choice Theory", in *The Concise Encyclopedia of Economics*, http://www.econlib.org/library/Enc/PublicChoiceTheory.html

Shawarby, Sherine Al- (2000), "Estimating the Impact of the Egyptian Exchange Rate on Exports", in Heba Nassar and Alfonse Aziz (eds.), *Egyptian Exports and Challenges of the 21st Century*, Center for Economic & Financial Research and Studies, Cairo University

Sherif, Khaled Fouad and Soos, Regina M. (1992), "Egypt's Liberalization Experience and Its Impact on State-Owned Enterprises", Chapter 4 in Iliya Harik and Denis J. Sullivan (eds.), *Privatization and Liberalization in the Middle East*, Bloomington: Indiana University Press

Stallings Barbara (ed.) (1995), *Global Change, Regional Response: The New International Context of Development*, New York: Cambridge University Press

Stubbs, Richard and Underhill, Geoffrey R.D.(2000), *Political Economy and the Changing Global Order*, Ontario: Oxford University Press

Sullivan (eds.), *Privatization and Liberalization in the Middle East*, Bloomington: Indiana University Press

Springborg, Robert (1989), *Mubarak's Egypt: Fragmentation of the Political Order*, Boulder and London: Westview Press

Stewart, Frances (1991), "The Many Faces of Adjustment", *World Development*, Vol.19, No.12, December 1991.

Stiglitz, Joseph (2000), "What I learned at the world economic crisis: The Insider", *The New Republic*, April 17, 2000, Washington, DC

Streeten, Paul (1995), "The Political Economy of Reform", Chapter 10 in Daniel M. Schydlowsky (ed.), *Structural Adjustment: Retrospect and Prospect*, London: Praeger

Sturzenegger, Federico and Tommasi, Mariano (eds.) (1998), *The Political Economy of Reform*, Cambridge, MA: The MIT Press

Sullivan, Denis J. (1992), "Extra-State Actors and Privatization in Egypt", Chapter 2 in Iliya Harik and Denis J. Sullivan (eds.), *Privatization and Liberalization in the Middle East*, Bloomington: Indiana University Press

Tarp, Finn (1993), *Stabilization and Structural Adjustment: Macro-economic Frameworks for Analysing the Crisis in Sub-Saharan Africa*, London: Routledge

Thiele, Rainer (2001), *The Social Impact of Structural Adjustment in Bolivia*, Kiel Working Paper No. 1056, Kiel Institute of World Economics

Tohamy, Sahar (1998), *Tax Administration and Transaction Costs in Egypt*, Working Paper No.33, Cairo: The Egyptian Center for Economic Studies

Toye, John F. (1991), "Is There a New Political Economy of Development?" in Colclough, C. and Manor, J. (eds.), *States or Markets? Neo-liberalism and the Development Policy Debate*, Oxford: Clarendon Press, 1991.

__________ (1996), "Structural Adjustment, Labour Markets and Employment Policy", Chapter 6 in Charles Harvey (ed.), *Constraints on the Success of Structural Adjustment Programmes in Africa*, Saint Martin's Press, LLC

Tripp, Charles and Owen, Roger (eds.) (1990), *Egypt Under Mubarak*, London and New York: Routledge

Tschirgi, Dan (ed.) (1996), *Development in the Age of Liberalization: Egypt and Mexico*, Cairo: The American University in Cairo Press

UNCTAD (1999), *Investment Policy Review: Egypt*, New York and Geneva: United Nations Conference on Trade and Development

Underhill, Geoffrey R. D. (2000), "Conceptualizing the Changing Global Order", Introduction in Richard Stubbs and Geoffrey R.D. Underhill (eds.), *Political Economy and the Changing Global Order*, Second Edition, Ontario: Oxford University Press

UNDP (1996 - 2000), *Human Development Report*, New York: United Nations Development Programme

UNRISD (1994), *Structural Adjustment in a Changing World*, Briefing Paper No.4, Geneva: United Nations Research Institute for Social Development

Wadouda and Wahby, Azza (eds.) (1996), *Privatization in Egypt: The Debate in the People's Assembly*, Center for Political Research and Studies, Cairo: Cairo University

Wahba, Mourad (1996), "Private and Public Economic Bases: The Egyptian Case", Chapter 5, in Dan Tschirgi (ed.), *Development in the Age of Liberalization: Egypt and Mexico*, Cairo: The American University in Cairo Press

Waterbury, John (1983), *The Egypt of Nasser and Sadat: The Political Economy of Two Regimes*, Princeton, NJ: Princeton University Press

Weaver, James H. (1995), "What is Structural Adjustment?", Chapter 1 in Daniel M. Schydlowsky (ed.), *Structural Adjustment: Retrospect and Prospect*, London: Praeger

Weiss, Dieter and Wurzel, Ulrich (1998), *The Economics and Politics of Transition to and Open Market Economy: EGYPT,* Development Centre Studies, Paris: The Organisation for Economic Co-operation and Development

Williamson, John (ed.) (1994), *The Political Economy of Policy Reform,* Washington, DC: Institute for International Economics

Williamson, John and Haggard, Stephan (1994), "The Political Conditions for Economic Reform", in John Williamson (ed.), *The Political Economy of Policy Reform,* Washington, DC: Institute for International Economics

World Bank (1981), *Accelerated Development in Sub-Saharan Africa: An Agenda for Action,* Report No.3358, Washington, DC

___________ (1989-99), *Annual Report,* Washington, DC

___________ (1995), *Structural and Sectoral Adjustment Lending: World Bank Experience (1980-1992),* Sector Study No. 14691, Washington, DC

___________ (2000), *The World Development Report 1999/2000: Entering the 21st Century,* Washington, DC

___________ (2001), *The World Development Report 2000/2001: Attacking Poverty,* Washington, DC

___________ (2002), *Arab Republic of Egypt: Poverty Reduction in Egypt – Diagnosis and Strategy,* Vol.1: Main Report, Report No. 24234-EGT

World Bank (2002), *Arab Republic of Egypt: Poverty Reduction in Egypt – Diagnosis and Strategy,* Vol.2: Annex Tables, Report No. 24234-EGT

WTO (1999), *Trade Policy Review: Egypt 1999,* Geneva: World Trade Organization

Journals, Magazines, and Newspapers

Al-Ahram, Cairo (http://www.ahram.org.eg)

Al-Ahram Weekly, Cairo (http://weekly.ahram.org.eg/)

British Journal of Middle Eastern Studies, London

Cairo Times, Cairo (http://www.cairotimes.com/)

Country Report: Egypt (Quarterly), London: Economist Intelligence Unit

MEED: Middle East Economic Digest (Weekly), London

The Middle East (Monthly), London: IC Publications Ltd.

The Middle East Journal (Quarterly), Washington, DC: Middle East Institute

Third World Quarterly, London: Carfax Publishing

Statistical Data

Central Bank of Egypt, *Annual Report*

__________________, *Economic Review* (Quarterly)

Ministry of Economy of Egypt (1999), *Quarterly Economic Digest*

Ministry of Economy and Foreign Trade (from 2000 on), *Monthly Economic Digest*

IMF, *International Financial Statistics* (Monthly)

World Bank, *World Development Report* (Annual)

The Author

Dr. Dong-Joo has been working as a researcher at the Korea Institute for Industrial Economics and Trade(KIET) since 1984, The KIET is a Korean government economic institute, which contributes to setting up industrial and trade policies. Dr. Joo has specialized in the economic affairs of Middle Eastern countries and some African affairs as well. In the meantime, he has produced many research papers and visited many Middle Eastern and African countries for fieldwork or conferences.

Academic Background

- 1982. BA, Hankuk University of Foreign Studies (Arabic Literature and Politics)
- 1992. MBA, HUFS (Management Information System)
- 1999. MA, University of Manchester (Development Studies)
- 2004. Ph.D, University of Manchester (Development Studies)

Job Career

- 1984-Present. Researcher and Research Fellow, KIET
- 2002. Specialist, Regulatory Reform Committee in the Office of the Prime Minister of Korea.
- 2003. Adjunct Professor, Hankuk University of Foreign Studies

Major Publications(Mostly in Korean)

- Economic Sanctions in the Middle East(1998)
- The Middle East Economy in the Era of the Arab-Israeli Peace(1995)
- Prospect of South African Economy after the Multi-Racial Election(1994)
- The Economy of the Arab Maghreb Countries(1991)
- The Economy and Business Environment of Iran(1985)

Contact: djjoo@kiet.re.kr

주동주
(朱東柱)

•약력•

한국외국어대학 아랍어과(1982)를 졸업하면서 정치학을 부전공으로 공부하였다. 이후 한국외국어대학교의 경영학(MIS) 석사(1992), 영국 맨체스터 대학의 국제개발학 석사(1999)와 박사학위(2004)를 취득하였다. 1984년 국책연구소인 산업연구원(KIET)에 입사한 이래 중동경제를 중심으로 개발도상국 문제를 연구해오고 있으며, 현재는 산업연구원의 국제산업협력실에 연구위원으로 근무하고 있다. 그 동안 중동과 개발도상국 문제에 관해 많은 저술을 냈으며, 정부와 기업의 정책에 자문활동을 해 왔다. 한국외국어대의 겸임교수로 강의하였으며, 2004년부터는 개인적으로 국제개발학을 공부하는 소규모 모임을 이끌어오고 있기도 하다.
(Email: djjoo@kiet.re.kr)

•주요저서•

「고유가시대의 대중동 산업협력 전략」(2006)
「신흥경제대국 BRICS와 한국경제」(2005)
　외 다수

개혁의 정치경제학

· 초판 인쇄　　2007 년 11 월 20 일
· 초판 발행　　2007 년 11 월 20 일
· 지 은 이　　주동주
· 펴 낸 이　　채종준
· 펴 낸 곳　　한국학술정보㈜
　　　　　　　경기도 파주시 교하읍 문발리
　　　　　　　파주출판문화정보산업단지 513-5
　　　　　　　전화　031)908-3181(대표) · 팩스　031)908-3160
　　　　　　　홈페이지　http://www.kstudy.com
　　　　　　　e-mail(출판사업부)　publish@kstudy.com

· 등 　 록　　제일산-115 호(2000. 6. 19)
· 가 　 격　　22,000 원

ISBN　　978-89-534-7729-2 93320 (paper book)
　　　　　978-89-534-7730-8 98320 (e-book)